Flash 5™
Primer

ISBN 0-13-031093-X

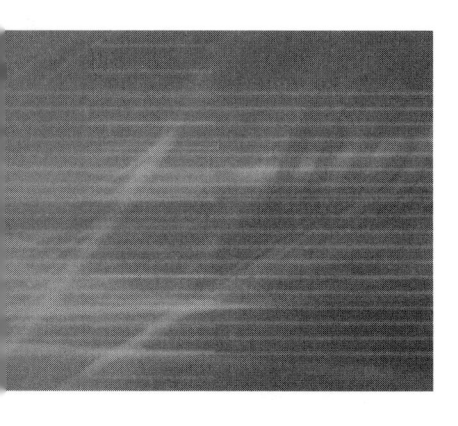

Prentice Hall PTR
The Primer Series

Flash 5 Primer

 . . . . Policano

Director 8 Primer

 . . . . Chominsky

Web Photoshop 6 Primer

 . . . . Miletsky

Photoshop 6 Primer

 . . . . Miletsky

Flash 5 Primer

JOHN POLICANO

PH PTR

Prentice Hall PTR, Upper Saddle River, NJ 07458
www.phptr.com

Library of Congress Cataloging-in-Publication Date
Policano, John.
    Flash 5 primer / John Policano.
       p. cm.
    ISBN 0-13-031093-X
     1. Computer animation. 2. Flash (Computer file) 3. Web sites--Authoring programs. I.
Title: Flash five primer. II. Title.

TR897.7 .P674 2001
006.6'96--dc21

                                                                                                   00-054858

Editorial/Production Supervisor: *Donna Cullen-Dolce*
Acquisitions Editor: *Tim Moore*
Editorial Assistant: *Allyson Kloss*
Developmental Editor: *Jim Markham*
Manufacturing Manager: *Alexis R. Heydt*
Marketing Manager: *Debby vanDijk*
Art Director: *Gail Cocker-Bogusz*
Interior Series Designer: *Rosemarie Votta*
Cover Designer: *Anthony Gemmellaro*
Cover Design Director: *Jerry Votta*

© Copyright 2001 by Prentice Hall PTR
Prentice-Hall, Inc.
Upper Saddle River, NJ 07458

All rights reserved. No part pf this book may be
reproduced, in any form or by any means, without
permission in writing from the publisher

The publisher offers discounts on this book when ordered in bulk quantities.
For more information, contact

    Corporate Sales Department,
    Prentice Hall PTR
    One Lake Street
    Upper Saddle River, NJ 07458
    Phone: 800-382-3419; FAX: 201-236-714
    E-mail (Internet): corpsales@prenhall.com

Flash is a trademark of Macromedia, Inc. All other product names mentioned in this book
are the trademarks or service marks of their respective companies, organizations, or owners.

Printed in the United States of America

10 9 8 7 6 5 4 3 2 1

ISBN: 0-13-031093-X

Prentice-Hall International (UK) Limited, London
Prentice-Hall of Australia Pty. Limited, Sydney
Prentice-Hall Canada Inc., Toronto
Prentice-Hall Hispanoamericana, S.A., Mexico
Prentice-Hall of India Private Limited, New Delhi
Prentice-Hall of Japan, Inc., Tokyo
Simon & Schuster Asia Pte. Ltd., Singapore
Editora Prentice-Hall do Brasil, Ltda., Rio de Janeiro

*To John Fischl, a great person,
friend, and grandfather*

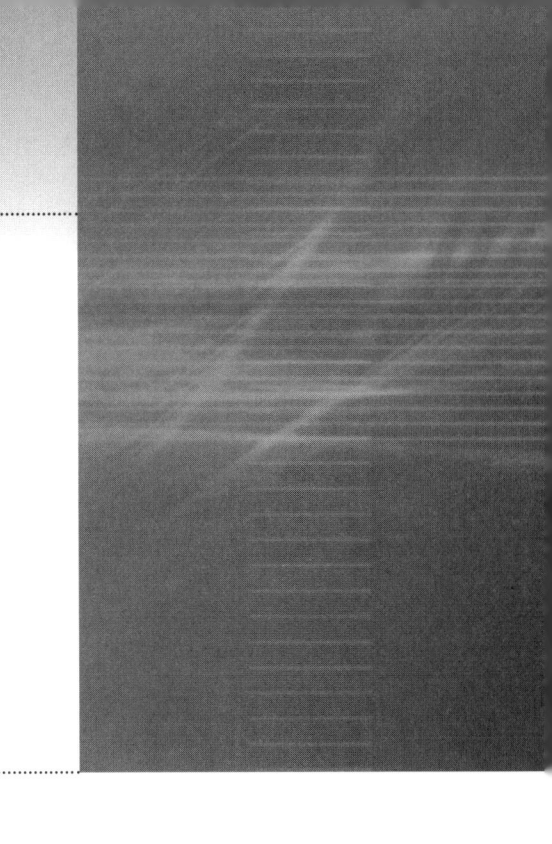

CONTENTS

INTRODUCTION . . . . **xxi**

ACKNOWLEDGMENTS . . . . **xxv**

CHAPTER 1

WHAT'S NEW IN FLASH 5? 1

Making Flash Work for You 2

Preferences 2

Keyboard Shortcuts 3

Understanding the Panels and Windows 4

Panels 4

Info Panel 4

Fill and Stroke Panels	4
Transform Panel	6
Align Panel	6
Mixer and Swatches Panels	7
Character, Paragraph, and Text Options Panels	8
Instance and Effect Panels	9
Clip Parameters Panel	10
Frame Panel	11
Sound Panel	11
Scene Panel	11
Generator Panel	12
Windows	12
Toolbar	13
Stage	14
Actions Window	14
Output Window	16
Movie Explorer Window	16
Debugger Window	16

New Library Features 17

Importing and Sharing Libraries	17

CONTENTS

    Create Permanent Libraries   18

    Importing your Movie as a Library   18

    Sharing Library Files across Multiple Movies   18

  Learning Interactions   19

  Smart Clips   21

Other New Features 24

  Make Font Symbols   24

  Import MP3 Files   25

  XML and Flash 5   25

CHAPTER 2

CREATING AND IMPORTING ARTWORK 27

Creating Graphics in Flash with Key Tools 28

  Oval   29

  Rectangle   30

  Pen   31

  Lasso   32

  Ink Bottle   34

  Paint Bucket   36

  Eraser   36

Shapes, Grouped Objects, Symbols, and Imported Bitmaps 38

Shapes 38

Grouped Objects 40

Symbols 41

Imported Bitmaps 42

Importing Artwork from Other Applications 46

From FreeHand to Flash 46

Preparing Your Illustrator Files for Flash 50

Making Your Bitmaps Vector-based Images with Adobe Streamline 51

Preparing Your Files with Fireworks 3 53

Exporting from Adobe Photoshop and Imageready 54

Finding the Right Graphics 55

CHAPTER 3

ANIMATING YOUR ARTWORK 57

Understanding the Timeline and Keyframes 57

When to Use Shape Tweening 59

Morphing a Circle into a Square 59

CONTENTS   xi

    Morphing a Circle into an "A"   61

    Animating the Shape of Letters   65

All You Need to Know About Motion Tweening 67

    Animating Position and Scale   67

    Fading the Instance of a Symbol   69

    Spinning Your Graphics   70

    Follow that Path   71

    Bouncing Ball   75

Creating a Movie Clip 77

    Pulsing Circle   77

Frame-by-Frame Animation 79

Using Video in Flash 80

CHAPTER 4

GETTING YOUR AUDIO IN SYNC 81

Adding Audio to Your Project 81

    File Formats You Can Use   82

    Setting Up Your Audio File   82

    Importing Your Audio File   83

Controlling Audio 84

Understanding the Sound Editing Controls   84

    Using the Time In/Out Controls   85

    Understanding Envelope Handles and Envelope Lines   86

    Looping Audio Clips   87

Event Sounds   89

Streaming Sounds   91

Using Shared Libraries for Your Audio Files   93

Choosing the Right Compression 95

CHAPTER 5

ALL YOU NEED TO KNOW ABOUT ACTIONSCRIPT 97

What Is ActionScript? 97

How Does ActionScript Work? 98

Frame Actions   98

Object Actions   98

Writing Your Own ActionScripts 98

The ActionScript Window   98

    Basic Actions   99

    Actions   99

Operators	101
Functions	102
Properties	102
Objects	103
ActionScript Syntax	103
Targeting Movie Clips	104
Writing and Using Variables	105
ActionScript Debugger	106
Local or Remote Debugging?	107
Debugger Features	108
Sample ActionScripts	109
Date Script	110
Change that Cursor	113
Control Your Volume	114
Email and ASP	118

CHAPTER 6

FLASH YOUR WEB SITE 123

Pre-Production Techniques and Hints 123

Understanding Movie Dimensions	123

Storyboarding	125
Organizing Your Files	125

Preparing Your Flash Movie 126

Creating an Interface 127

Creating Buttons	127
Using Movie Clips to Add Animation to Buttons	130

Establishing Navigation 132

Organizing the Timeline	132
Applying Button Actions	134
Changing the Behaviors of Buttons	135

Organizing the Sections of the Site 137

Using Movie Clips for Sections	137
Home Page Section	*137*
Save Time; Reuse Elements	138
Banners Section	*139*
Web Sites Section	*141*
Screen Savers Section	*144*

Printing from Flash 145

Setting Up a Printable Document	145
Making a Movie Print	147

Troubleshooting Your Site 150

Bringing Your HTML Site to Life 150

Adding a Splash Screen to Your Site 151

CHAPTER 7
CREATING GAMES 153

ShapeMatch 153

Creating the Graphics   154

    Background   *155*

    Score Board   *155*

    Reset Button   *156*

    ShapeMatch Graphic   *157*

    Grid   *157*

    Tiles   *158*

    You Win!   *161*

Adding the Code   161

Flash Tennis **168**

Creating the Graphics   168

    Walls   *169*

    Background   *171*

Score Bar	171
Ball	173
Paddles	174
Adding the Code	175
Player Paddle	175
Computer Paddle	175
Ball	176

CHAPTER 8

Exporting Your Files from Flash 181

Exporting Movies 181

About the SWF File Format	182
Load Order	184
Generate size report	184
Protect from import	184
Omit Trace actions	184
Debugging Permitted	184
Password Field	184
JPEG Quality	184
Audio Stream and Event	185

CONTENTS

    Override sound settings   185

    Version   185

  Flash for Video   185

    Exporting Quicktime Movies   185

Exporting a Single Frame 187

Publishing Your Movie 188

  Using the Publish Feature   188

    Template   188

    Dimensions   196

    Playback   196

    Quality   197

    Window Mode   198

    HTML Alignment   198

    Scale   199

  Using Dreamweaver   199

  Using the Macromedia Flash Deployment Kit   200

Understanding the HTML Behind Your Movie 203

  Creating Basic HTML for a Site   203

  Using Javascript Plug-in Detection   204

  Plug-in Detection Using Flash   206

CHAPTER 9

SHRINKING YOUR FILE SIZE 207

Finding Trouble Spots 207

Bandwidth Profiler — 208

Streaming Graph — 208

Frame by Frame Graph — 209

Size Report — 212

Optimizing Imported Bitmap Files 214

Affecting File Size with Fonts 215

Streamlining Shapes 216

Using MP3 Audio Compression 218

CHAPTER 10

TIPS AND TECHNIQUES 221

Using Javascript to Open and Close Browser Windows 221

Opening a Window — 222

Closing a Window — 223

Working with Framesets 224

Layering Movies 226

    Audio in a Level   226

    Turning that Audio On and Off   228

    Faking Video in Flash   231

Loading Screens 235

Pausing Your Movie 237

All You Need to Know About Masks 241

    Spotlighting Effect   241

    Building a Wipe with a Mask   241

Text Fields and Forms 243

    Using External Text Files   243

    HTML Text in Flash   245

    Scrolling Text   245

    Using Text Files to Hold Your URLs   247

    Using Forms for Calculations   248

Dragging Items 250

    Dragging a Movie Clip   250

    Dragging Products to a Shopping Cart   252

Swish: A PC-only text animator 257

Projectors 259

Screen savers 259

Index 261

INTRODUCTION

Macromedia Flash has exploded onto the Web development scene. Every day more Web developers and companies choose to use Flash on their site in one form or another. This book offers a way for you to sharpen and expand you skills by adding Flash to your resume.

TARGET AUDIENCE

This book is for anyone interested in creating dynamic and more interesting sites—particularly intermediate to advanced developers. If you are not part of this group do not be scared off because there is something in here for you as well. You will need to work a little harder to understand some of the concepts, but the benefits to you and your career are worth it. Trust me: I have spent many late nights learning programs.

It doesn't matter if you are a designer or a programmer, you will find the examples in this book helpful. Flash works well with most of today's programs, such as Macromedia's FreeHand, Fireworks, and Dreamweaver, and Adobe's Photoshop, and Illustrator. If you work with these programs, it will be easier for you to pick up and understand Flash.

WHAT YOU WILL FIND IN THIS BOOK

This book will show you how to build Web sites, games and other applications using Flash by covering all the components of Flash and how they can be used in various situations you might encounter.

Chapters 1 through 5 go into depth on topics like creating graphics, importing graphics, animating, using audio, and writing ActionScripts. Chapter 1 focuses on what has changed since Flash 4 and what is new with Flash 5. Chapter 2 shows you how Flash works with graphics. You will see how some of the tools work and what makes them unique. You will also learn how to import your graphics from many of today's popular graphics applications. Chapter 3 shows you how to animate the graphics that you have created or imported into Flash. You will learn about Shape Morphs and animating your graphics along a path. Chapter 4 deals with audio and goes into depth on how Flash works with audio. You will learn how to import audio and how to control the audio once it is imported. Chapter 5 gives you a look at ActionScript, which is the programming language used in Flash. There are examples that feature some of the new ActionScripts and include explanations of how the code needs to be written.

Chapters 6 and 7 give you examples on building whole projects. Chapter 6 will lead you through the building of an entire site and it even offers some tips on how to spruce up your current site by adding Flash. Chapter 7 shows you how to make games using Flash. This chapter features *ShapeMatch*, a classic memory game, and Flash Tennis, which is based on the classic arcade game Pong. These games include lengthy instructions on how to build the graphics and ActionScripts to make the games work.

Chapters 8 and 9 deal with the topics of exporting your file from flash and how to trim the file size of your final product. Chapter 8 gives you insight into the Publish feature in Flash as well as how to write your own code from scratch or with Dreamweaver. Chapter 9 shows you how to get a detailed look into your file and how to trim the file size of your final movie.

Chapter 10 gives you a range of examples that will fit almost any need. You will find examples that show you how to control audio with ActionScript, pause your movie, preload you file, use HTML in Flash, create scrolling text fields, and create movie clips that you can drag around the screen. These are just a few of the great examples you will find in this chapter.

BEFORE YOU BEGIN

You should be aware of a few things before you begin reading this book. You will notice there are Figures, Tables, Tips, Notes, and Warnings throughout the book.

CONVENTIONS

- Figures and Tables—Figures often show you how things are supposed to look and other times will show you how menus need to be set up. Tables will help you by listing file formats, accepted tags, etc.
- Tips—These tips and tricks will help you make your project better or help you work faster.
- Notes—These sections are more detailed explanations of what is being said in an example or paragraph. They should be read for more insight into the current topic.
- Warnings—These comments are designed to warn you about areas where most people are prone to make mistakes. You will find these useful when you are troubleshooting your site for mistakes.

ONLINE HELP

I have posted some of the examples from the book online at www.jpgraphics.net. Please check back often, as I will continue to add new examples when I get the free time.

You can also contact me with questions or comments at Flash5Primer@jpgraphics.net. If you would like to see an example that is not in the book or not online, please feel free to email me and I will try to post it as soon as I can.

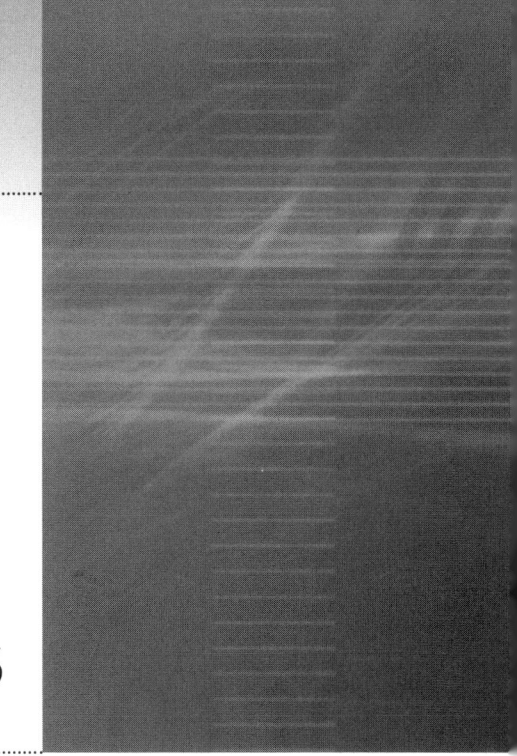

ACKNOWLEDGMENTS

This is a long list, and I don't want to leave anyone off. So to be safe, I am going to start off by saying I am sorry if I missed anyone and promise to add your name in the next revision of the book. Let's dive in and acknowledge the people that played a direct role in helping me get this book to press.

First, I would like to thank Dennis and Jason of PFS New Media for introducing me to Tim Moore, my acquisitions editor. Thanks to Tim for giving me a shot at writing. Next, I need to thank Jim Markham, my development editor, for helping me organize the book and make it the best it can be. Thanks to Erik Poulsen, my tech reviewer for helping me tighten up the book from the technical aspect. For helping me down the homestretch, I have to thank Donna Cullen-Dolce, my production editor.

This is a special group of people without whose vast knowledge this book would not have turned out as well. The first person had to put up with my questions since I started in the industry and has always been there for me when I needed his help. Jose Rodriquez (www.JRVisuals.com) has not only been a great help with this book but in my career. Thanks again, Jose, for all your help, especially in creating Flash Tennis! Next, I have to thank Mike Keszkowski (www.sourcecodecentral.com) for allowing me to use his ASP code in one of my examples in the book. Also, I would like to thank Mike for providing me with all the code for the message board and email applications that I will be making part of my site. I can't forget Darin Galgano and Jeff Martini, whose input helped me set up the content of the book.

The following group of people had to put up with me on a daily basis: My Mom and Dad, Eric, James, Kelley, and Kelley's family. I love you all. Thanks for all your support and for putting up with me while I was writing till all hours of the night.

Next, I need to thank the staff of JMCP Touch Interactive for being so flexible with my hours and supportive of me while I was writing.

I also need to thank my close friends Bob, Jen, Bill, Jaime, Steve, and Derek. You put up with my constant complaining about writing and my excuses when I couldn't hang out on weekends because I needed to work on the book. You all mean so much to me. Thanks a lot for being there.

chapter 1

WHAT'S NEW IN FLASH 5?

Because Flash 5 is a *major* upgrade from Flash 4 that offers so many improvements, it might be easier to write about what hasn't changed. I understand that this would not be helpful, so this chapter introduces all of the features that are new or have been improved in Flash 5. The features introduced in this chapter are used in different scenarios throughout the book, which is why it is important to become at least familiar with the functions of each of the panels and windows.

This chapter covers ways to customize Flash to help you work faster. This chapter also provides useful insight into the new panels and windows that you will need to know about to work in Flash 5. The panels and windows play a major part in how efficiently you will be able to work. The better you understand the function of each, the faster and better you will be able to create your own projects.

The chapter winds up with looks at the upgraded libraries and some of the new features. The libraries have been revamped in Flash 5 to offer new symbols and audio clips. If you are familiar with Flash 4, you will notice that more libraries have been added to Flash 5. These libraries are called Learning Interactions and Smart Clips. They contain some useful features that are covered in this chapter as well as later in the book. The new features that are introduced at the end of this chapter are creating font symbols, importing MP3 files, and using XML with Flash.

So, without further delay, let's look at the new Preferences menu as well as the Keyboard Shortcuts menu.

MAKING FLASH WORK FOR YOU

In Flash 5, you have more preferences than in Flash 4, and you have the ability to edit and create keyboard shortcuts for any menu item. You will see how changing some of these preferences and creating a few keyboard shortcuts will help you work faster and more efficiently.

PREFERENCES

I am only covering a few of the preferences that I feel are going to help you most when you are working. To see the preferences in Flash 5, you have to go to a new place in the menus. Choose Edit -> Preferences to bring up the Preferences window you see in Figure 1-1. You will notice right away there are more options than in Flash 4.

Flash has tabs that break down the Preferences window into three categories: General, Editing, and Clipboard. There are some slight differences between the Preferences windows, but nothing really significant. The most noticeable difference is a platform-specific issue dealing with printing. The menu is Printing Options, and it can only be found in the PC Preferences window under the General tab. For those who have used Flash 4, you might find the ability to set the selection style and frame drawing back to the way they worked in Flash 4 useful. Some people really do not like the

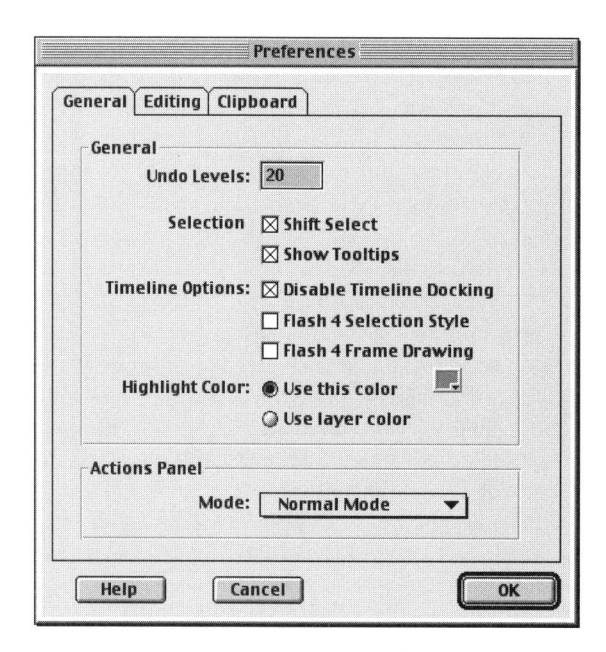

Figure 1-1 New Preferences window in Flash 5.

way that Flash 5 selects frames, so this will help them adjust to the new version. The Selection Style and Frame Drawing options are located in the Timeline section under the General tab of the Preferences window.

When you look at the menus under the Editing tab, you should notice the addition of the Assistant menu from Flash 4 into this window. The Assistant menu contained items such as Connect Lines, Smooth Curves, and Click Accuracy. All of the menus that now reside in the Preferences window under the Editing tab have retained all their features. The only difference is that the Snap to Grid feature has been removed. Other than that, you still have the ability to change the settings of the remaining menus to help you when you are designing and editing images. Also, there are settings for the new Pen tool. I personally like to make sure that all the options in the Pen Tool section are checked because they all make it easier to use the Pen tool. How to use the Pen tool is covered in Chapter 2.

When you look at the menus under the Clipboard tab, you will see a new section for FreeHand. This feature will keep the text that is imported from FreeHand as text blocks, basically leaving them editable. This is a great time-saver if you use FreeHand. This completes our look at the preferences for Flash.

KEYBOARD SHORTCUTS

This is a great new feature in Flash which allows you to edit and add new keyboard shortcuts. All you have to do is choose Edit -> Keyboard Shortcuts (Figure 1-2).

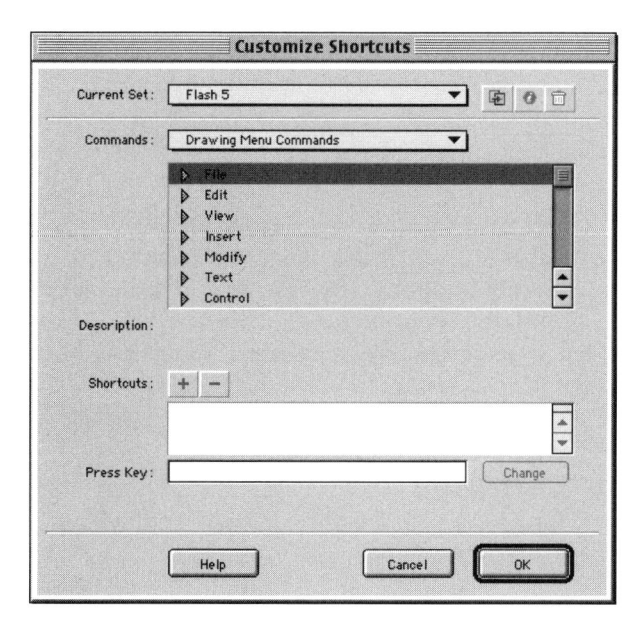

Figure 1-2 Customize Shortcuts window.

This window allows you duplicate the standard set for Flash 5 and make changes to it. You can customize any menu while you are in Drawing mode or Test Movie mode. You can also customize keys that will jump to any of your drawing tools. This is one feature that can help speed up your production time.

UNDERSTANDING THE PANELS AND WINDOWS

In Flash 5, Macromedia has combined the windows, Inspectors, and new menus to make up all the panels. If you are familiar with Flash 4, you will remember the Inspectors that consisted of Object, Frame, Transform, and Scene. These have all been incorporated into panels in one form or another, except for the Frame Inspector. This function is now a window called Movie Explorer, which we will cover later in this chapter.

PANELS

When you open Flash for the first time, the panels will show up in their default positions. If you look in the Window menu, you will see two menus in the Panels section that are called Panel Sets and Save Panel Layout. The functions of these menus are pretty self-explanatory; they allow you to save the panels in any layout that you like. This is great when you are working in an office environment where the computers are shared. If someone changes the layout of your panels, you can bring up your layout by selecting it from the Panel Sets menu.

There are 17 panels in Flash: Info, Fill, Stroke, Transform, Align, Mixer, Swatches, Character, Paragraph, Text Options, Instance, Effect, Clip Parameters, Frame, Sound, Scene, and Generator. I am going to run through these panels quickly to give you an idea of what each one does.

Info Panel

The Info panel (Figure 1-3) will show you the width, height, and X and Y position of a selected graphic that is on the Stage. The X and Y position of the symbol by default shows you the position of the upper left corner of the graphic. This can be changed to the center by clicking in the center of the box graphic located next to the X and Y windows. The bottom left side of the panel shows you the RGB color values of all shapes, but not of grouped objects, symbols, and bitmaps. You can also find out the X and Y position of the cursor at the bottom right of the Info panel.

Fill and Stroke Panels

The functions of these panels speak for themselves. The Fill panel lets you select the color and type of fill you want to use on a shape. (Figure 1-4) You have a choice of

CHAPTER 1 • WHAT'S NEW IN FLASH 5?

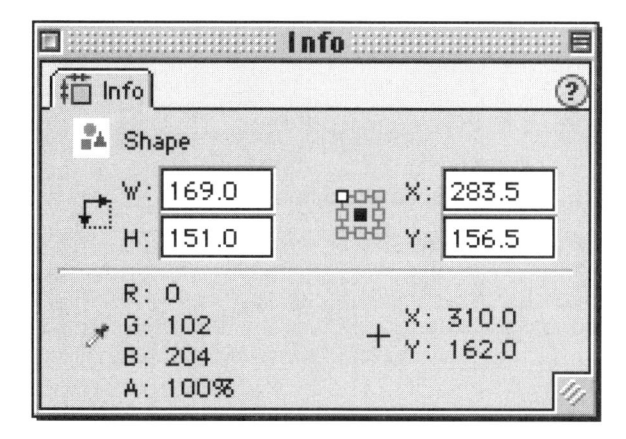

Figure 1-3   Info panel.

None, Solid, Linear Gradient, Radial Gradient, and Bitmap. At the right corner of the menu, you can add gradients you have created into the Swatches panel.

The Stroke panel lets you select the color, type, and thickness of the stroke you apply to an image. "Stroke" is a term used for the outline of an image. The stroke can be manipulated to create a thick or thin border around an image. This is very helpful when you want a shape to stand out over a background that has a similar color. Figure 1-5 shows the types of strokes that are available in Flash.

> **Warning**
> If you are concerned about the final file size of your product, then I would use strokes that are not solid sparingly. Because of their complex shapes, they add quickly to your final file size.

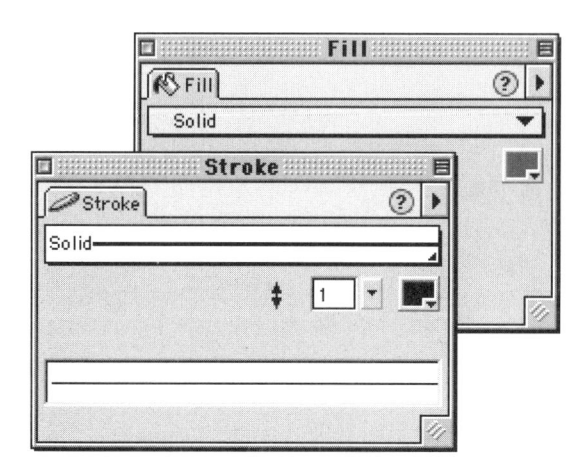

Figure 1-4   Fill and Stroke panels.

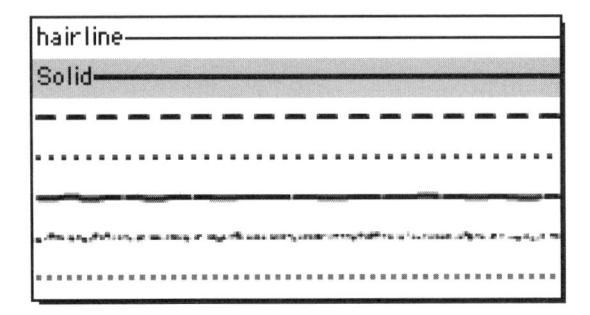

Figure 1-5 Types of strokes available in the Stroke panel.

Transform Panel

The Transform panel (Figure 1-6) allows you to control the width, height, rotation, and skew of a graphic. There are two cool, almost hidden features in this panel. At the bottom right corner of the window, you will see two buttons. The one on the left copies images and sets them to the same settings. It will place the copy right on top of the original. The button on the right will reset the copy or the original back to its original state if it is a symbol or object.

Align Panel

The Align panel is very helpful when you are creating graphics in Flash (Figure 1-7). I only wish that more applications had an Align tool that was this useful. As you can see by Figure 1-7, you have the ability to align your graphics vertically and horizontally to each other or the Stage. You can also distribute, space, and match the size of

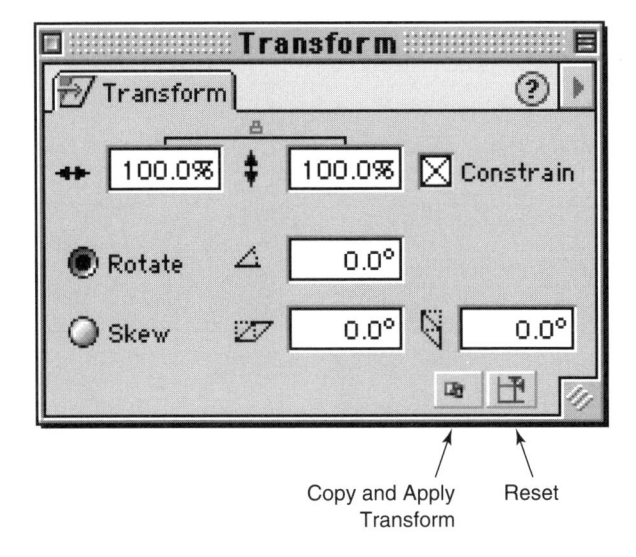

Figure 1-6 Transform panel.

CHAPTER 1 • WHAT'S NEW IN FLASH 5?

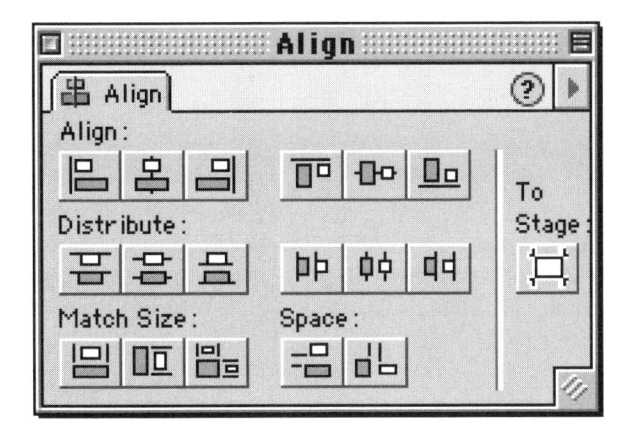

Figure 1-7   Align panel.

graphics. These features are very useful when you are creating buttons and other types of navigation elements.

Mixer and Swatches Panels

The next panels on our list are the Mixer and Swatches panels (Figure 1-8). These two panels are where you can create and save all of your colors. In the Mixer panel, you can choose the colors for the stroke and fill of an object. You can choose these colors from the RGB, HSB, or Hexadecimal color mode. You can even alter the Alpha (transparency) of the colors. If you find a color you think you will be using often, you can save it in the Swatches panel.

The Swatches panel is a storage area for all the swatches you have created and the default color palette of Flash. In the arrow menu, you can select from Duplicate

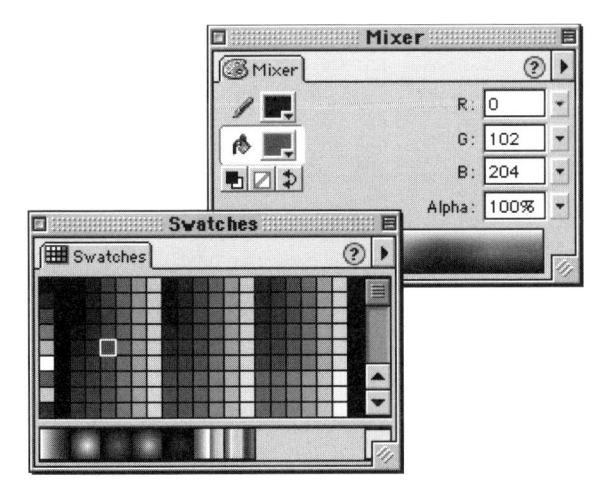

Figure 1-8   Mixer and Swatches panels.

Swatch, Delete Swatch, Add Colors, Replace Colors, Load Default Colors, Save Colors, Save as Default, Clear Colors, Web 216, and Sort by Color. This gives you the flexibility to customize your palette for certain jobs or to the way you work.

Character, Paragraph, and Text Options Panels

These panels work hand in hand, so I have grouped them together (Figure 1-9) in one section. The Character panel allows you to choose the font, size, tracking, kerning, color, script, and URL for your text. The Tracking feature allows you to control the spacing in between selected letters. The Kerning checkbox allows you to either use or not use the particular font's built-in kerning information. The Script feature sets the type to normal, superscript, or subscript. In the URL field, you can type in a URL and make the text work as a text link. This is very similar to a hyperlink in an HTML page. The URL entered in this field will not be visible to the viewer of the file; it will merely provide the address for the text to link.

The Paragraph panel allows you to customize how you want a paragraph of text to appear: aligned left, center, right, or justified. You can also set the line spacing and indentation of the text.

The Text Options panel is one of more important panels if you are working with text fields and/or imported text. The main menu in this panel allows you to choose from Static Text, Dynamic Text, and Input Text. You can use the Static Text option for any graphics and text you are creating that will not be affected by the user or another source. You will want to select Dynamic Text if you are planning to import text from an outside source. Notice how the menus change when you select the Dynamic Text option (Figure 1-10). You now have the choice of forcing the text to stay on one line or allowing it to go to multiple lines. The main difference between single-line and multi-line mode is whether you want Flash to wrap the text or not. The Variable field is very important because this is how you will name the field and have the external source send the text. There is also the option to allow HTML text in the field. I go over this in greater detail in Chapter 10. You can let your text have a black border and white background if you want the traditional text field look. You also have the option of letting

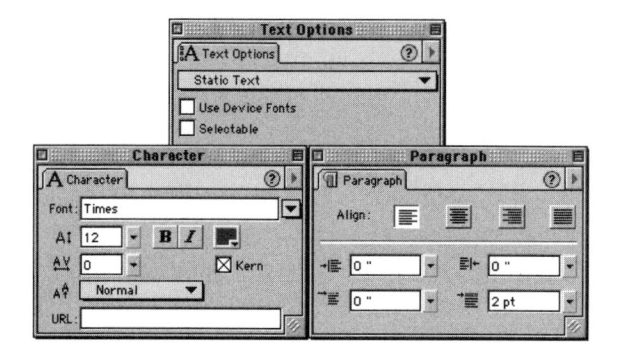

Figure 1-9   Text Options, Character, and Paragraph panels.

CHAPTER 1 • WHAT'S NEW IN FLASH 5?

Figure 1-10 The Text Options panel with Dynamic Text selected.

your text be selectable or not. The last option in this window is the Embed Fonts menu, and it allows you to select specific or all characters, numbers, and letters to be embedded into a Flash movie.

Instance and Effect Panels

These panels (Figure 1-11) only work with symbols, which I discuss in greater detail later in the book. When you click a symbol that is on the stage, you will see the Instance panel change to reflect the symbol and its behavior. For example, when you

Swap Symbol Edit Symbol Duplicate Symbol Edit Actions

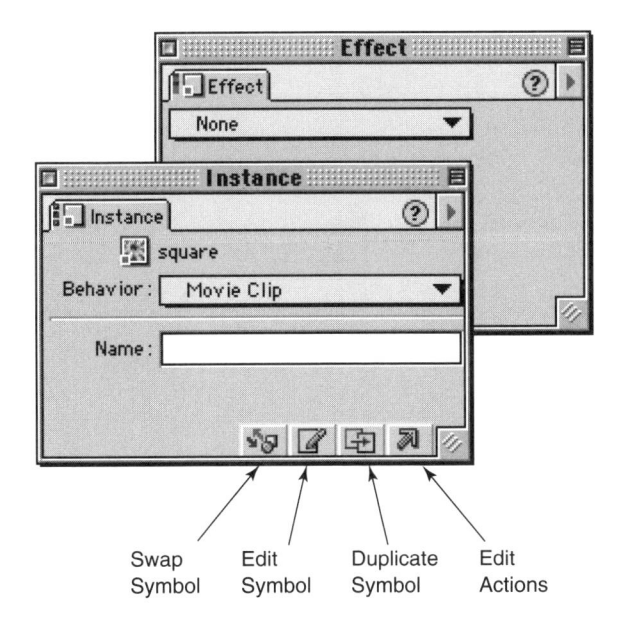

Figure 1-11 The Instance and Effect panels.

click a Movie Clip symbol, you will see the panel update to show the Behavior as Movie Clip and the name of the movie if there is one. This Name field is used for ActionScript so that you can use movie clip actions.

You will notice four buttons at the bottom of the panel. The first button is the Swap Symbols button. This is very useful when you need to update a graphic on the Stage. All you have to do is select the symbol, click this button, and choose another symbol from the library. The next button is the Edit Symbol button, which sends the clip into Symbol Editing mode so you can edit it in its Timeline. The third button is the Duplicate Symbol button, which allows you to duplicate a particular symbol and rename it. The last button is the Edit Actions button, which opens the Actions window with the actions for that symbol, if there are any.

The Effect panel is used to apply one of the built-in effects to a symbol. You can choose from None, Brightness, Tint, Alpha, or Advanced as your effect. Using these effects, you can reuse a symbol and have it look different in every instance by changing its color and/or transparency.

Clip Parameters Panel

The Clip Parameters panel is used when you are working with Smart Clips. When you select a Smart Clip that is on the Stage, you will see the Clip Parameters window update with some parameters and a description (Figure 1-12). I will discuss Smart Clips in greater detail later in this chapter.

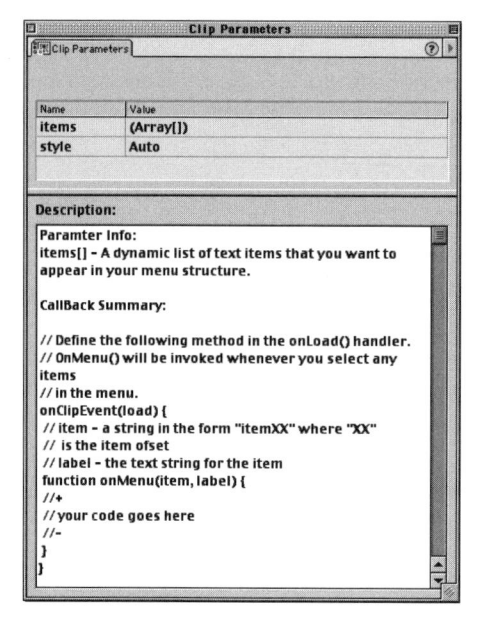

Figure 1-12 Clip Parameters panel when selecting a Smart Clip.

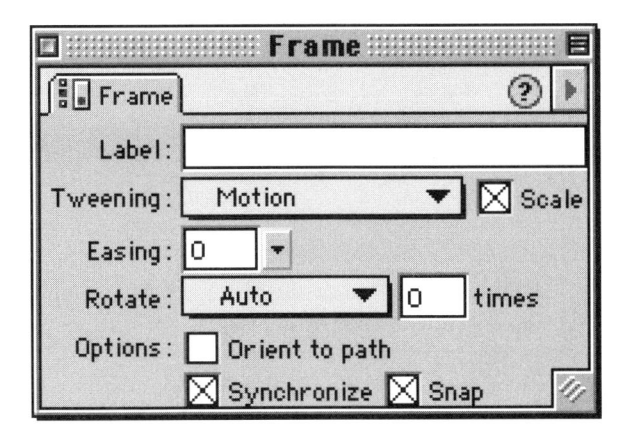

Figure 1-13 Frame panel with Motion Tweening selected.

Frame Panel

The Frame panel, as you might have guessed, works with frames (Figure 1-13). This window allows you to set frame labels and tweening between two keyframes. Tweening is discussed in more detail in Chapter 3.

Sound Panel

The Sound panel is used for adding, selecting, and editing audio tracks (Figure 1-14). The features of this window are described in greater detail in Chapter 4.

Scene Panel

The Scene panel is used to help you keep track of multiple scenes (Figure 1-15). With the three buttons at the bottom of the window, you can duplicate, add, and delete scenes. You can also drag scenes around to change the order in which they will appear.

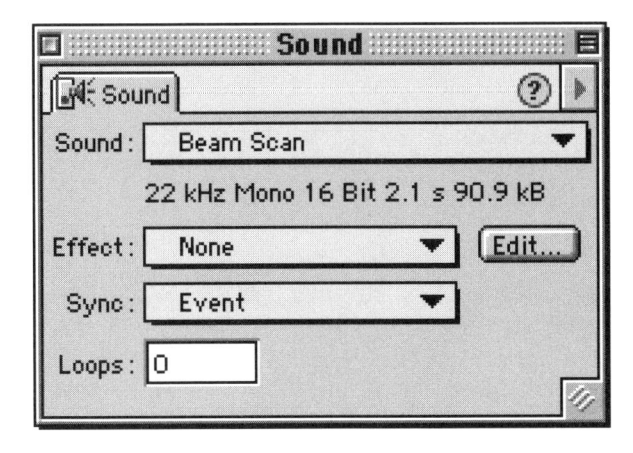

Figure 1-14 Sound panel.

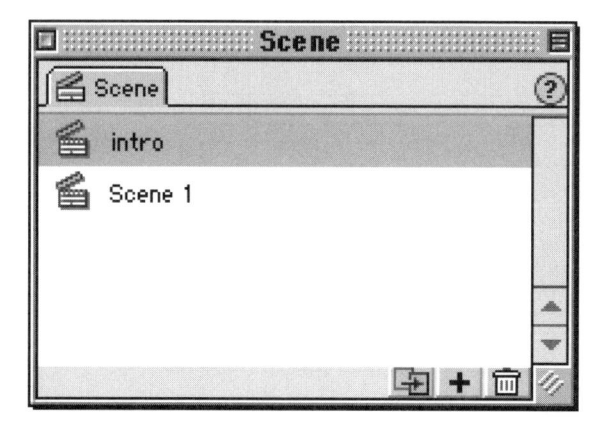

Figure 1-15   Scene panel.

Since you can control all the scenes but one by using ActionScripts, you really only need to make sure that you have your intro scene on top.

Generator Panel

The Generator panel can only be used if you have downloaded or installed the Generator templates from Macromedia (Figure 1-16). You can use this panel to set up your generator objects that you place on the Stage.

If you do not have the templates installed, you will see the panel in Figure 1-17.

This completes our look at all the new panels. Now we are going to see all the new windows and libraries in Flash 5.

WINDOWS

This section covers all the new features added to the windows, as well as covering the new windows that have been added. The new windows are the Movie Explorer and Debugger. First, we will cover the changes to the Tools (Toolbar), Stage, Actions, and Output windows, then we will move on to the new windows.

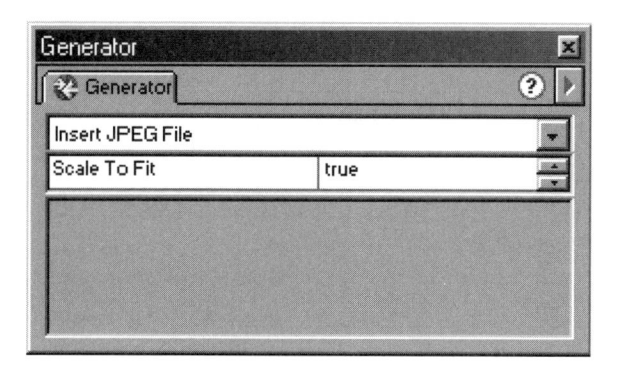

Figure 1-16   Generator panel with templates installed and in use.

Figure 1-17   Generator panel without templates installed.

Toolbar

First on our list of the revamped interface is the Toolbar (Figure 1-18). This change to the Toolbar was done to make users of other Macromedia software feel more comfortable using Flash.

The first thing you will notice is that the Toolbar is much more organized because it is broken down into sections: Tools, View, Colors, and Options. The next thing you will probably notice is the addition of two new tools. The Pen and Subselect tools are used for creating or editing shapes by their points. The Colors section definitely makes life easier for me because it is a lot like Illustrator. This section gives you the option to set the fill and stroke to black and white, no color, or swap the colors—all of this with the three buttons located at the bottom of the Colors section.

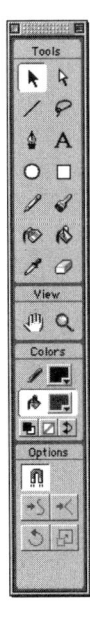

Figure 1-18   The new Toolbar.

Stage

Next you will notice the Stage window and its new menu located at the bottom right corner (Figure 1-19). This menu is called the Launcher Bar and it contains links to the Info, Mixer, Character, and Instance panels, as well as links to the Movie Explorer, Actions, and Library windows. You can also hide any of these panels or windows by using the Launcher Bar. The bottom left corner of the window features a menu that shows you the magnification level of the Stage. You can adjust how magnified the Stage is by selecting or typing in a new percentage.

If you choose View -> Rulers, you will notice that you can now create guides by dragging off of the rulers. These guides can be locked down or they can be editable. By default, the guides are set up to be editable and to have objects snap to them. This is another great addition to the Stage window.

Actions Window

The Actions window received a major overhaul in Flash 5 (Figure 1-20). You will notice right away the difference and how much easier it is to write and look at code in the new window because it is expandable.

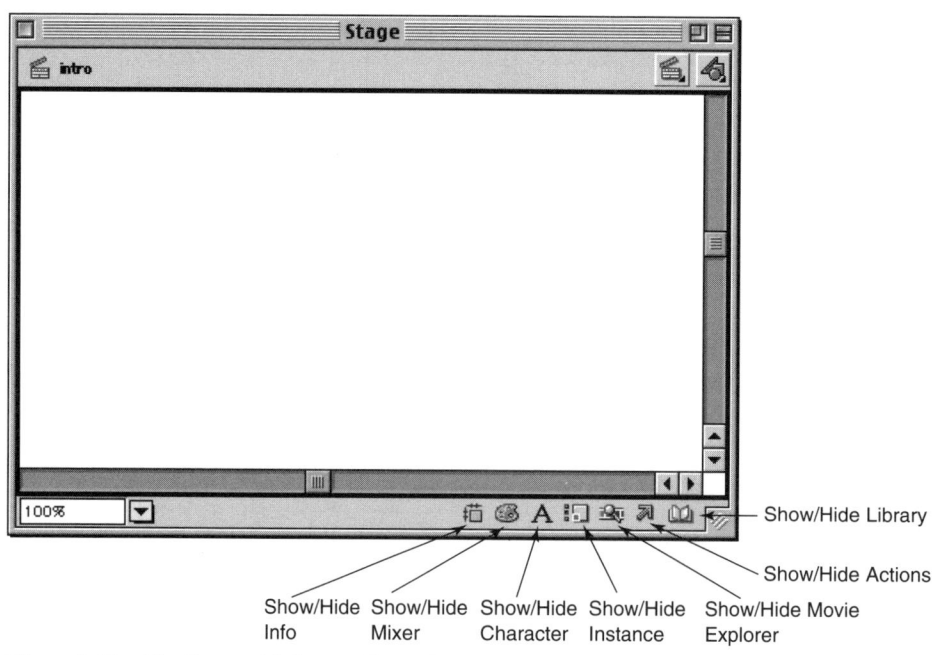

Figure 1-19   The Stage with its new Launcher Bar and Magnification menu on the bottom.

CHAPTER 1 • WHAT'S NEW IN FLASH 5? 15

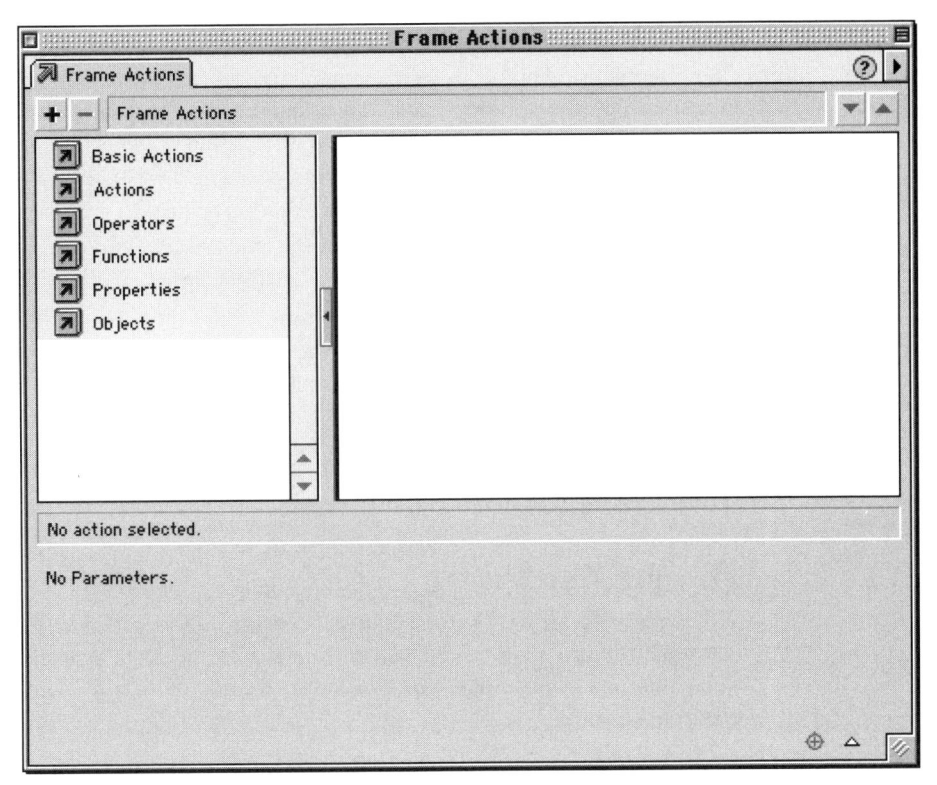

Figure 1-20   Actions window.

The biggest change to this window is the expansion of ActionScript, which I cover in Chapter 5. If you click on the right arrow menu, you will see some options that we did not have before. Most of these options will make it easier for you to learn and work with ActionScript. First, we have Normal and Expert modes, which allow for different styles of working. If you are a beginner, I definitely suggest that you leave this set to Normal mode because it will show you where you need to fill in a variable or clip name. The next section of this window is set up to help you edit and fix your code. The Check Syntax option is great because it tells you exactly where your code has a problem. The third section deals with importing and exporting scripts. You might like to work in another application when you are coding, so Flash allows you to import files into the Actions window. The last section is all about working in the window. The colored syntax will make it much easier for you to read and learn ActionScripting. The Show Deprecated Syntax option will highlight older actions that have been replaced by newer actions.

Output Window

The Output window is the simplest window, but it is very helpful, especially when you are in Test Movie mode because you can have all the variables and objects of a movie listed in the window. All you have to do is choose Debug -> List Objects of List Variables.

Movie Explorer Window

The Movie Explorer window allows you to list all the elements of a movie (Figure 1-21). The Show menu allows you to turn on and off what gets shown in the window below it. For example, you have the ability to look at all the text, symbols, ActionScript, imported sounds and bitmaps, frames, and layers. If this is too much, you can just do a search for the item you are looking for using the Find feature. A good use for the Movie Explorer window is to create a site map when you have multiple people working on a site. This will allow people to find trouble areas more quickly and speed up your production time.

Debugger Window

To debug your movie, you can choose Control -> Debug Movie (Figure 1-22). This will open your movie into Test Movie mode with the Debugger active. As you are clicking through your movie, you will have the opportunity to check your symbols, variables, and scripts.

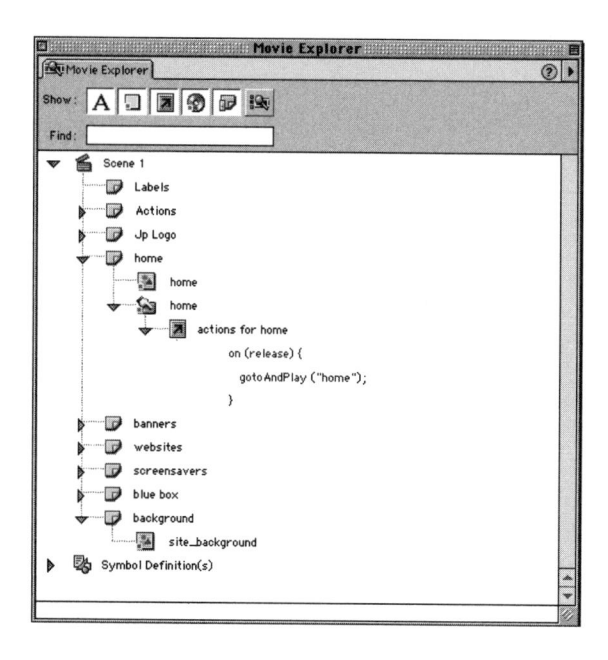

Figure 1-21 Movie Explorer window.

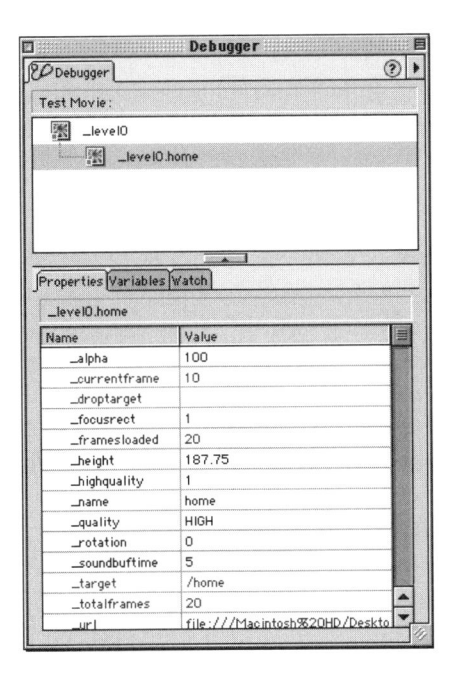

Figure 1-22   The Debugger window in use, looking at the properties of a movie clip.

NEW LIBRARY FEATURES

There are some new libraries included in Flash 5 and they are located in Window -> Common Libraries. The Buttons, Graphics, Movie Clips, and Sounds libraries are straightforward, but worth looking at for ideas. There are some cool buttons and sounds in these libraries. You can now also add your very own libraries permanently into Flash as well as share libraries between projects and movies. The two libraries that need more explanation are Learning Interactions and Smart Clips. We will start with how to import and share libraries, then we will move onto the new libraries.

IMPORTING AND SHARING LIBRARIES

There are really three things about libraries that are discussed in this chapter, so I will define them up-front so there will be no confusion as you are reading through this section. The first thing that is covered is how to create a permanent library from one of your files. The second section covers how to import a movie as a library. The third shows you how to set up a file to share some of its library items with other movies and then how to make another movie call this movie to retrieve the symbols. This should clear things up so that you will understand the difference between the next three sections.

Create Permanent Libraries

To create permanent libraries, you will need to move the symbols that you want to place in the Library into one movie file. I suggest that this file be stripped of all the files and animation that are not needed for the symbols that are going to be part of the Library. Once you have finished creating the final movie file, all you have to do is move the file into the Library's folder that is located in the Flash 5 Program folder on your hard drive. You do not need to restart Flash for this to take effect. The Library will automatically show up in the Common Libraries menu.

Importing your Movie as a Library

Sometimes you will need to borrow graphics from another movie file that you have created, but you do not want to make this file a permanent Library file. This is a very simple task; all you have to do is choose File -> Open as Library. This will open only the Library of the movie file you choose.

Sharing Library Files across Multiple Movies

This is a feature that will save you time and reduce your file size. This will also speed the download time of the site, because once the file loads for one movie, it will be loaded already when the next movie goes to use it. For this to work, you will need to follow the steps below, first setting up the sharing movie and then setting up the movie that will be calling the sharing movie. This example uses symbols, which are covered in more detail in Chapter 2.

1. Open a new file.
2. Choose Insert -> New Symbol; this will create a symbol.
3. Set the Behavior of the symbol to Graphic.
4. Choose Window -> Library to open the Library.
5. Control + click (right-click on a PC) on the symbol in the Library.
6. Select Linkage from the menu that appears; this opens the Symbol Linkage Properties window (Figure 1-23).

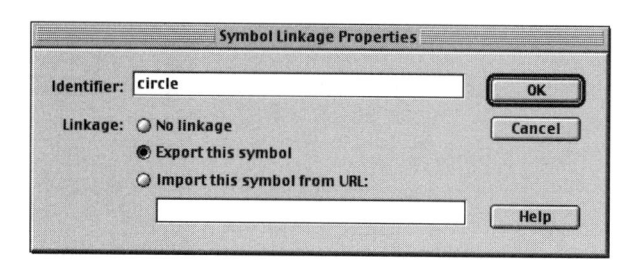

Figure 1-23   Symbol Linkage Properties window.

7. Choose Export this symbol in the Linkage section of this window.
8. Give the symbol a name that you can call it by when you go to import it.
9. Save the file and export a SWF file.

This completes our sharing movie. Now we will move onto our movie that will be calling this sharing movie to get this file. Make sure that you close the sharing movie before you begin the next example.

1. Open a new file.
2. Choose File -> Open as Shared Library. This opens the Library file of the shared movie.
3. Drag the symbol from the Library onto the Stage of the new movie.
4. If you open the Library of the new movie, you will see the symbol in the Library.
5. Control + click (right-click on a PC) on the symbol in the Library.
6. Select Linkage from the menu (Figure 1-24).
7. You will see that the file is set up to be imported from the SWF file of the movie. You should just make sure that the name and URL for the shared movie are correct. If the movies are in the same directory, all you need is the name of the SWF file in this field.

To test this file, open the movie in Test Movie mode (choose Control -> Test Movie).

LEARNING INTERACTIONS

This is really a cool library because you have six pre-built interactive questions. These questions are actually Smart Clips that you can customize to show a question and accept an answer (Figure 1-25).

When you open the Clip Parameters panel, you will be able to enter any questions and answers that you want (Figure 1-26). Also available in this menu are options to set the number of tries someone has to answer the question and the feedback that they will

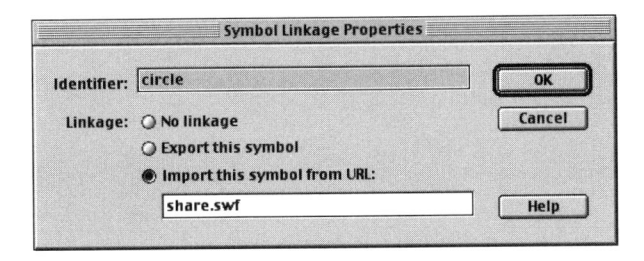

Figure 1-24 Symbol Linkage Properties window for the movie that is importing the shared file.

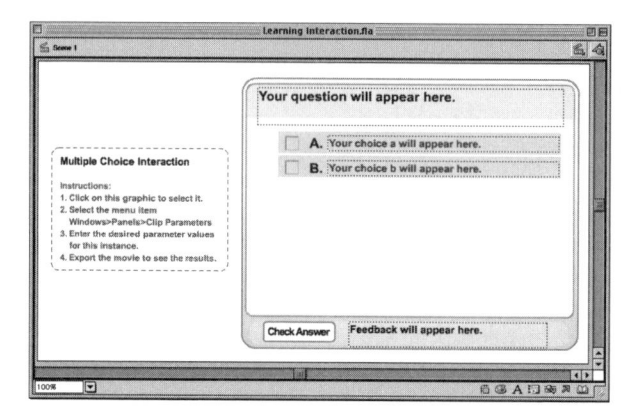

Figure 1-25   Multiple-choice interaction movie clip.

receive whether they are right or wrong. If you click the Tracking tab, you will see some menus that will be used only if you are collecting and sending these variables to an outside source like Active Server Pages (ASP) or Perl. If you are, you will want to click the Knowledge Track button and set up a variable that will refer to this question in the Objective ID field. The Weighting field refers to the amount of points a person will receive for answering a question correctly. When you click the Navigation tab, you will have options to turn the navigation off, enable the next button, or allow the question to automatically go to the next frame when it is completed.

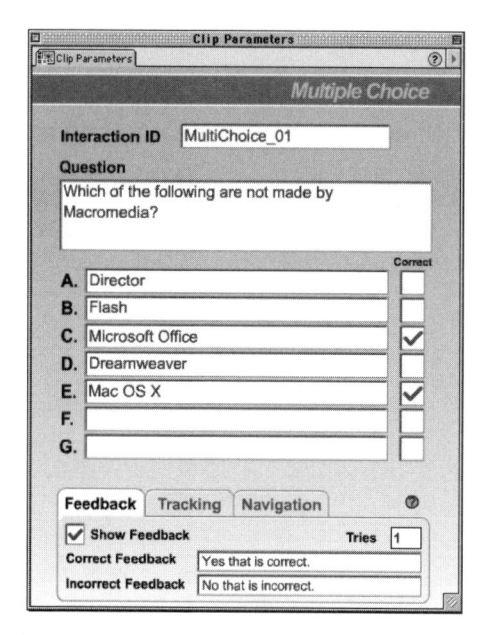

Figure 1-26   Clip Parameters panel for the Multiple Choice Interaction Movie Clip.

SMART CLIPS

Here you have the choices of the Checkbox, Radio Button, and List menus (Figure 1-27). All three of these menus have very complicated movie clips that are combined with ActionScript to detect the user's computer type and set up the buttons accordingly. For example, all the buttons have PC and Mac versions of their graphics so they will fit into a page no matter what system the end-user has. These clips are not as easy as I thought they would be to use, but I have figured out a way to work with them so I can get the results I want.

This example has some more advanced topics, like using Smart Clips and variables. These are covered in greater detail later in the book. This example is here to show how Smart Clips work and to show how you can work them into your files.

1. Open a new file.
2. Choose Window -> Common Libraries -> Smart Clips.
3. Drag the Menu clip onto the Stage from the Smart Clips Library window.
4. Select the Menu clip on the Stage.
5. Choose Window -> Panels -> Clip Parameters; this opens the Clip Parameters panel (Figure 1-28).
6. In the Clip Parameters panel, double-click the Array text that is in the Value column next to the item text. This opens a Values window (Figure 1-29).

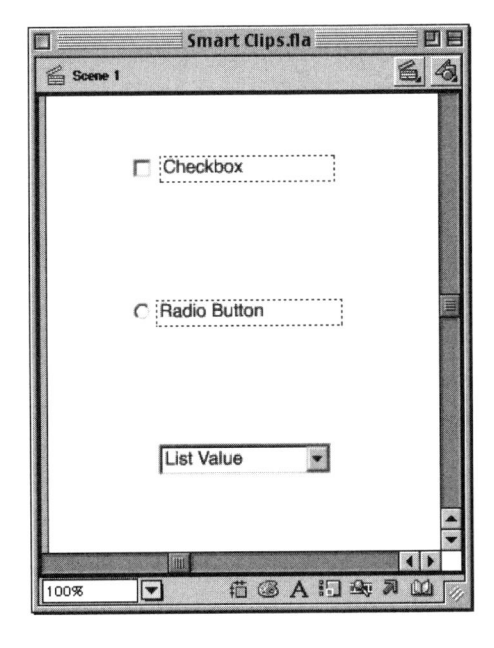

Figure 1-27 Smart Clips that are available in Flash 5.

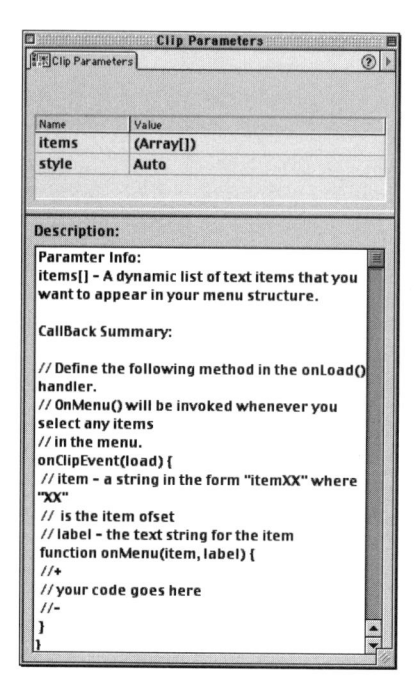

Figure 1-28 The Clip Parameters panel for the Menu clip.

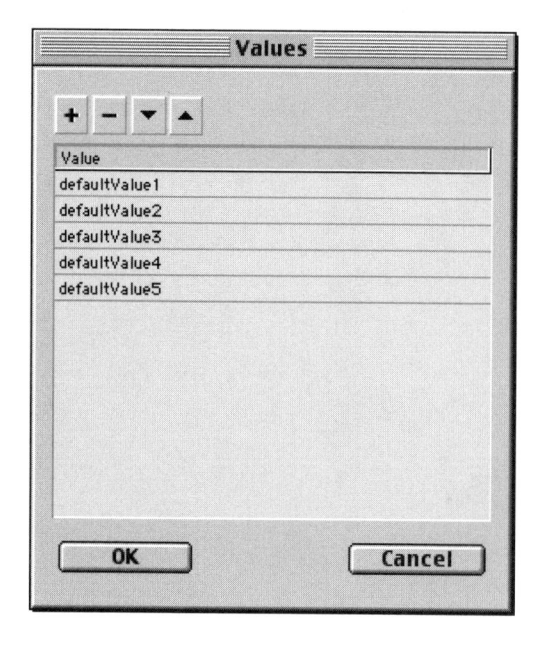

Figure 1-29 The Values window for the Menu clip.

7. The Values window is where you will set up the list that you want to appear in the pull-down menu.

> **Note:** The Style menu allows you to choose how the clip appears on the users machine. When this is set to default, the menu will check to see what system it is on and show the appropriate clip. You can also choose to lock the clip into either Mac or PC if you have a bias toward one or the other.

8. Choose Control -> Test Movie. This will allow you to test your movie to make sure the items appear correctly.
9. While in Test Movie mode, choose Debug -> List Variables.
10. This opens the Output window with the variables listed for the menu (Figure 1-30).
11. You will notice on about the fourth line that it will say something like:

    Variable **_level0.instance7.currentValue** = "defaultValue3"

    EBP: Parenthesis not present in script.

12. The bold part of this is the variable that you can use to find out what has been selected from the menu.

Now that you know how to get a variable for a menu, you can apply this to any ActionScripts that you need. You can duplicate the Menu clip on the Stage and Flash will automatically assign it a new variable that you can check in the same way we did with the first clip.

Figure 1-30 The variables for the Menu clip listed in the Output window.

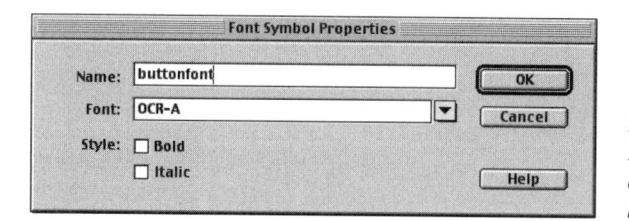

Figure 1-31 Font Symbols Properties window, where you can choose a Font and Style to be shared as a symbol.

OTHER NEW FEATURES

This section covers the leftover new features that did not fit so nicely into the previous sections of this chapter. I guess you could consider this sort of a miscellaneous section. We are going to be covering how to make font symbols, importing MP3 files, and XML and Flash.

MAKE FONT SYMBOLS

This is great when you have a text-heavy site that uses a few different movies. This is the same concept as sharing library files; basically, what this does is make a font of your choice a shared library item. Sometimes you just do not want to trust that an end-user has the fonts you want to use in your site and you do not want to embed the font in every movie. This will allow you to embed the font into one movie and the other movies can link to it for the font symbol.

1. Open a new file.
2. Choose Window -> Library; this opens the Library window.
3. Click on the menu in the top right-hand corner of the Library window.
4. Choose New Font (Figure 1-31).
5. Choose any font you want from the Font pull-down menu and give the font symbol a name so you will recognize it in the Library.
6. Control + click (right-click on a PC) on the new text symbol in the Library.
7. Choose Linkage from the menu (Figure 1-32).

Figure 1-32 Symbol Linkage Properties window.

8. Choose Export this symbol in the Linkage section of this window.
9. Give the symbol a name that you can call it by when you go to import it. The Identifier does not need to be the same as the name of the symbol.
10. Export the movie and save the file.

That completes our sharing movie. Now we need to set up our movie that will be linking to this movie to get the font symbol. Make sure that the shared movie created above is closed before you begin the next step.

1. Open a new file.
2. Choose File -> Open as Shared Library.
3. Select the shared movie you just created above.
4. The Library of this movie will appear with the file that has been set up to be shared.
5. Select the font symbol and drag it into the Library of the new movie.
6. Control + click (right-click on a PC) on the font symbol you just placed into the new file's Library.
7. Choose Linkage.
8. Double-check that the linkage properties are correct for this file.

This completes the sharing of this font. Now when you go to use the font in this new movie, it will not add to the file size of the movie because it will be linking out to the shared movie for the font.

IMPORT MP3 FILES

This is a good feature for people who like to use a lot of audio in their sites. The ability to import MP3 files will keep the working file and final movie file much smaller. Importing audio is covered in greater detail in Chapter 4.

XML AND FLASH 5

Flash 5 has integrated some XML action scripts that will allow you to communicate directly with XML from Flash. This will be a great feature to use in the future, and I guess that it will be good to learn now so you have a good understanding when XML is more widely accepted. The problem with this is that XML is only really supported on a PC using Internet Explorer 5.5 or higher. You can download the Flash Enterprise Kit for IE 5.5 from Macromedia to see some examples of how using XML will help you to better your site.

chapter 2

CREATING AND IMPORTING ARTWORK

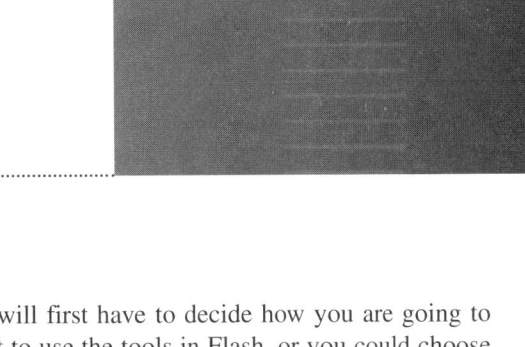

To build a project using Flash, you will first have to decide how you are going to create the graphics. You might want to use the tools in Flash, or you could choose one of the many design programs available such as Photoshop, Illustrator, FreeHand, or Fireworks.

This chapter starts off by showing you how similar Flash is to other programs that you may use. I have highlighted some key features of the Oval, Rectangle, Pen, Lasso, Ink Bottle, Paint Bucket, and Eraser tools. The next part of the chapter covers the four types of graphics found in Flash (shapes, grouped objects, symbols, and imported bitmaps). The chapter wraps up with an in-depth look at importing graphics from today's popular graphics applications.

This chapter will show you some tips for using the tools in Flash that will aid in your designing for Flash as well as speed up your production time. Understanding the tools will help you to work more efficiently—this is why I compare some of the tools in Flash to tools from other programs. These tools have similar functions to the tools found in Photoshop, Fireworks, Illustrator, and FreeHand.

You will also learn when and how to best use the different types of graphics found in Flash. For example, you will learn the benefits of the Movie Clip symbol and when it is best to use the Button symbol. You will learn which file formats work best when imported into Flash and which applications best prepare these imported files. This chapter covers these programs and shows you how to use them to create transparent bitmap files, such as GIF and PNG files, and import them into Flash. If you need higher resolution images, there are sections on PICT, BMP, and JPEG files. Enough build-up, let's jump right into it by learning about the key tools in Flash.

CREATING GRAPHICS IN FLASH WITH KEY TOOLS

The Oval, Rectangle, Pen, Lasso, Ink Bottle, Paint Bucket, and Eraser are the key tools I have selected because they are similar to those of other programs and will help you create your design (Figure 2-1).

However, some of these tools do not act like you would expect. For example, the Eraser tool that works like the eraser tool found in Photoshop. There is even a Pen tool that will make you think you are working in Illustrator. Knowing the features of these tools will also speed your production time. So, let's learn more about these tools and how they will help you work in Flash.

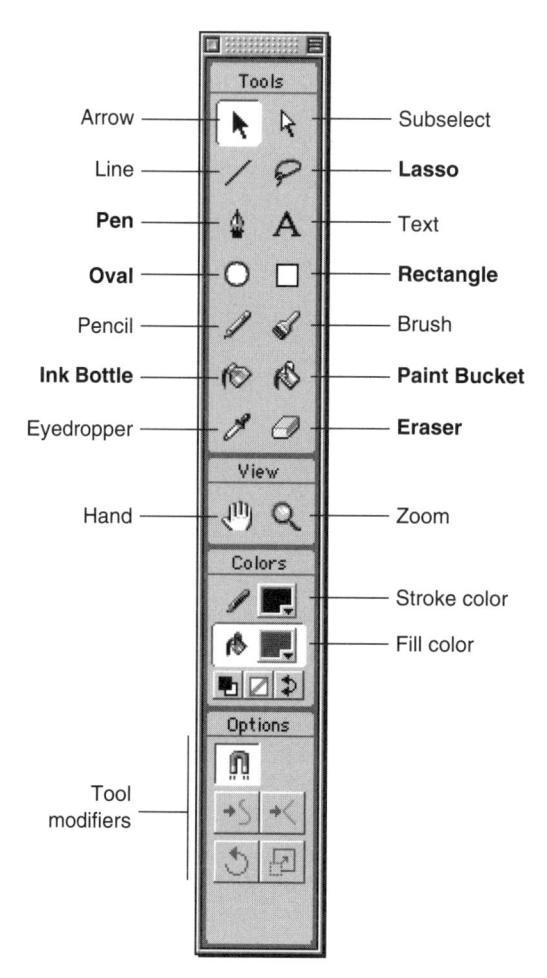

Figure 2-1 The tools we are covering in this chapter are called out.

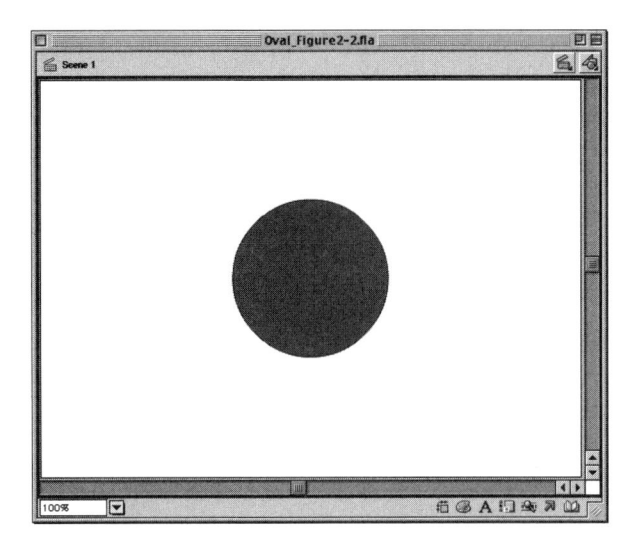

Figure 2-2   Circle drawn on the Stage with the automatic outline.

OVAL

This may seem like a very basic tool, but there are a few features worth covering. To best illustrate the features of the Oval, I will walk you through a couple of steps. Sometimes when using the Oval tool, you will want to create a perfect circle. To do this, you hold the Shift key when you are drawing an oval on the Stage. You will notice that the oval is constrained to a perfect circle no matter which way you move your mouse. This example will show you how to make a circle with a stroke.

1. Open a new file.
2. Select the Oval tool from the Toolbar.
3. Draw a circle on the Stage by holding the Shift key while you drag the Oval tool.

Notice that the circle automatically has a stroke on it (Figure 2–2). If you look at the Colors section of the Toolbar, you will see two color swatches. The top one represents the stroke, which by default is black, and the bottom swatch represents the fill, which is blue by default. To draw an oval without a stroke, you can select the stroke color (top swatch) and click the No Color icon (Figure 2-3).

Sometimes, you will also find the need to make an oval with just a stroke and no fill. To do this, you can just set the fill swatch to blank or no color and select the color you desire for the oval's stroke. You can also select the appearance of the stroke for the oval in the Stroke panel (Figure 2-4). The Stroke panel has menus that allow you to change the stroke style, stroke height, and stroke color.

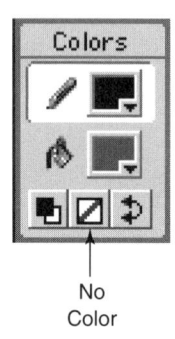

Figure 2-3 *The No Color icon is located under the fill color, in between the Default Colors icon and the Swap Colors icon.*

RECTANGLE

All of the features from the Oval tool also apply to the Rectangle tool. The Rectangle tool has one option that the Oval tool does not, however. This option is the Round Rectangle Radius menu, which lets you set the radius of the corners of the rectangle. This menu is located in the Options section of the Toolbar, which is under the Colors section. This option is only available when you have the Rectangle tool selected. A very common use for the Round Rectangle Radius option is for buttons. Many Web sites that you see have rectangular buttons with rounded corners. This example will show you a quick way to make this shape.

1. Open a new file.
2. Select the Rectangle tool from the Toolbar.
3. Click the Round Rectangle Radius button; this opens the Corner Radius text box.
4. Type 20 in the Corner Radius window and click OK.
5. Draw a rectangle on the Stage (Figure 2-5).

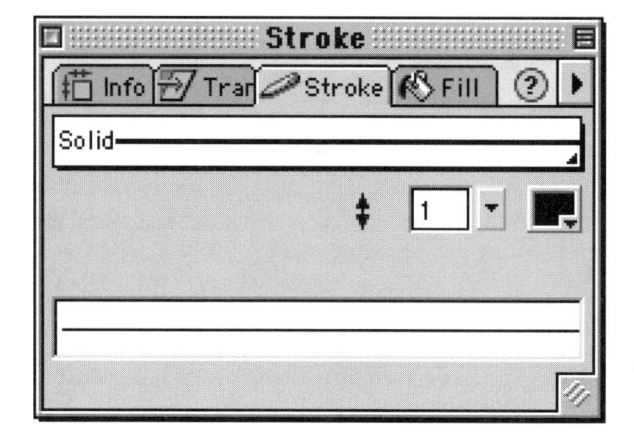

Figure 2-4 Stroke panel used for changing the look of the outline or lines you are creating.

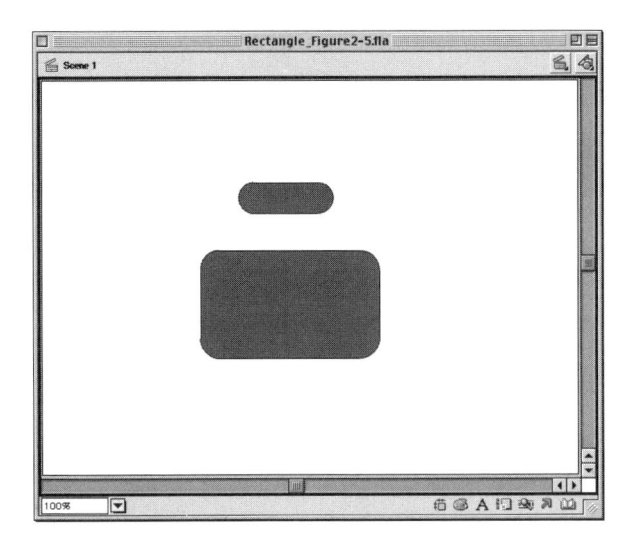

Figure 2-5   Two rectangles drawn with the Round Rectangle Radius field set to 20.

You will notice that the smaller rectangle looks like a pill, whereas the larger rectangle has a much different look with the same setting for the radius. The only drawback to this feature is there is no way to change the radius of the corners after you have drawn the rectangle. You will have to use trial and error to figure out what works best for each situation.

PEN

The Pen tool is new to Flash 5 and it incorporates some of the features that you might be familiar with if you use Illustrator or FreeHand. This tool allows you to draw with points so you can adjust the curve of a line more easily. This is known as drawing with Bezier points, which allow you to control a shape even after you have drawn it. You can always go back into a shape and select one of the points and change its position or angle. This is covered in the second example of this section. The first example will show you how to use the Pen tool to create a simple line. You can reuse the document from the previous example; all you have to do is select the image from the Stage and delete it.

1. Select the Pen tool.
2. Click on the left side of the Stage.
3. Press the Shift key and click on the right side of the Stage (Figure 2-6).
4. Press the Escape key or choose another tool to stop the Pen tool from trying to draw more points.

The examples in Figure 2-6 show lines and the use of points to control the lines and the arcs of the lines. You can make the Pen tool draw a perfectly straight line by pressing

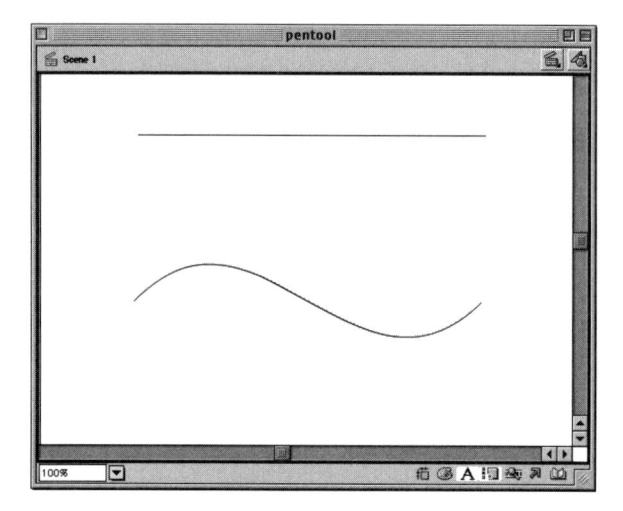

Figure 2-6 Examples of the Pen tool making straight lines and curved lines.

the Shift key when you click on the Stage. When holding the Shift key, the line you draw can be horizontal, vertical, or at a 45-degree angle. This next example will show you how to make a curved line like the one in Figure 2-6. You can reuse the document from the previous example by selecting the image from the Stage and deleting it.

1. Follow the instructions for creating a line with the Pen tool.
2. Choose the Subselect tool from the Toolbar.
3. Select the right point. The point will appear as a hollow square when you select it.
4. Option-click (or Alt-click on a PC) on the right point and press the Shift key while you drag down. This will allow you to drag a tangent handle off the point and add an arc to the line.
5. Select the left point.
6. Option-click (or Alt-click on a PC) on the left point and press the Shift key while you drag up on the tangent handle.

The outcome of this example should look like the curved line in Figure 2-6. As you can see, this tool allows you a lot of control over the images and lines that you create in Flash.

Lasso

The Lasso tool will help you when you are designing in Flash because it will give you the flexibility to edit vector shapes that you do not have in other programs. This is not just a selection tool, it is a powerful editing tool. The Lasso has two options under the

CHAPTER 2 • CREATING AND IMPORTING ARTWORK

Options section of the Toolbar. They are the Magic Wand and the Polygon. The Magic Wand is only used when you are trying to select a section of an imported bitmap file. The Polygon option of the Lasso tool allows you to make selections using straight lines. The following example will show you the Polygon option. To reuse the document from the previous example, all you have to do is select the image from the Stage and delete it.

1. Choose the Oval tool.
2. Set the stroke to No Color.
3. Draw an oval on the Stage.
4. Choose the Lasso tool.
5. Select the Polygon option.
6. Draw a triangle in the oval with the Lasso tool. When you have finished drawing your triangle, double-click on the shape to close it.
7. Choose Edit -> Cut to cut the triangle selection out of the oval (Figure 2-7).

You can delete, move, or change the color of a selection. Figure 2-7 shows the triangle deleted out of the center of your oval. This is very useful when you want to edit a more complicated image such as an illustrated character. Another great option of the Lasso tool is the Magic Wand. This option can be used when you are trying to edit bitmap images that you have imported. You can break apart an image by using Command + B (Control +B on a PC). Then you can use the Magic Wand to select and delete the edges or certain colors from the image.

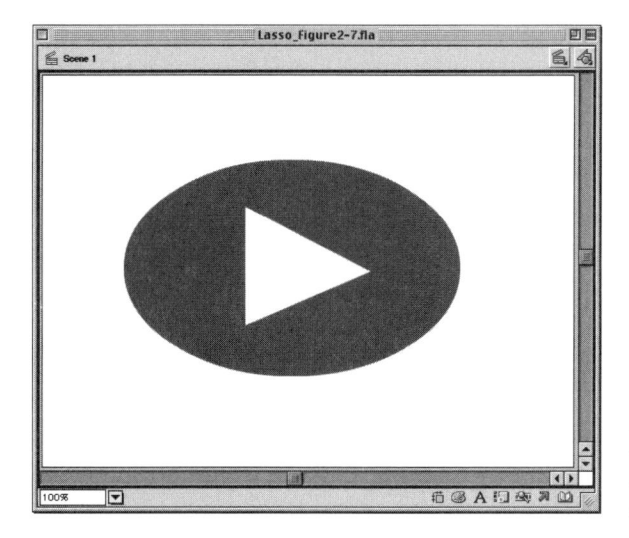

Figure 2-7   An oval with a triangle cut in it, which was created from the Lasso tool selection.

> **Note:** To break apart a letter, choose Modify -> Break Apart. You can also use Command + B (Control + B on a PC). This breaks the characters down into shapes so they cannot be edited with the Type tool after they are broken. This is further discussed later in this chapter in the "Shapes, Grouped Objects, Symbols, and Imported Bitmaps" section.

INK BOTTLE

The Ink Bottle tool is used to add a stroke or change the color, thickness, and style of an existing stroke or line. To use this in an example, we will follow the instructions for drawing a circle on the Stage, but we will draw the circle without a stroke. Reuse the document from the previous example by selecting the image from the Stage and deleting it.

1. Draw a circle without a stroke.
2. Select the Ink Bottle tool.
3. Change the stroke color in the Stroke panel so that the outline color is black and the thickness of the line is 4 points.
4. Click the circle that is on the Stage with the Ink Bottle tool. (Figure 2-8)

This tool is great for adding an outline to a shape that you have created. It also comes in handy when you decide that the outline you have created is too thick or not thick enough. Another great use for Ink Bottle is to create outlines for text. Reuse the document from the previous example by selecting the image from the Stage and deleting it.

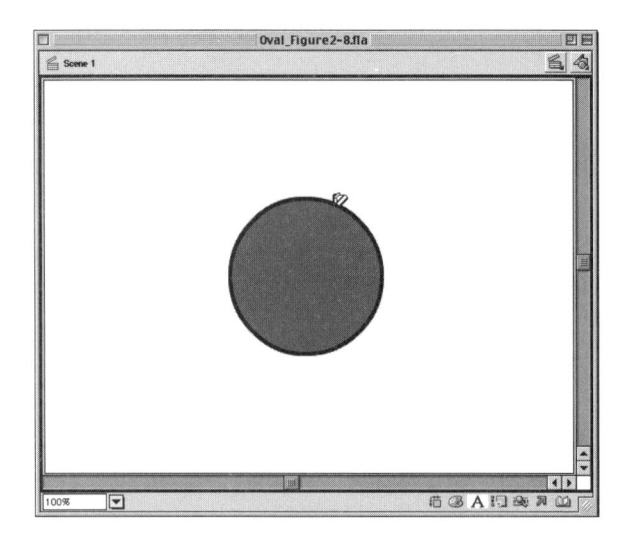

Figure 2-8 Circle with the added outline from the Ink Bottle tool.

CHAPTER 2 • CREATING AND IMPORTING ARTWORK

1. Select the Type tool from the Toolbar.
2. Choose Window -> Panels -> Characters.
3. Set the Font height (size) to 70.
4. Click on the Stage and type the letter "A".
5. Select the Arrow tool from the Toolbar; this will select the text. You can tell that the text is selected by the blue bounding box around the letter.
6. Break apart (Command + B or Control + B on a PC) the letter so that it is a shape.
7. Select the Ink Bottle tool.
8. Tap the letter "A".
9. Press the Delete key to delete the fill of the letter (Figure 2-9).

> **Warning**
> When you are creating an outline for text, make sure that you get all sides of the letter. For example, when you apply an outline to the letter "A", it will apply the outline to the outside of the letter. You need to tap the inside area of the "A" so the inside outline is created. Also, it is advised that you use a thin point size when creating outlines for fonts. I usually select 0.5 as my line weight.

The result of the example is the outline of the letter "A". This is a very useful feature, and it is the only way that you can create an outline for text in Flash.

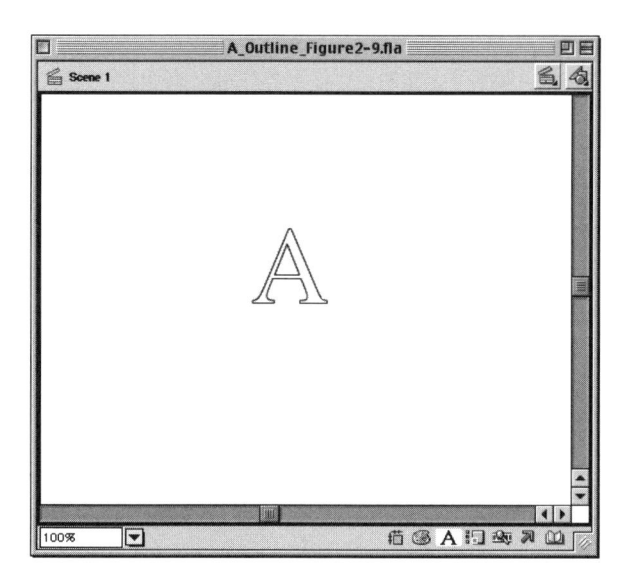

Figure 2-9 Outline of the letter "A" created with the Ink Bottle tool.

Paint Bucket

The Paint Bucket tool works pretty much the same in Flash as it does in other programs. There is one difference that I want to bring to your attention. In the Options section, you will see a menu that allows you to choose Don't Close Gaps, Close Small Gaps, Close Medium Gaps, and Close Large Gaps. This is great when you are trying to fill in outlines that have gaps in them (Figure 2-10). To reuse the document from the previous example, select the image from the Stage and delete it.

1. Select the Pen tool from the Toolbar.
2. Set the Pen tool option to Smooth in the Options section of the Toolbar.
3. Draw an oval, but stop just before completing it.
4. Select the Paint Bucket tool.
5. Set the Gap Size option to Close Large Gaps.
6. Click inside the oval you have drawn.

Eraser

The Eraser tool is an unlikely tool to find in a vector-based program. Flash treats vector graphics almost like a bitmap-based program with the Eraser tool. It allows you to erase any part of the shape you are working with. You have the ability with this tool to select the size and shape of the brush that you will be erasing with. To reuse the document from the previous example, select the image from the Stage and delete it.

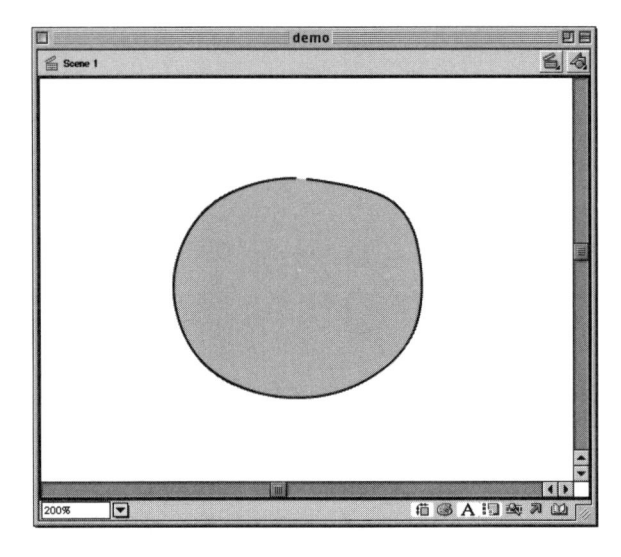

Figure 2-10 Paint Bucket tool filling an oval that has a gap at the top.

CHAPTER 2 • CREATING AND IMPORTING ARTWORK

1. Select the Rectangle tool.
2. Set the Round Rectangle Radius option in the Toolbar to "0" so that you draw a square without rounded corners.
3. Draw a square on the Stage. Hold the Shift key while drawing to make a perfect square.
4. Select the Eraser tool from the toolbar.
5. Drag the eraser across the square (Figure 2-11).

One of the most interesting options of the Eraser tool is the ability to select what you want to erase. You can erase fills, lines, selected fills, and inside graphics.

1. Use the graphic from the previous example, with the Eraser tool still selected.
2. Change the Eraser's mode in the Options section to Erase Fills.
3. Drag the eraser over the square (Figure 2-12).

You will notice that when you drag over the square with the Eraser tool, it only erases the fill and leaves the outlines unaffected.

The Eraser tool has another option that is very helpful—the Faucet. The Faucet is located next to the Eraser Mode button. The Faucet is great for getting rid of any line or fill you click. It is a quick and easy way to get rid of the fills for graphics for which you do not want to ruin the outlines. This is ideal when you have created outlines for text and you are having a hard time deleting the fills. This is also good for getting rid of numerous fills or lines.

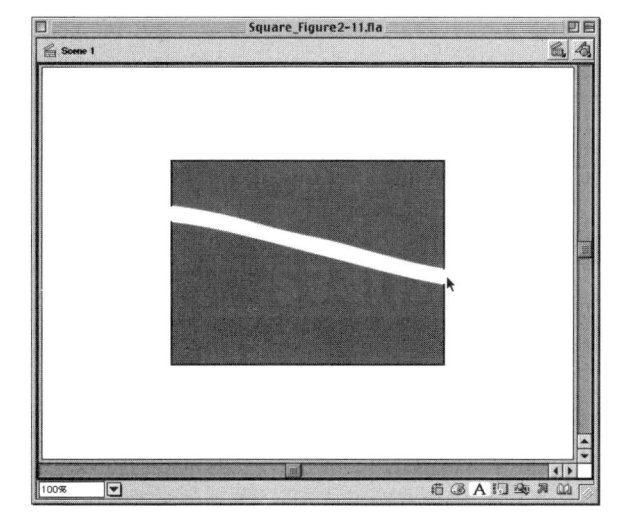

Figure 2-11   A demonstration of the Eraser tool erasing the fill as well as the outline of a square.

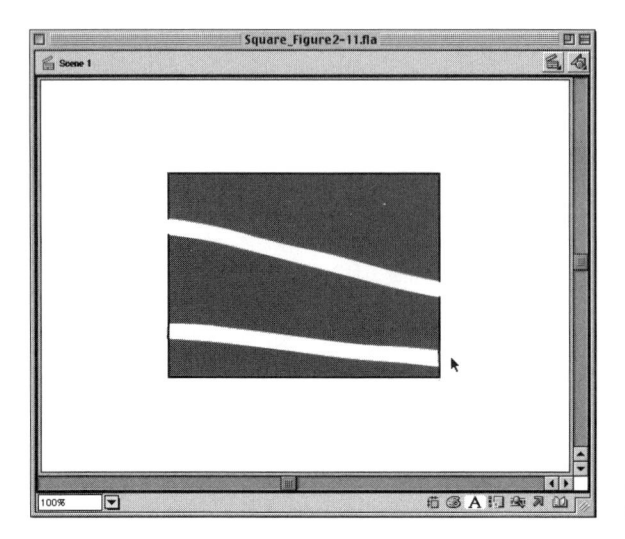

Figure 2-12 Eraser tool erasing only the fill of a rectangle.

1. Use the graphic from the previous examples, with the Eraser tool still selected.
2. Select the Faucet from the Options section of the Toolbar.
3. Click in the middle filled section of the square; this will delete this section.

SHAPES, GROUPED OBJECTS, SYMBOLS, AND IMPORTED BITMAPS

When you create or import graphics in Flash, the graphics can be placed into one of four categories: shapes, grouped objects, symbols, and imported bitmaps. A shape is a basic graphic that is usually created within Flash. Grouped objects are shapes or imported vector artwork, which are treated as a single graphic. The symbol is the most used category because of its versatility. Flash offers some useful features that make it easier to work with imported bitmaps. The following sections of this chapter go into greater detail about these types of graphics and will give you a better understanding of how Flash works.

SHAPES

The shape is the most basic of graphics in Flash. When you use the Oval, Rectangle, Pen, or other tools in Flash to create graphics, you are creating shapes. This type of graphic is completely editable, and when it is selected, it looks like the first example in Figure 2-13.

CHAPTER 2 • CREATING AND IMPORTING ARTWORK

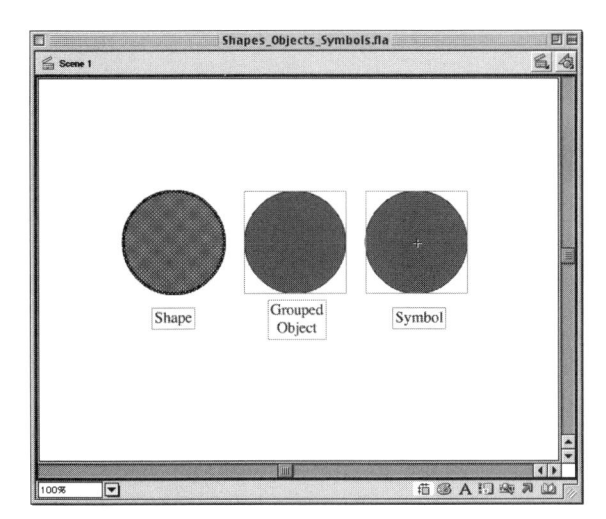

Figure 2-13 Examples of a shape, grouped object, and symbol when selected.

You will notice that when you select a shape, it has a checker-boxed, almost grayed-out, look. Some advantages to using a shape are that you can select part of the graphic and you can edit the shape's color or outline easily. You can change the look of a shape by using the Arrow tool to drag on a side, or corner and pull it outward, or you can use the Subselect tool to edit the shape's points.

1. Open a new file.
2. Draw a circle.
3. Select the Subselect tool.
4. Use the selection tool to highlight the circle (Figure 2-14).

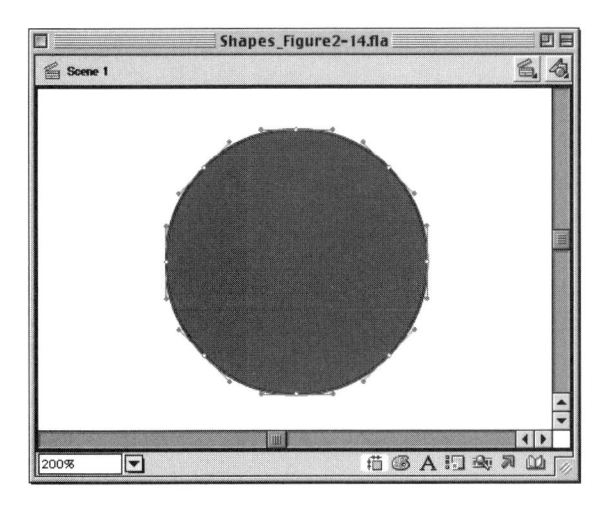

Figure 2-14 A circle that has been selected by the Subselect tool, showing the editable points of a shape.

These are features that are unique to shapes. Only shapes can be edited using the Sub–select tool, so this is the biggest advantage of the shape over the other types of graphics.

> **Any shapes on the same layer that overlap will be automatically joined. If the shapes are the same color, you will not be able to separate them. If the shapes are different colors, you will be able to separate them, but you will lose any part of the bottom shape that was overlapped.**

GROUPED OBJECTS

The next type of graphic is a grouped object. This looks like the example in Figure 2-13 when it is selected. Notice the selection is a square around the image. To create a grouped object from your shapes, you can either choose Modify -> Group or you can use the keyboard shortcut Command + G (Control + G on a PC). Once you have done this, the graphic cannot be edited unless it is ungrouped. To ungroup a grouped object, you can either choose Modify -> Ungroup or use the keyboard shortcut Shift + Command + G (Shift + Control + G on a PC).

1. Use the graphic from the previous example.
2. Select the Arrow tool from the toolbar.
3. Choose Modify -> Group to group the object.

> **What is the difference between the Break Apart and Ungroup features? When you use the Break Apart feature, you can break apart any graphic. The Ungroup feature will only restore images to the state from which they came. For example, if you started with text that was grouped, it will only be broken down to the text blocks that you started with. To break the text down further, you must use the Break Apart feature (Command + B or Control + B on a PC). This will reduce the text to shapes.**

Most vector images when they are imported from other applications will come in as grouped objects. One of the advantages to grouping shapes is the ability to keep shapes from being edited or deleted when they are all on the same layer. It is important to know that when you have shapes and grouped objects on the same layer, the grouped object will always appear on top of the shape.

Symbols

The symbol has the most advantages of all the graphics that can be created. You will notice that it looks like a grouped object when it is selected (Figure 2-13), except that it has a crosshair in the center of it. When you create symbols, they are stored in the Library.

> **Note:** The Library in Flash is like a folder where your symbols, imported graphics, and audio clips are kept. When you choose a symbol to use on the Stage, you are using an instance of the graphic in the Library. An instance is a reference to the symbol in the Library. This means that no matter how many instances you create from this symbol, the file size of your project will not get any bigger since Flash will only need to load the symbol once.

When you are using an instance of a symbol from the Library, the main symbol is not affected, even when the properties of an instance have been modified. Properties of a symbol include things like size, position, and effects. To create a symbol, you can either select the graphic and choose Insert -> Convert to Symbol or use the keyboard shortcut F8. You can also create a symbol in Symbol Editing mode by choosing Insert -> New Symbol or by using the keyboard shortcut Command + F8 (Control + F8). Symbol Editing mode is used to create or edit your symbols. When you are editing symbols in this mode, all of the instances of the symbol will be updated. This is a great time-saver when you need to tweak or change buttons or images that you have used throughout a site.

> **Tip:** Symbols have three behaviors: Graphic, Button, and Movie Clip. The Graphic behavior is used for static images, but can hold animation. The drawback is you cannot assign actions to it like the Movie Clip and Button behaviors. The main advantage to the Movie Clip behavior is that you can assign a name to it. This will allow you to access it through ActionScripting. The Button behavior is used strictly for buttons because it has a Timeline set up with the states of the button. Examples of each of these behaviors are used throughout the book. You can change the behavior of a symbol at any time for any instance on the stage or in the Library. The problem with updating a behavior in the Library is that it does not update the symbol on Stage. So if you are using the symbol multiple times, you will have to edit the behavior of each instance of the symbol. This is best used for a button you do not want to be active or a movie clip that you do not want to loop anymore.

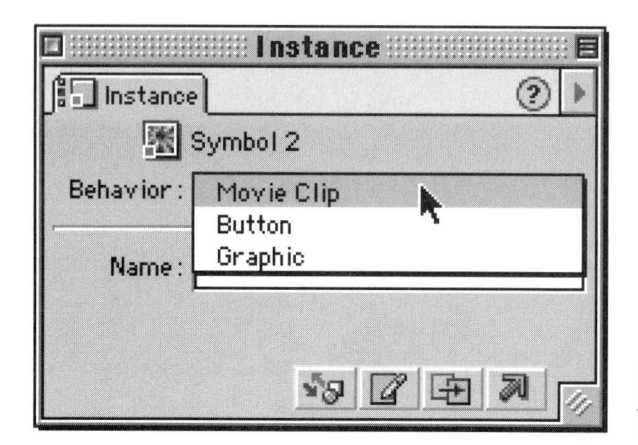

Figure 2-15 The Instance panel showing the available behaviors.

If you select a symbol on the Stage, you can look at the Instance panel. The Instance panel allows you to change the behavior of the symbol (Figure 2-15). You can also Swap Symbols, Edit Symbols, Duplicate Symbols, and Edit Actions that have been assigned to symbols in this panel.

You can also apply some effects to a symbol by selecting the symbol and opening the Effect panel (Figure 2-16). The Effect panel will allow you to change the Brightness, Tint, Alpha, and Advanced color combinations of the symbol. These are all great features that can be used in static images or combined into animations, which are covered in Chapter 3.

IMPORTED BITMAPS

You will probably encounter a client or occasion when you will need to use a bitmap image in your Flash movie. There are a few things that you must keep in mind when you are working with bitmaps in Flash. This section will cover the good and bad

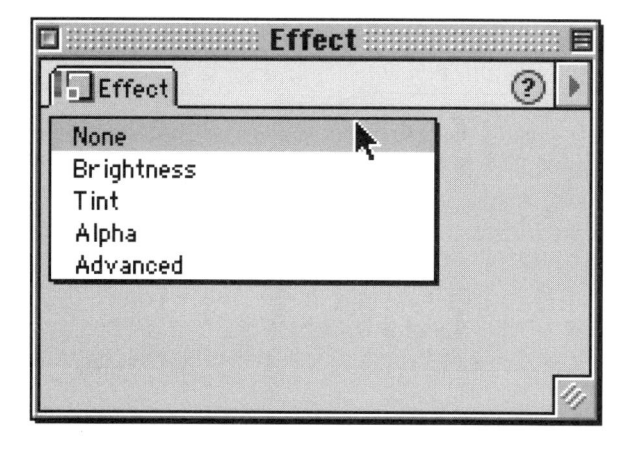

Figure 2-16 The Effect panel showing the available effects.

CHAPTER 2 • CREATING AND IMPORTING ARTWORK

points to using these types of images. One good thing to know is when bitmaps are imported, they are automatically placed on the Stage and in the Library. This is very helpful because this means that you will be able to use this image more than once without affecting the file size of the movie. In this respect, the bitmap image is like a symbol, but this is where the similarities end. If you want to fade or tint a bitmap, you will need to convert it into a symbol (press F8 to convert a graphic to a symbol). By doing this, you will give the bitmap almost all the features of a symbol. One major drawback to bitmaps is they cannot be made larger without losing quality. One feature of the bitmap that is very helpful is the ability to launch an external application to edit the graphic and have it updated automatically in Flash. For this example, I took a screenshot of the Flash 5 splash screen. You can also take a screenshot of the screen that opens when you choose About Flash from the Apple menu (the About screen is located under the Help menu on a PC).

> **Tip:** Taking screenshots on a Mac vs. a PC is very different. On the Mac, you first press the Caps Lock key to turn Caps Lock on. Then, you press Shift + Command + 4 and click on the window that you want to capture. The screen capture is placed in the root of your hard drive and is saved as a PICT file. On a PC, you press the Print Screen button. Then you need to open Photoshop or another image editing program and paste the screenshot into a new file.

1. Open a new file.
2. Choose File -> Import or Command + R (Control + R on a PC) to import your screen capture of the Flash 5 splash screen.
3. Choose Window -> Library to open the Library window.
4. Press Control + click (right-click on a PC) on the screenshot you imported to open a context menu.
5. Choose the application that created the file or another application in which to edit the graphic (Figure 2-17). This launches the application and allows you to create a new file or edit the original.
6. When you have completed editing the file, choose Update (Fireworks) or Save (Photoshop) from the File menu.

Notice that when you switch back to Flash, the file has already been updated. Another way to update or replace a graphic is to open the Bitmap Properties window (Figure 2-18). You can do this by double-clicking on the Bitmap icon in the Library window. Choose Update from this window. You will notice the statistics of the graphics get updated as well as the graphics themselves. This will only work if you have not changed the location of the graphic or Flash movie. If you have changed the location, you can use the Import option, which will allow you to search your computer for the graphic.

Figure 2-17   Context menu for a bitmap image in the Library window.

A bitmap image can also be broken apart like a grouped object so that it will look and act like a shape. One main advantage to this is the ability to edit the shape of a bitmap.

1. Use the file from the previous example.
2. Choose the Arrow tool and select the bitmap on the Stage.
3. Press Command + B (Control + B on a PC) to break apart the file.
4. Click anywhere away from the image on the Stage to deselect the image.
5. Use the Arrow tool and drag the left side toward the center (Figure 2-19).

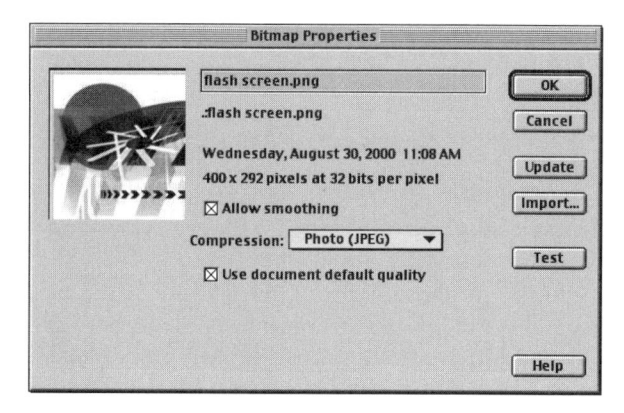

Figure 2-18   Bitmap Properties window.

CHAPTER 2 • CREATING AND IMPORTING ARTWORK

Figure 2-19   Bitmap image edited after it has been broken apart.

One drawback to this method of editing the file is that you cannot make the bitmap larger than the shape that has been imported. Once you have broken the image down, it acts like a fill and will tile when you try to make the shape larger (Figure 2-20).

Some people might consider this to be a benefit if you need to tile a bitmap as a background for a page. You can use the Eyedropper tool to select the bitmap, when it is broken, and use it as a fill. You will notice that the fill swatch in the toolbar updates to a thumbnail of the image. Now you can use the Paint Bucket tool to fill in any shape you want with the image (Figure 2-21).

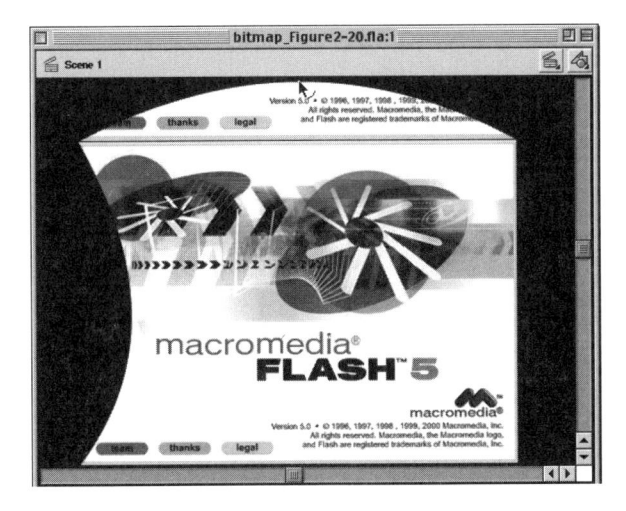

Figure 2-20   Bitmap image acting like a fill when the top edge is moved up.

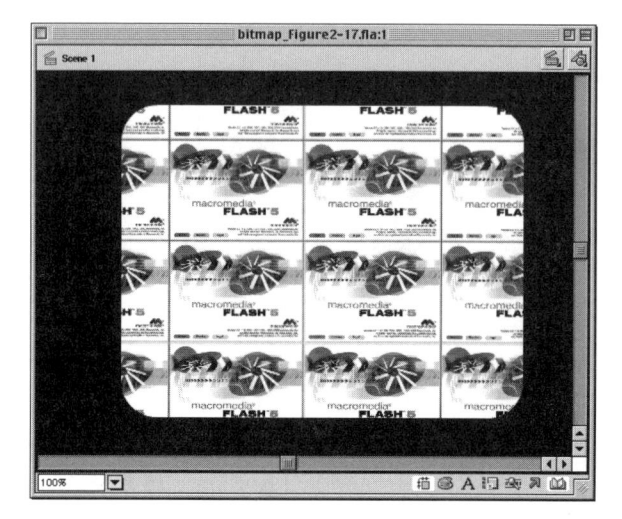

Figure 2-21   Bitmap used as a fill for a rectangle.

IMPORTING ARTWORK FROM OTHER APPLICATIONS

Flash does not have all the features that many of today's graphic applications do. I have created this section to help you understand how to prepare your files for Flash. Everyone has their favorite programs they like to work in; this is why Macromedia allows you to import many different file types (Table 2-1). If you have Quicktime 4 installed, you will also be able to import the files from Table 2-2. These tables cover the most popular file types you would be importing and what platform they can be used on. Note that there are a few file types which only work on a particular platform.

Exporting files in a Flash-friendly format from graphics applications is getting easier because a majority of companies have accepted the Flash SWF file format as standard. Before you know it, all the programs you use will allow you to export your files in the SWF file format. You will notice as you read through this section that a few programs already have the ability to export their files in this format. These programs include FreeHand, Fireworks, and Illustrator. The following sections cover ways of exporting files from graphic applications into formats that are easily imported and work best with Flash.

FROM FREEHAND TO FLASH

Flash now accepts FreeHand files. That's how I had to start this section because I always thought it was strange that Flash did not allow you to import FreeHand files when Macromedia owns both software packages. I will also cover how to export your file from FreeHand as an SWF file. This used to be the best way to get your graphics

CHAPTER 2 • CREATING AND IMPORTING ARTWORK

Table 2-1 Files Accepted by Flash without Quicktime 4 and the Platforms That Accept Them

File Type	Platform
Macromedia FreeHand (version 7.0 and newer)	Mac and Win
Adobe Illustrator (version 6.0 and earlier)	Mac and Win
Flash/FutureSplash Player	Mac and Win
AutoCAD DXF	Mac and Win
Bitmap	Win
Enhanced Metafile	Win
GIF/Animated GIF	Mac and Win
JPEG	Mac and Win
PICT	Mac
PNG	Mac and Win
Windows Metafile	Win

out of FreeHand and into Flash. First, I am going to cover how you can import your FreeHand files. Flash actually gives you a lot of control when you are importing the files. If you select a FreeHand file when you are importing into Flash, you will get the FreeHand Import window (Figure 2-22).

This window allows you to choose many options to make sure that your file comes across exactly as you need it to. First, you can select if the pages of your FreeHand file will be mapped to keyframes or scenes, and if your layers will be mapped to layers, keyframes, or flattened. Second, you can choose not to bring in all your pages if you have multiple pages. The last section has three options: you can include invisible layers,

Table 2-2 Files Accepted with Quicktime 4 and the Platforms That Accept Them

File Type	Platform
MacPaint	Mac and Win
Photoshop	Mac and Win
PICT	Win (as a bitmap)
Quicktime Image	Mac and Win
Quicktime Movie	Mac and Win
Silicon Graphics	Mac and Win
TGA	Mac and Win
TIFF	Mac and Win

48 **CHAPTER 2 • CREATING AND IMPORTING ARTWORK**

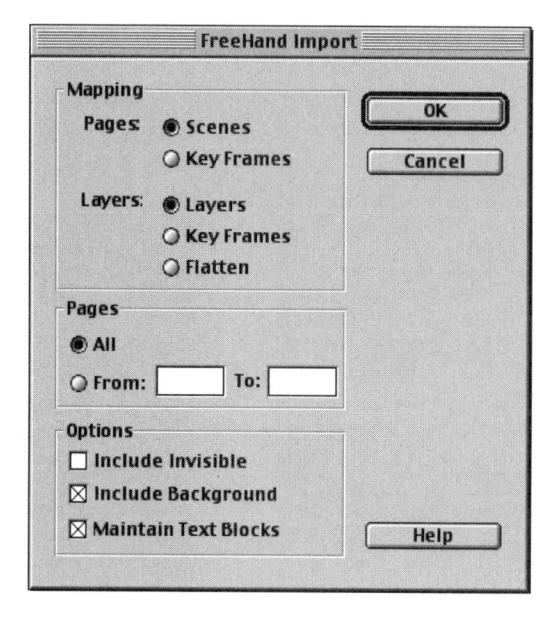

Figure 2-22   FreeHand Import window in Flash.

include a background layer, and maintain text blocks. The last option listed strikes me as the most useful. Finally, you do not have to retype your text from your storyboards to the final project.

> **Warning:** Make sure that you work in RGB when you are in FreeHand or your files will not come across as you expect. If you have already started working in CMYK, you should convert all your colors over yourself because Flash does not do a good job of converting CMYK to RGB.

> **Tip:** If you are having problems with colors not coming across as you want them to, try exporting as an SWF file. I have had better luck keeping my image color close when I have exported from FreeHand as an SWF file.

If you prefer, you can still export your file as an SWF file from FreeHand by following these simple steps.

1. Choose File -> Export.
2. Select the Flash SWF file format.
3. Click the Options button, which allows you to control the outcome of your file by opening the Flash Export window (Figure 2-23).

CHAPTER 2 • CREATING AND IMPORTING ARTWORK

> **Note:** The settings in the Flash Export window will affect file size and image quality. For most shapes, you will be able to save file size and go with the maximum path and image compressions. Choose OK after you have adjusted your settings in the Flash Export window. Choose Export from the Export Document window.

This will save an SWF file that is ready to be imported into Flash. To import SWF files into Flash, choose File -> Import, then add the files you would like to import. Static images will come into Flash as grouped objects. Animated images will come into Flash as symbols and frame-by-frame animations. If you do not want to keep exporting from FreeHand and importing into Flash, then copy and paste the images between the two programs. This works for most images, but you are always safer working with SWF files or FreeHand files.

There are some great features in FreeHand 9 that will help you put your graphics a step ahead of those not using this program. For example, the new Perspective feature will allow you to animate your text and graphics as if they were in 3-D space and you will be able to directly export the animation as an SWF file. This is something you cannot do in other vector-based programs.

Figure 2-23   FreeHand's Flash Export window.

Preparing Your Illustrator Files for Flash

There are a few ways that you can bring graphics into Flash from Illustrator. The first way is to just copy and paste a graphic over from Illustrator into Flash. This works some of the time, but colors and gradients usually do not come across very well. The second way that you can bring files into Flash from Illustrator is to save your file out as an Illustrator file (AI or EPS) and import the file into Flash.

> **This works best if the file is saved as an Illustrator 6.0 file because Flash does not support Illustrator 7.0 and higher.**

The third and best way to export files from Illustrator is to use the Flash Writer plug-in. If you are using Illustrator 9, it comes with the ability to export Flash SWF files, so you will not need to download the Flash Writer plug-in. Both of these work very similarly but there are a few differences worth pointing out. First, I will cover the Flash Writer plug-in for people who are using Illustrator 8. You can download this plug-in for free from the Macromedia Web site: http://www.macromedia.com/software/flash/download.

Once you have this plug-in installed, you can export from Illustrator as a Flash SWF file. If you go to the File menu of Illustrator and choose Export, you will see the Flash Player SWF option. This opens a window where you will be able to choose settings for your SWF file (Figure 2-24). A good feature from these settings is Export Layers as Separate Files. If you have created your artwork on different layers, then you will really appreciate the ability to bring them in as separate elements. Once you have saved SWF files from Illustrator, you can import them into Flash easily and with their colors intact.

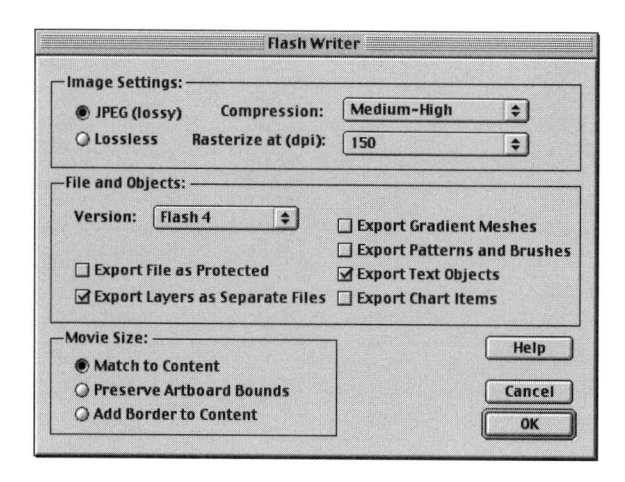

Figure 2-24 The Flash Writer export window in Adobe Illustrator 8.

CHAPTER 2 • CREATING AND IMPORTING ARTWORK 51

> **Warning:** If you are planning to use SWF files in Flash, make sure you do not check the Export File as Protected box. If this box is checked, you will not be able to import the SWF file into Flash.

Now I will cover exporting from Illustrator 9. Basically, these features work the same, but Illustrator 9 has a few features that will help make your life a little easier when you are trying bring your files into Flash. When you are in Illustrator 9, you need to choose File -> Export. In this window, select the Flash SWF file format and click Export. This will bring up the Flash (SWF) Format Options window (Figure 2-25).

Notice that this window looks different from the Flash Writer window. This window is a little more basic, but it really only includes what is important. The top section of the window has the Export Options. Here you have a choice of exporting your file as one SWF file, or making your layers export as frames in one file or as separate files. The only other difference is the ability to make your images into symbols automatically. After this, the windows are very similar.

MAKING YOUR BITMAPS VECTOR-BASED IMAGES WITH ADOBE STREAMLINE

Adobe Streamline is great when your client hands you black and white sketches and wants them put on the Web. It is also great for converting artists' inked boards into animations on-screen. This example shows the steps to laying the groundwork for an

Figure 2-25 Flash (SWF) Format Options window from Illustrator 9.

Figure 2-26   Black and white scan of inked boards for Oxy campaign. Visuals provided courtesy of Oxy® © 2000 SmithKline Beecham.

animation I did for SmithKline Beechham's Oxygen Campaign. The files I started with were inked frames for a television commercial.

1. All you need to do is scan the boards so they look like the images in Figure 2-26.

> **To get sharper lines with less distortion, try scanning the images at a higher resolution. I have found that 300 ppi is a good resolution to start at. Next, I like to bring the image into Photoshop to adjust the levels and sharpen the edges of the lines. Then, I change the resolution to 72 ppi.**

2. Now import the image into Streamline and let it trace the scan. To get the best results, set Streamline to the settings shown in Figure 2-27.

3. Once it is done, save the traced art as an Illustrator 6.0 or 7.0 file and import this into Flash.

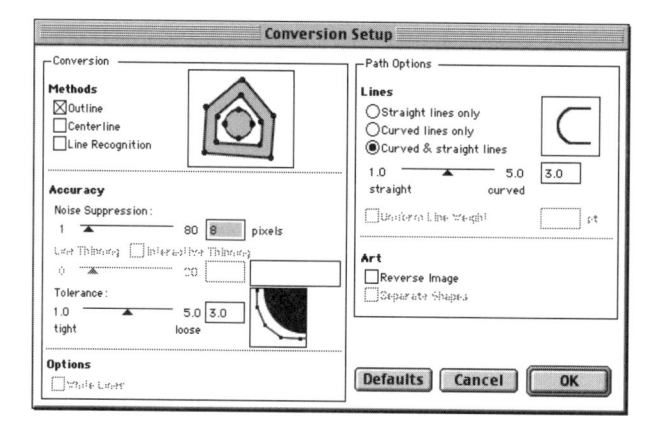

Figure 2-27   Streamline's Conversion Setup window.

CHAPTER 2 • CREATING AND IMPORTING ARTWORK   53

Figure 2-28   Colored frame from the Oxy campaign. Visuals provided courtesy of Oxy® © 2000 SmithKline Beecham.

The great thing about this is that now you can break apart this image and color it any way that you want (Figure 2-28).

Streamline takes what used to be an all-day ordeal of tracing elements and makes it a five-minute joy. Streamline produces the best results when tracing black and white images.

PREPARING YOUR FILES WITH FIREWORKS 3

With Fireworks, you have the ability to export in many formats that Flash will accept. For animations, you can use animated GIFs or you can use the Flash SWF file format. It is best to use the SWF file format whenever possible. Even with still graphics, you can use the SWF format.

1. To export from Fireworks in the SWF format, choose File -> Export Special -> Flash SWF.
2. You will see the Export Special window. Choose Setup. This brings up the Flash SWF Export Options window (Figure 2-29).
3. Choose the options that best suit your needs and then click OK.

Fireworks also has the ability to export in the PNG file format. Most images that you would normally make into GIFs can be made into smaller 8-bit PNG files. You will notice that you have the same options with an 8-bit PNG file as you do with a GIF. With Flash 5, you have more flexibility when you are importing PNG files. When

Figure 2-29 Flash SWF Export Options window from Fireworks.

you import a PNG file, you will see the Fireworks PNG Import Settings window (Figure 2-30). You have the option of importing all the editable objects like images, text, and guides. You also have the option to flatten the image when you import it. These are great features that will save you a tremendous amount of time. The ability to import editable text into Flash is a great feature.

EXPORTING FROM ADOBE PHOTOSHOP AND IMAGEREADY

When exporting your images from Photoshop or Imageready, you can choose from many file formats that are accepted by Flash. For the best results, when exporting files that have transparencies, use GIFs. PNG (8-bit) files are problematic with these two

Figure 2-30 Fireworks PNG Import Settings window.

programs, and 24-bit PNG and PICT files are very bulky in file size. If you do not need transparent files, then you can use JPEG, GIF, or PNG files. The Save for Web feature is the best way to export your graphics from Photoshop because it will show you an optimized preview of each file. This will allow you to see the final product before you have saved it out. Imageready has a similar feature built into it. For a more in-depth look at Photoshop and GIFs, look at Jason Miletsky's *Web Photoshop 6 Primer.*

FINDING THE RIGHT GRAPHICS

One of the hardest things to do when you are working on a project is to find the right graphics. This is made a lot easier when you find a company like Nova Development who sells packages of clip art. The recommended package is the Art Explosion 750,000 for the Macintosh and the 600,000 for the PC. Both of these packages are jam-packed with useful clip art images that can be imported directly into Flash because they are in Illustrator EPS format for the Macintosh and WMF format for the PC.

chapter 3

ANIMATING YOUR ARTWORK

One of the best features of Flash is its ability to animate your graphics. With Flash, you have the ability to rotate, scale, morph, change color, and even fade out an object. There are three types of animation in Flash: Shape Tweening, Motion Tweening, and frame-by-frame. This chapter covers the three types of animation with examples that will show you how to morph a shape, animate an instance of a symbol, and animate along a path. The only drawback of animating in Flash is that it is processor-dependent. This means that a person who has a Quadra or 486 will not see the animation as smoothly as a person who has a G4 or Pentium III. But, if you use it in the right way, you can create new and exciting elements for your Web site that will entertain visitors as well as convey your message.

UNDERSTANDING THE TIMELINE AND KEYFRAMES

To understand how to animate, you have to understand the Timeline and how to work with it. The Timeline window is broken down into two sections (Figure 3-1).

The left side has the names of the layers and useful menus pertaining to layers. Along the top, you have the Show/Hide All Layers button, Lock/Unlock All Layers button, and the Show All Layers as Outlines button. These buttons affect all the layers when they are clicked. To apply these functions to an individual layer, just click in the column of the functions you wish to apply, next to the layer. In the bottom left

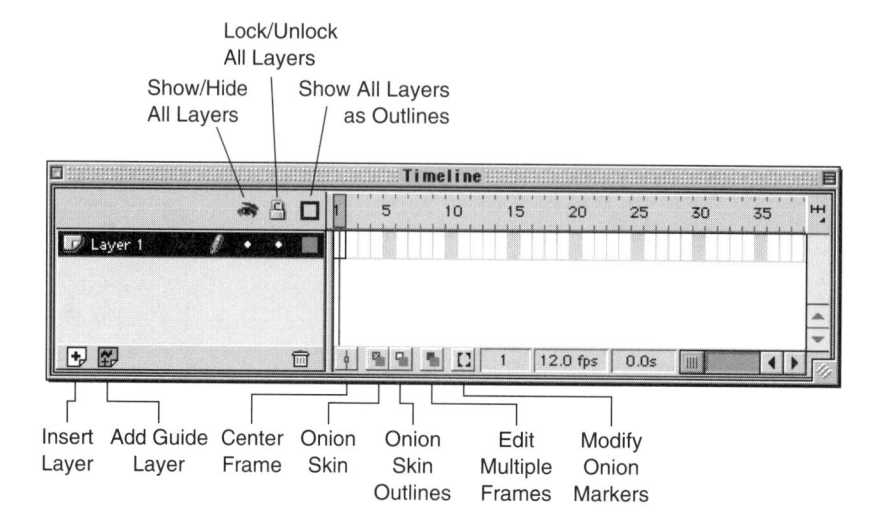

Figure 3-1 Timeline with the names of all the major characteristics, buttons, and menus.

corner of the window, you will see the Insert Layer and the Add Guide Layer buttons. To the right of the Add a Guide button, there is a Trash Can icon, which is the Delete Layer button.

The right side of the Timeline window consists of the Onion Skinning buttons (located in the bottom left section of this window) and frames, which are pieces of time. The buttons at the right side of the window are the Center Frame, Onion Skin, Onion Skin Outlines, Edit Multiple Frames, and Modify Onion Markers buttons. The Center Frame button will center the Playback Head in the Timeline window. The Onion Skin button will show all the frames of an animation that are in between the Onion Markers that appear when you click this button. The Onion Skin Outlines button has the same effect as the Onion Skin button, but all the frames except the one that is selected appear as outlines. The Edit Multiple Frames button allows you to select frames with Onion Markers and edit them. The Modify Onion Markers button is a menu that lets you set some preferences for the Onion Markers. These preferences are Always Show Markers, Anchor Onion, Onion 2, Onion 5, and Onion All. These features are all used in examples throughout this chapter. At the right side of the window you will see the Playback Head, which is the red line with a box on top, highlighting the frame that it occupies.

A keyframe is a point that is placed on a frame in the Timeline. A keyframe can be set to represent the start, end, or a change of a graphic on a layer. For example, when you open a new project in Flash and look at the Timeline (Figure 3-1), you will see Layer 1 with an empty keyframe.

As soon as you draw on this layer, a solid circle appears, representing the object you have drawn (Figure 3-2). This is the starting keyframe for the graphic you have

CHAPTER 3 • ANIMATING YOUR ARTWORK 59

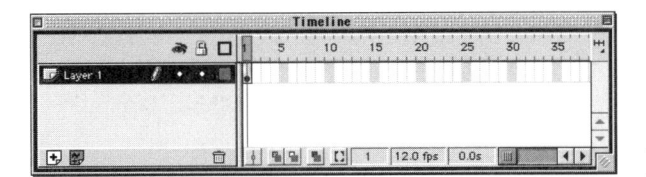

Figure 3-2 Timeline with a filled keyframe in the first frame.

just made. Move down the Timeline by clicking on a frame and choose Insert -> Keyframe. This keyframe can now represent another instance of the graphic. For example, whatever you do to this image in this frame will only affect this instance. With that said, let's dive right into our first type of animation, Shape Tweening.

WHEN TO USE SHAPE TWEENING

Shape Tweening is best used for changing the shape of a graphic. This is most commonly used for changing shapes into text or changing the shape of text. You cannot, however, change the shape of symbols, grouped shapes, or bitmap images. You must break down symbols and grouped shapes to be able to use shape tweening on the shapes. The following examples are going to show you a few scenarios and tricks on how to use Shape Tweening.

MORPHING A CIRCLE INTO A SQUARE

First, we are going to start with a very simple animation, which will allow you to morph a circle into a square. Once we have completed this, we will move on to a few more complicated shape morphs.

1. Open a new file.
2. Draw a circle without a stroke on the Stage.
3. In the Timeline, add a keyframe on Frame 10 (press F6 to insert a keyframe).

> **Tip:** There are multiple ways to insert a keyframe. You can choose whichever way is easiest for you. One way, and my favorite, is pressing the F6 key. This works for both the Macintosh and on a PC. Another way is to Control + click (right-click on a PC) in the frame in which you wish to insert the keyframe and select Insert Keyframe from the menu.

4. While in Frame 10, delete the graphic of the circle from the Stage.
5. Draw a square without a stroke in Frame 10.
6. Click in between the two keyframes to highlight the frames between them.
7. Choose Window -> Panels -> Frame to open the Frame panel.

> **Note:** There are two other ways to open the Frame panel. The first way to get to the Frame panel is to press Command + F (Control + F on a PC). You can also click and hold on a frame in between keyframes and select the frame from the Panels section of the context menu. On the PC, you can right-click to get to the context menu.

8. Select Shape from the Tweening pull-down menu in the Frame panel (Figure 3-3).

> **Note:** When using Shape Tweening, I have found that you get the best results when you use the Distributive Blend Type. This is the default setting in the Tweening menu. You can leave the Easing option set to "0"; this is covered in more detail later in this chapter.

9. To see your animation, go to the Controller window (choose Window -> Controller, or on a PC, choose Window -> Toolbars -> Controller) and play the animation.

When you look at the Timeline, you will see a line and arrow connecting the two keyframes (Figure 3-4). This means that Flash is tweening the positions of the graphic in between the two keyframes.

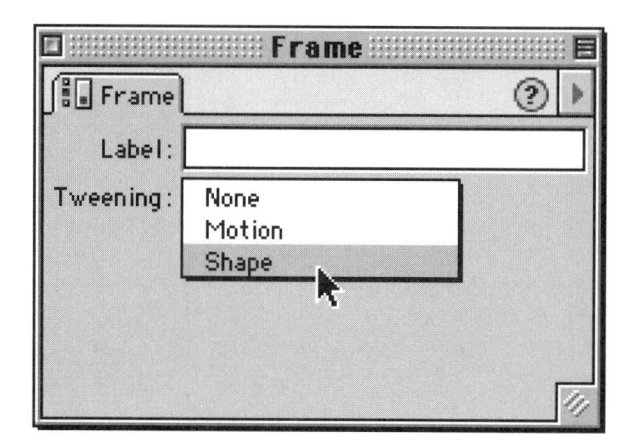

Figure 3-3 The Frame panel with Shape Tweening being selected.

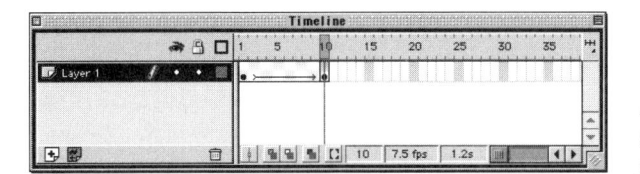

Figure 3-4 Timeline showing Shape Tweening between two frames.

Your animation should show the circle morphing into a square (Figure 3-5).

> **Tip:** There are a few ways to test a movie you have created. One is by choosing Control -> Test Movie. Another is by pressing Command + Return (Control + Enter on a PC). This will export a looping version of the animation that you have created.

Well, we have completed a simple morph. Now it is time to move onto something a little more difficult. This next section will show you how to make a circle morph into the letter "A". This is probably more useful than the circle to the square, but as the saying goes, you have to crawl before you can walk.

Morphing a Circle into an "A"

This section will make use of Shape Hints, which allow us to make a smoother transition from a circle to an "A". To start this example, we will use the file from the previous example.

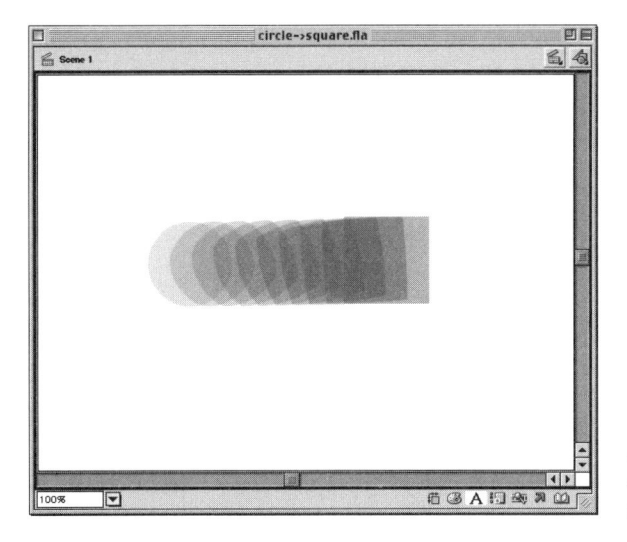

Figure 3-5 Shape tween from a circle to a square, including all the frames in between.

1. Go to Frame 10 and delete the square graphic from the Stage.
2. Choose Window -> Panels -> Character to open the Character panel if it is not open already.
3. For this example, set the Font to Times New Roman. Set the Font Height to 72.
4. Select the Text tool.
5. Type the letter "A".
6. Select the Arrow tool; this should select the letter.
7. Use Command + B (Control + B on a PC) to break the "A" down to a shape as explained in Chapter 2.
8. Click in between the two keyframes to highlight the frames between them.
9. Choose Window -> Panels -> Frame to open the Frame panel if it is not open already.
10. Select Shape from the Tweening pull-down menu in the Frame panel; leave the Easing and Blend options at their default settings.
11. Choose Control -> Test Movie to play the movie. Figure 3-6 shows the frames of the animation using the Onion Skin feature. This is covered later in the chapter.

When you play the animation now, you will notice that you do not get a very appealing tween from the circle to the "A". There are a couple of steps we can go through to make the animation better.

1. Add a keyframe in Frame 2 (press F6 to insert a keyframe).
2. Select the Eraser tool.

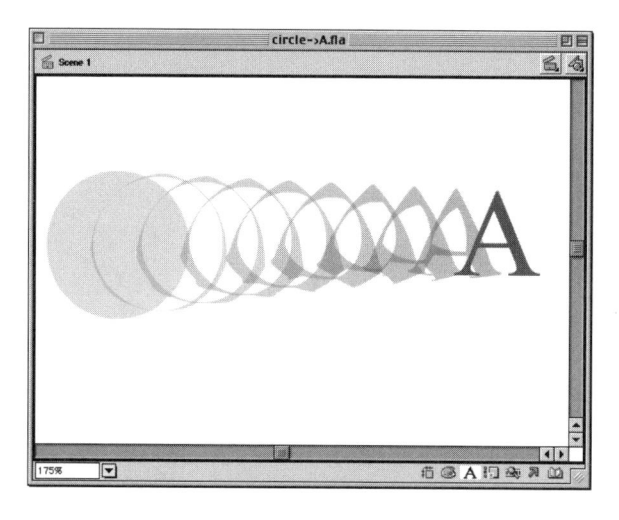

Figure 3-6 Shape tween from a circle to an "A", including all the frames in between.

CHAPTER 3 • ANIMATING YOUR ARTWORK 63

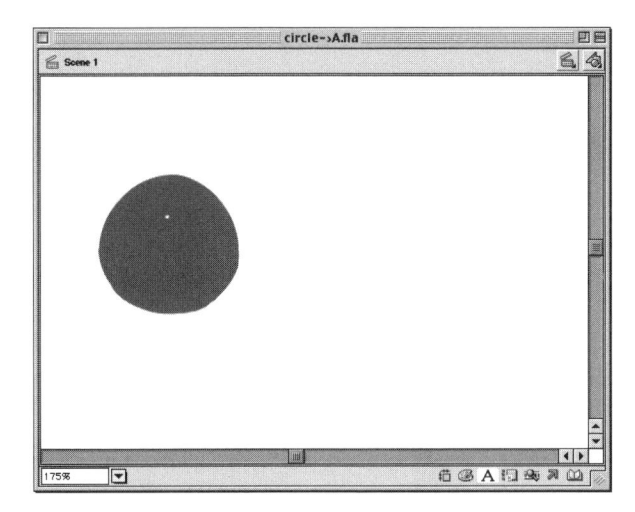

Figure 3-7 Circle after hole has been made with Eraser tool.

3. Select the smallest circle brush size available from the Options section of the Toolbar.
4. Go to the Stage and use the Eraser tool to poke a hole in the circle at about the same spot where the hole in the "A" would be (Figure 3-7).

This has helped, but our animation still is not as clean as it could be. What we need are Shape Hints. Shape Hints are placed on your starting shape and ending shape. They represent points of the starting shape that you want to become certain points of the ending image. To add Shape Hints to our animation, we will start with the circle in Frame 2 because this is our new starting shape.

1. Go to Frame 2.
2. Choose Modify -> Transform -> Add Shape Hint.

> **To create a Shape Hint, you can also use the keyboard shortcut Shift + Command + H on the Macintosh (on a PC, the shortcut is Control + Shift + H). If you feel you will be using this feature a lot, I suggest you create a keyboard shortcut for this action as covered in Chapter 1.**

3. You will see a little red circle with an "a" in it appear on the Stage. Each time you insert a Shape Hint, you will get a red circle with the next letter of the alphabet.
4. Move the first circle to the lower left of the circle.
5. Add more hints to help Flash; place the hints around the circle in the spots where the example in Figure 3-8 displays them. (I have added 10 Shape Hints for this example.)

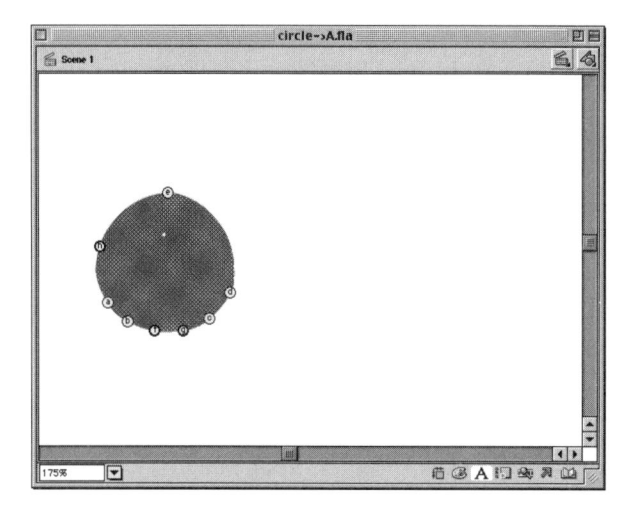

Figure 3-8   Circle with Shape Hints added.

6. Now go to Keyframe 10 to set up Shape Hints for the "A".
7. You will notice that Flash has put all of the Shape Hints in the center of the image on top of one another. Move them to their spots according to Figure 3-9.

To figure out where you would like to place Shape Hints on an image, just imagine the "A" over the circle in the starting frame. Then, for the ending frame, you can use the Onion Skin feature. This will show you all the frames between the start and end Onion Markers (Figure 3-10). When you are in Onion Skinning mode, you should

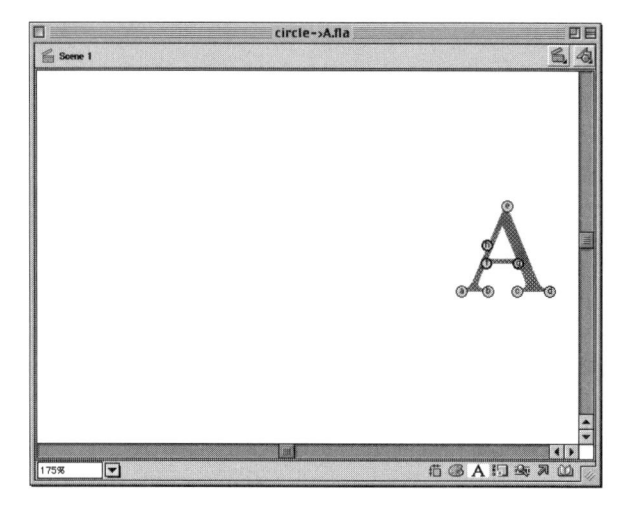

Figure 3-9   "A" with Shape Hints added.

CHAPTER 3 • ANIMATING YOUR ARTWORK 65

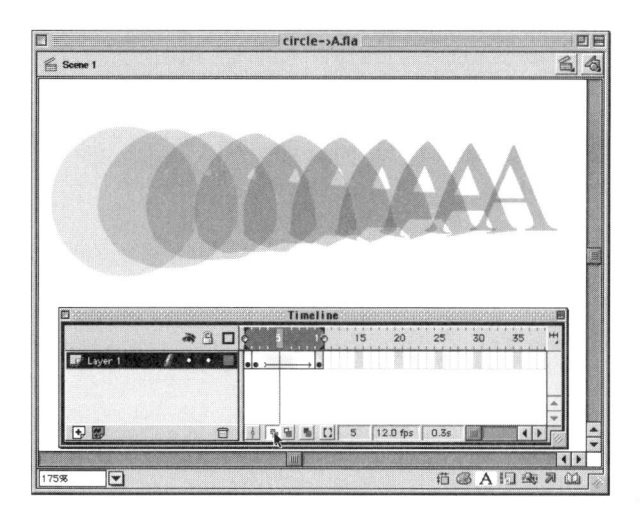

Figure 3-10   Circle to "A" morph with Onion Skin feature turned on.

notice the frames leading up to the "A" update as you place Shape Hints on the "A". This will help you make a better and quicker morph. You also should watch out because too many or misplaced hints can ruin a morph.

ANIMATING THE SHAPE OF LETTERS

Well, we have mastered changing a circle into a letter, so now we are going to move onto changing letters into different letters. This example will instruct you to mock up a text logo. To allow you to follow more closely, the Font and Font Height settings are provided.

1. Open a new file.
2. Select the Type tool.
3. In the Character panel, set the Font as Verdana and the Font Height to 100.
4. Type the word "LOGO".

> **Note**: The best way to create layers is by clicking the Insert Layer button on the bottom left of the Timeline window. You can also choose from one of the following ways: The first way to insert a layer is to choose Insert -> Layer; the next way is to Control + click (right-click on a PC) in the Timeline on the layer name, then choose Insert New Layer from the context menu.

5. Choose the Arrow tool.
6. Press Command + B (Control + B on a PC) to break apart the old logo.
7. Click the Insert Layer button so that you end up with one layer for every letter of the word "LOGO". You should have four layers.
8. Click on "O" and choose Edit -> Cut.
9. Paste the letter into one of the empty layers. To paste the letter in the correct spot, you can either use Shift + Command + V (Shift + Control + V on a PC) or you can choose Edit -> Paste in Place.
10. Repeat Steps 8 and 9 for the remaining letters.
11. Go to Frame 10 and highlight all the layers in that frame.
12. Press F6 to add keyframes in this frame for all of the layers.
13. Delete the old logo from all the keyframes in Frame 10.
14. Select the Type tool.
15. In the Character panel, set the Font to Georgia and the Font Height to 100.
16. Type the word "LOGO".
17. Select the Arrow tool.
18. Break apart the logo letters.
19. Cut and paste the letters in the layers that match up with the letters of the old logo.
20. Choose Window -> Panels -> Frame to open the Frame panel.
21. Apply a shape tween to each layer.
22. Choose Control -> Test Movie to play your movie.

Figure 3-11 shows the starting and ending frames with some of the intermediary frames that Flash created. If you want to sharpen the transition between the letters, you can add Shape Hints to some of the letters. The next section explains how to use the most popular animation technique available in Flash, Motion Tweening.

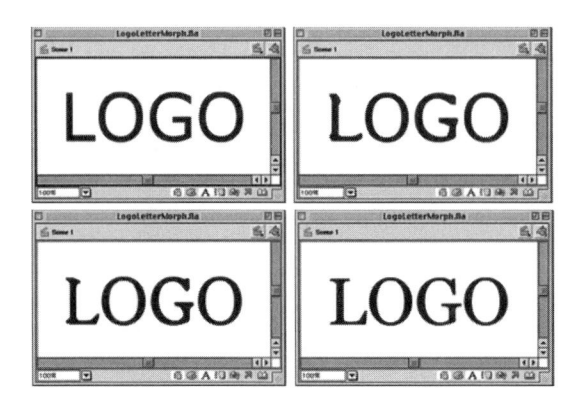

Figure 3-11   Letter morph from one font to another.

ALL YOU NEED TO KNOW ABOUT MOTION TWEENING

Motion Tweening is used for grouped objects and symbols. The main difference with the tweening of grouped objects and symbols is that you cannot animate instances of grouped objects. This is another reason why you should make most of your elements symbols. The following examples cover simple through more advanced types of animation used in many sites on the Web.

ANIMATING POSITION AND SCALE

This example covers animating a symbol or grouped object using Motion Tweening. We will animate the position and scale of an object.

1. Open a new file.
2. Create a square on the left side of the screen.
3. Click and highlight the square's keyframe in the Timeline.
4. Choose Insert -> Create Motion Tween (this will automatically create a symbol for the square and place it in the Library).

> **Note:** There are two other ways you can create a Motion Tween. The first is to Control + click (right-click) on the keyframe and select Create Motion Tween. The second way is to open the Frame panel and select Motion from the Tweening menu. You will need to have the frame highlighted in the Timeline before you select Motion Tweening in the Frame panel. With all but the last example, the graphic will be made into a symbol if it is not one already.

5. Go to Frame 10 and insert a keyframe (press F6).
6. Use the Arrow tool to select the square.
7. Move the square in Frame 10 from the left side of the screen to the right side. To drag an object straight, hold the Shift key while dragging.
8. Choose Window -> Panels -> Transform to open the Transform panel.
9. Highlight the square and make it larger by 150% (Figure 3-12).

> **Note:** When working in the Transform panel, make sure that you check the Constrain box next to the width and height boxes. This way, you can be sure that your object will scale evenly.

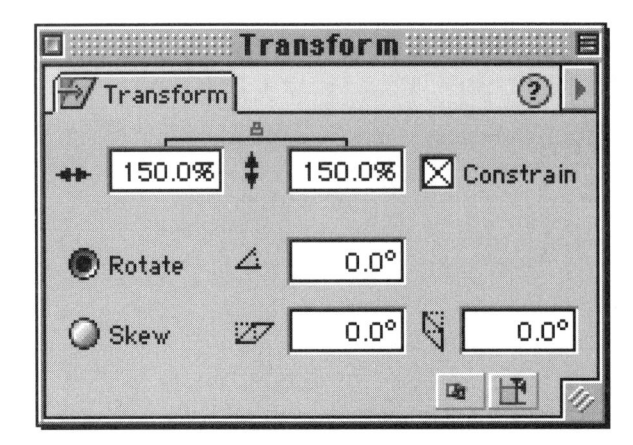

Figure 3-12 Using the Transform panel to make an object larger by 150%.

Our animation now shows the square getting larger as it moves across the screen (Figure 3-13).

Now let's get a little bit more involved. Let's change the transparency of the square as it moves across the screen.

> **Tip:** Since Flash is processor-dependent, you should always try to Tint an object instead of using Alpha transparency. This will make playback smoother and most of the time you can achieve the same effect.

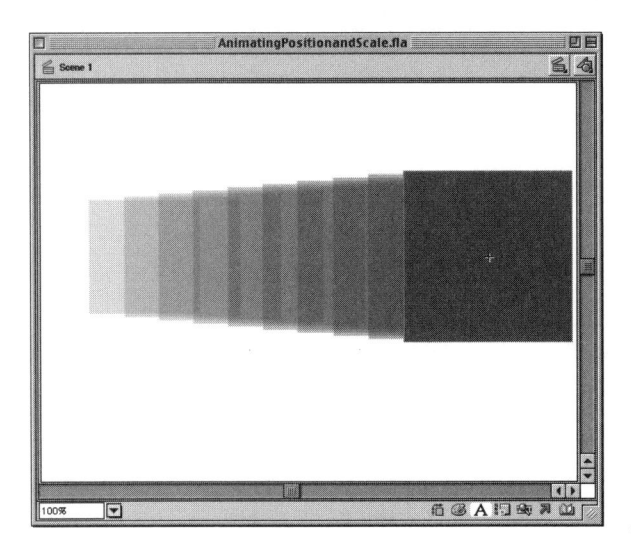

Figure 3-13 Square moving from left to right.

CHAPTER 3 • ANIMATING YOUR ARTWORK 69

FADING THE INSTANCE OF A SYMBOL

This example will show you how to make a symbol fade out as it moves across the Stage. We will create the fade by using the Tint or Alpha effect on the instance of a symbol. For this example, we will use the file from the previous example.

1. Go to Frame 10.
2. Choose Window -> Panels -> Effect. This will bring up the Effect panel.

> **Note**: The following is another example of how you can open the Effect panel. Control + click (or right-click on a PC) on the symbol. This will bring up the context menu and you can choose Panels -> Effect.

3. Select Tint from the pull-down menu in the Effect panel.
4. Set the Tint Color to white and double-check that the tint amount is set to 100% (Figure 3-14).

This was another fairly simple example, but we can use this as a basis for one of the most common animations that you will see on Flash sites, the pulsing button. This example is in the section about movie clips later on in this chapter.

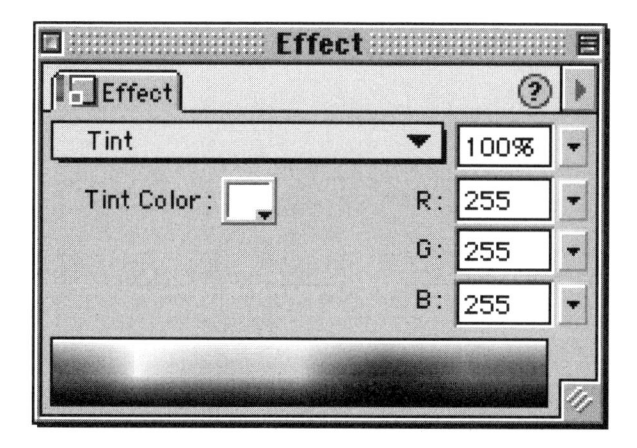

Figure 3-14 Effect panel with the Tint Color set to white.

SPINNING YOUR GRAPHICS

Rotating objects is another way to draw attention to your graphics, with limited effort on your part because Flash will automatically rotate an object if you rotate one of the keyframes. We are going to use text in this example because most of the time when you are animating something, it will be text.

1. Open a new file.
2. In the Character panel, set the Font to Times New Roman and the Font Height to 72.
3. Select the Type tool and type "Flash 5".
4. Select the keyframe for the text in the Timeline and Control + click (right-click on a PC).
5. Select Create Motion Tween from the context menu.
6. Insert a keyframe in Frame 10 by highlighting the frame and pressing F6.
7. Highlight the first keyframe of the text.
8. Use the Transform panel to rotate the text 135 degrees (a random number I chose for this example).

Flash automatically tweens the frames between the angle of the text in Frame 1 to the angle of the text in Frame 10 (Figure 3-15).

To make the rotation go in a certain direction, go into the Frame panel and set the rotation from the pull-down menu to either CW (clockwise) or CCW (counter-clockwise).

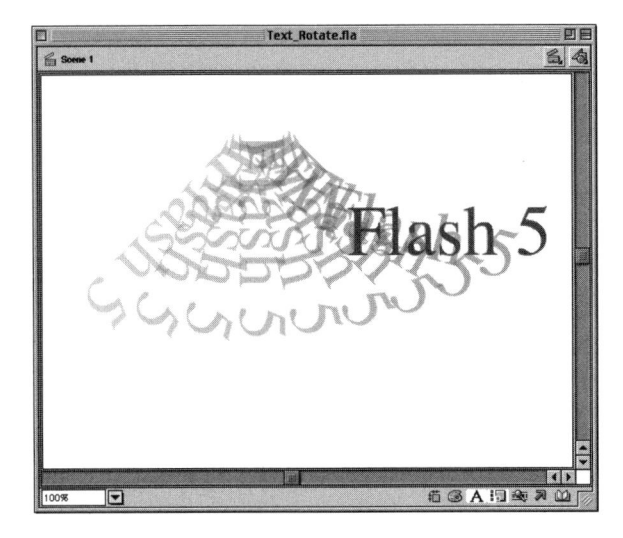

Figure 3-15 Onion Skin view of text being rotated across the screen.

CHAPTER 3 • ANIMATING YOUR ARTWORK

You will also be able to set how many times you would like the image to spin in a chosen direction (Figure 3-16).

> **When making objects rotate, sometimes you will need to add more frames to your animation to get your desired effect. If you have too few frames, the object will not look like it is spinning, but more like it is jumping back and forth.**

This is basically all there is to moving, scaling, rotating, and fading a symbol or grouped object in Flash. The next few examples will cover some techniques that will incorporate some of these features into more involved animations.

FOLLOW THAT PATH

Once in a while, you will find the need to have something animated along a path. You might be creating a site that has airplanes flying around, or some other object that needs to follow a path to look more realistic. In this example, I will show you how to make a plane follow a path that I have created.

1. Open a new file.
2. Choose Window -> Common Libraries -> Movie Clips.
3. Drag the Biplane movie clip from the Movie Clip Library onto the Stage.
4. Select the biplane.
5. Set the scale of the plane to 40% in the Transform panel.
6. Highlight the biplane's layer.

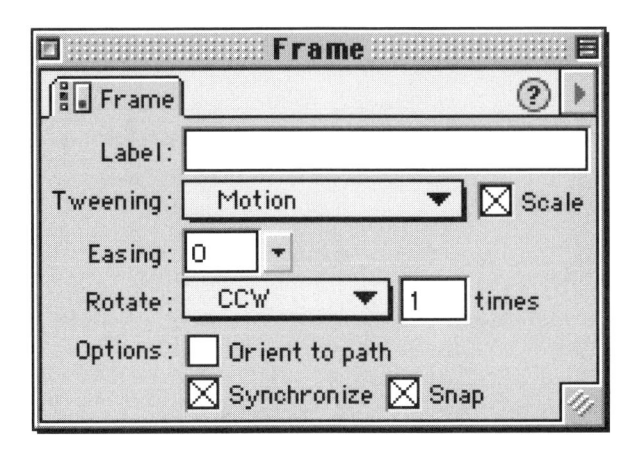

Figure 3-16   Frame panel with Tweening set to Motion and Rotate set to CCW 1 time.

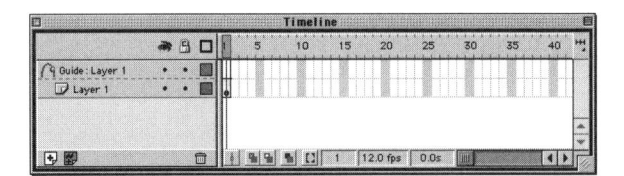

Figure 3-17 Timeline with a Motion Guide layer.

7. Choose Insert -> Motion Guide. This places a layer above the selected layer with the Motion Guide symbol in front of the layer's name (Figure 3-17).

> **There are two other ways to add the Motion Guide layer. The first is to Control + click (right-click on a PC) on the layer's name and select Add Motion Guide. The other is to click the Add Guide Layer button that is in the Timeline window next to the Insert Layer button.**

8. On this layer, draw a wave like the one in Figure 3-18 with the Pencil tool.

> **When using the Pencil tool to draw a smooth line, set the menu in the Options section of the Toolbar to Smooth. You can also smooth the line out after you have finished by using the Arrow tool to select the line. Then, click the Smooth button from the Options section of the Toolbar.**

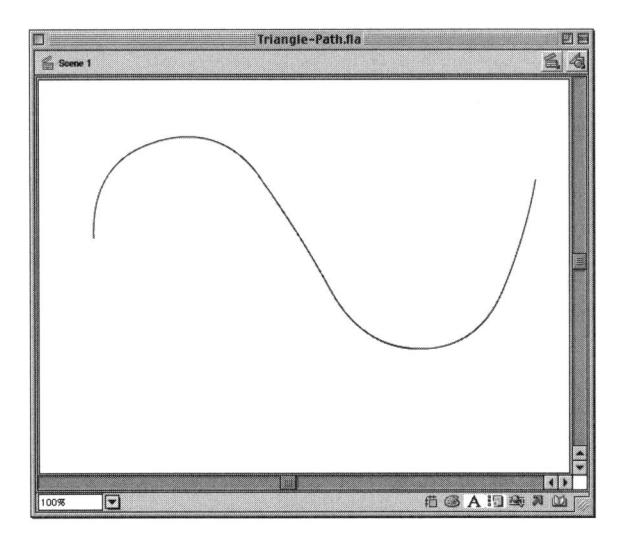

Figure 3-18 Picture of the path that the biplane will be animated along.

CHAPTER 3 • ANIMATING YOUR ARTWORK

9. On the Stage, select the biplane and drag it toward the line. You will see a hollow circle in the center or corner of the triangle when you are dragging it across the Stage. The plane will snap to the line (motion guide) when it gets close to it.

> **Note:** Make sure that the Snap to Grid feature is selected from the View menu. If Snap to Grid is enabled, it will have a check mark next to it.

10. Control + click (right-click) on the biplane's keyframe and select Create Motion Tween from the menu.
11. Move down the Timeline to Frame 10 and insert a keyframe (press F6) on the biplane's layer.

> **Note:** When you do this, you will notice that the Motion Guide layer is no longer visible. To make the layer visible, it needs to be extended to Frame 10. There are a couple of ways to do this: 1) Choose Insert -> Frame while Frame 10 is highlighted in the Guide layer; 2) Control + click (right-click) on Frame 10 in the Guide layer and select Insert Frame.

12. Click on Frame 10 on the Guide layer to highlight it and press F5 to extend the layer.
13. Select the biplane in Frame 10.
14. Move the biplane until it snaps to the end of the line. You will notice when you get close to the line and let go of the biplane that it will snap into place on the line.

If you preview the movie now, you will see the biplane moving along the line (Figure 3-19), but I think the biplane should follow the line like it was flying through the air.

Using the file from the previous example, follow these steps to make the biplane follow the path.

1. Select the biplane in Frame 1.
2. Rotate the plane -90 degrees in the Transform panel. Repeat this step for the Biplane movie clip in Frame 10.
3. On the biplane's layer, click in between the keyframes to highlight the animation.
4. Choose Window -> Panels -> Frame if the Frame panel is not open already.
5. In the Options section of the Frame panel, select Orient to Path.

74 CHAPTER 3 • ANIMATING YOUR ARTWORK

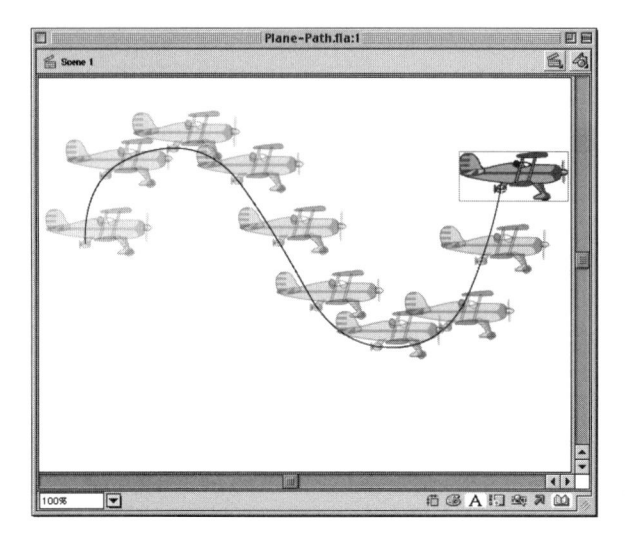

Figure 3-19 View of biplane following a path with Onion Skin feature on.

6. Choose Control -> Test Movie. You will see that the biplane is always pointing forward (Figure 3-20).

Well now that you have mastered the Guide layer, let's make our animation a little more involved. The next example will use paths to make a ball bounce across the screen.

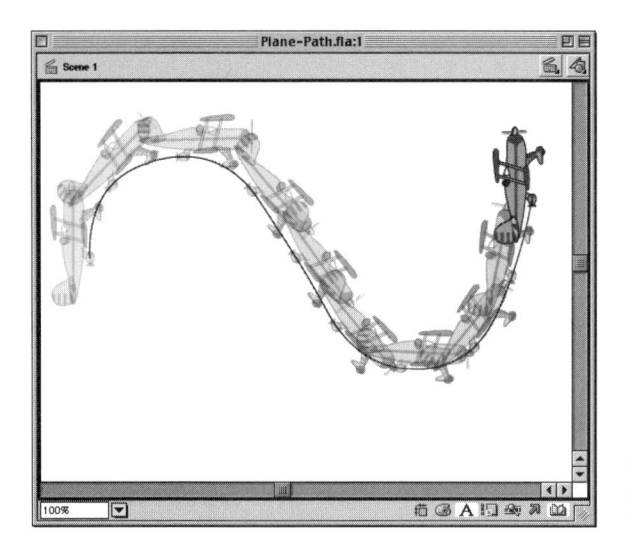

Figure 3-20 View of the biplane following a path with the Onion Skin feature on.

BOUNCING BALL

The bouncing ball is a perfect way for you to learn the Guide layer. This example will show that using the Easing feature will help your animation look more realistic. The Easing feature allows you to make an animation slow down or speed up as it leaves or enters a keyframe.

1. Open a new file.
2. Draw a circle.
3. Select the Paint Bucket tool.
4. Set the fill color to the blue-black radial gradient.
5. Choose Window -> Panels -> Fill to open the Fill panel if it is not open already.
6. Drag the blue marker (in the Fill panel) over a little to the right.
7. Insert a new marker at the beginning of the gradient range by clicking to the left of the blue marker.
8. Set the gradient color of this new marker to white using the pull-down color palette at the right of the gradient range.
9. Using the Paint Bucket tools click in the upper left part of the circle. This will fill the circle with the gradient and give it a 3-dimensional look.
10. Control + click (right-click) on Frame 1 and select Create a Motion Tween.
11. Control + click (right-click) on the layer's name and select Add a Motion Guide.
12. Use the Pencil tool to make a Motion Guide like the "V" shape in Figure 3-21.

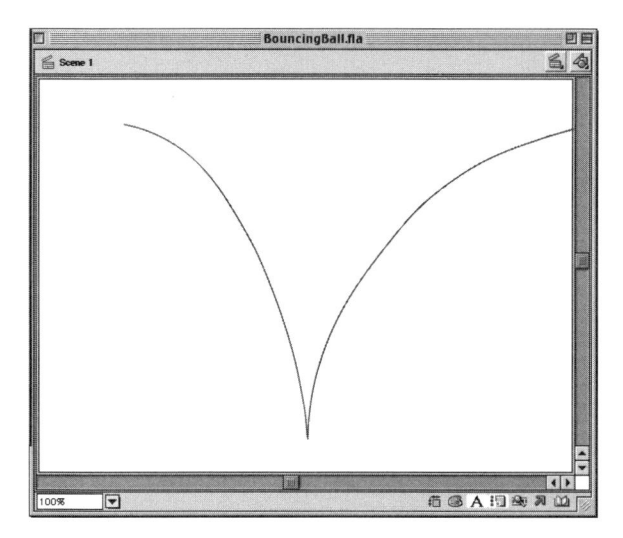

Figure 3-21   Path used for the bouncing ball.

13. Extend the Guide layer to Frame 20 by clicking on Frame 20 and pressing F5.
14. Add keyframes to Frames 10 and 20 of the circle's layer (press F6).
15. The circle in Frame 1 should be moved and snapped to the left side of the "V".
16. The circle in Frame 10 should be moved and snapped to the bottom point of the "V".
17. The circle in Frame 20 should be moved and snapped to the right side of the "V".
18. The next step is to change the easing of the ball in the Frame panel.
19. Click on the keyframe in Frame 1 on the circle's layer. In the Frame panel, change the Easing to −75. This will make the ball move faster as it is approaching the keyframe in Frame 10.
20. Click on the keyframe in Frame 10 on the circle's layer. In the Frame panel, change the Easing to 75. This will make the ball slow down as it reaches its ending point, Frame 20.

> **Tip:** If you use the Onion Skinning tool for the previous example, you will see the circle's position in every frame. This will help you understand the Easing feature that we have used. As you can see by Figure 3-22, the ball is much closer together in the starting and ending frames of the animation.

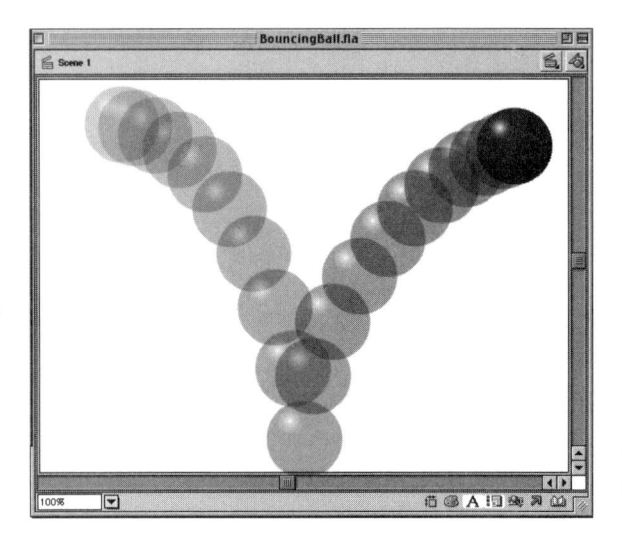

Figure 3-22 Onion skinned view of the ball bouncing, showing the effect of easing an animation.

CHAPTER 3 • ANIMATING YOUR ARTWORK 77

CREATING A MOVIE CLIP

A movie clip is a behavior of a symbol. One of the main advantages to using movie clips is that your animation can still be looping even when the main Timeline has stopped. This is most commonly seen in buttons on Flash sites that are pulsing to draw attention to them while the rest of the site is static. It is also a good idea to make certain animations into movie clips that you know you will be using again. This way, you will have the same file used in all your buttons, which helps keep the file size down.

PULSING CIRCLE

The following is a good example of something you might use as a movie clip for a button. This animation will help you draw attention to a button or graphic on your site. This example will show you how to make a looping movie clip that will add a pulsing effect to part of your site.

1. Open a new file.
2. Choose Insert -> New Symbol. This opens the Symbol Properties window. You can also use Command + F8 (Control + F8 on a PC) to create a new symbol.
3. Name your clip and choose Movie Clip as your symbol's behavior.
4. Select the Oval tool.
5. Draw an oval on the Stage that only has a stroke.
6. Control + click (right-click) on the first keyframe and select Create Motion Tween; this will automatically create a graphic symbol for the oval's stroke and place it into the Library.
7. Add a keyframe in Frame 6 (press F6 to insert a keyframe).
8. Highlight the keyframe in Frame 6.
9. Choose Window -> Panels -> Effect to open the Effect panel if it is not open already.
10. Set the Alpha (transparency) to 0%. The reason we are using Alpha in this example is because this movie clip might be placed over other images or different colored backgrounds. So, using the Tint effect in this example would not be the best idea.
11. Go to the Transform panel.
12. Set the Scale of the oval's stroke to 150%.
13. Create a new layer.
14. Select all six frames of the animation.

15. Press Option (Alt on a PC) and drag the animation so that its first frame is on Frame 3 (Figure 3-23) of the new layer. You will see a plus sign (+) in the Hand cursor; this means that you are copying the animation.
16. Click on Scene 1 at the top left-hand corner of the Stage window. This will bring you out of the Symbol Editing mode.
17. Choose Window -> Library to open the Library.
18. Drag the movie clip for the oval's outline onto the Stage.
19. Create a new layer.
20. Place the oval's stroke graphic symbol that was created by Flash from the Library onto the Stage in this new layer.
21. Select both the oval graphic and the movie clip using the Arrow tool.
22. Choose Window -> Panels -> Align.
23. Click the Align Horizontal Center and Align Vertical Center buttons; this will align the two images to each other.
24. Lock the movie clip's layer by clicking in the Lock column next to its layer.
25. Select the oval's outline graphic.
26. Break apart the oval's outline symbol by pressing Command + B (Control + B on a PC).
27. Fill the middle of the oval with a color, then delete the outline.
28. Choose Control -> Test Movie.

When you test this movie, you will see that the oval looks like it is shooting pulses out (Figure 3-24).

This type of animation is very simple and can add a great touch to a site. If you have already created an animation and you want to make it into a movie clip, it is very easy.

1. Select all the frames in the first layer. The best way to select all the frames in a layer is to click on the name of the layer.
2. Press Option + Command + C (Control + Alt + C on a PC).
3. Create a new Movie Clip symbol.
4. Highlight the first layer.

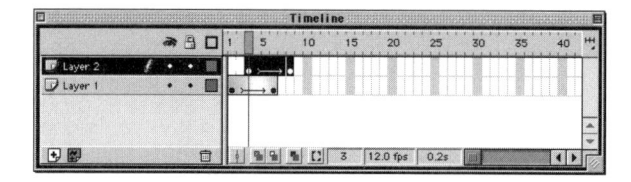

Figure 3-23   Timeline showing the copying of one layer to a new layer.

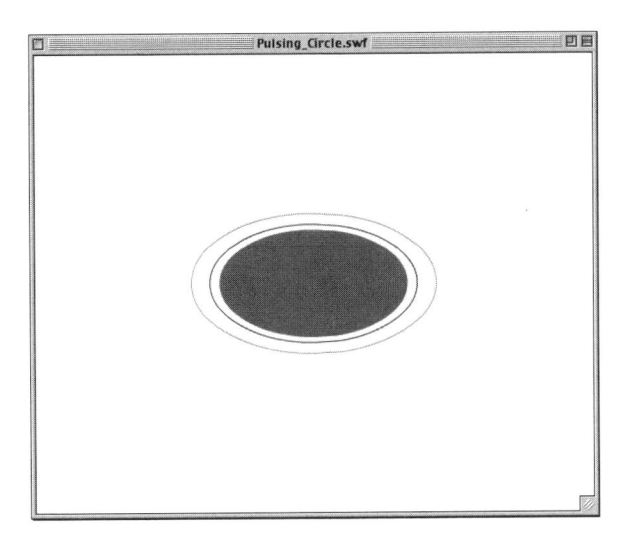

Figure 3-24 Pulsing oval that uses a movie clip to allow for the outlines to continually loop.

5. Paste all the frames into the Movie Clip Timeline by pressing Option + Command + V (Control + Alt + V on a PC).
6. Repeat Steps 1-5 for all the layers of your animation. Make sure that you add a new layer for every layer you are copying over.

> **Warning:** If you are copying an animation that is using Shape Hints, your Shape Hints will have to be redone.

FRAME-BY-FRAME ANIMATION

This is the most laborious of all the types of animation you can do in Flash because each frame must be created individually. But sometimes, it is the best and only way to create animated characters. I'm not saying that this is the only way to create animated characters. You can certainly use Motion and Shape Tweening for some character movement, but other movements are best done as frame-by-frame. The following is a good example of when you might need to use frame-by-frame animation to get the desired effect. If you have multiple frames of characters interacting with each other like those in Figure 3-25, use frame-by-frame animation.

Prepare the graphics and import them as a sequence. The trick to importing files as a sequence is to have them in numerical order. Then, when you are importing the images, just import Frame 1. Flash will notice that the file is part of a numbered

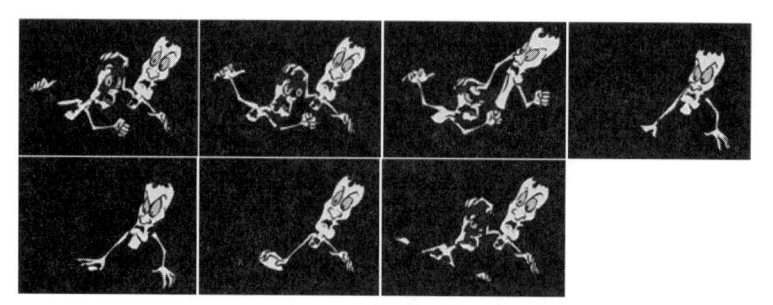

Figure 3-25 Sequence of stills to be used as a frame-by-frame animation. Visuals provided courtesy of Oxy® © 2000 SmithKline Beecham.

sequence and ask you if you want to import all the files as a sequence. Your Timeline should look like the one in Figure 3-26.

You can see how this would quickly add to the file size of your movie and why it is wise to try and stay away from overusing this type of animation.

USING VIDEO IN FLASH

Unfortunately, Flash does not allow you to use movie files like Quicktime, AVI, and MPEG. Even though it has the ability to import Quicktime files, these files will not show up when you export in the Flash SWF format. This feature is only for use when exporting as a Quicktime movie. You can, however, fake video in Flash. What you can do is break your movie file down into a sequence of frames to be used as a frame-by-frame animation. This can make your file size very large, so it is advisable to not try and import full frame video at 30 fps. You should probably try something no bigger than half that size (320x240), at about 8 fps. Chapter 10, "Tips and Tricks," will cover other ways to fake video.

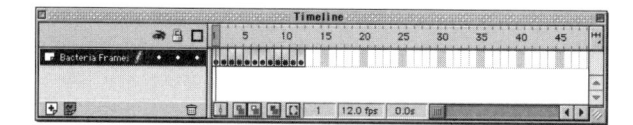

Figure 3-26 The Timeline of a frame-by-frame animation.

chapter 4

GETTING YOUR AUDIO IN SYNC

"Audio" is a word that either makes a person cringe or one that a person warmly embraces. If you are one of the former, then this chapter is for you. Here, I'll show you how easy it is to work with audio in Flash. We will cover topics like importing, controlling, compressing, and exporting. This chapter will help you to become more comfortable importing audio by discussing programs and techniques that will help you to set up your audio files to work better with Flash. You will learn the differences between the two types of sounds in Flash, Streaming and Event sounds. For the more advanced, we will delve into ActionScripts that can control your audio. The chapter wraps up with a section that discusses the types of compression available and the best way to set up your audio when exporting your file as a Quicktime movie. Now that I have teased you with the contents of this chapter, let's move on to the first section.

ADDING AUDIO TO YOUR PROJECT

Okay, you have decided to use audio in your site. Whether you use a music bed or an effect when you roll over a button, you will need to prepare the file. This section will cover the accepted file types, setting them up, importing them, and using Shared Libraries for your audio.

FILE FORMATS YOU CAN USE

Before you import audio, you need to make sure your audio clips are saved in a file format that is accepted by Flash. If you have Quicktime 4 or a newer version installed on your machine, you will be able to import more file types than in previous versions of Flash. Table 4-1 shows the accepted file formats, the platforms they work on, and which files require Quicktime 4.

Macromedia has allowed you to work more efficiently by allowing you to use more file types than previously allowed. This also decreases the time needed to set the files up to be imported.

Table 4-1 File Formats Accepted by Flash

File Formats	Platform	Quicktime 4 Required?
WAV	Mac and PC	Yes/No
AIFF	Mac	No
MP3	Mac and PC	No
Sound Designer II	Mac	Yes
Quicktime Movies (sound only)	Mac and PC	Yes
Sun AU	Mac and PC	Yes
System 7 sounds	Mac	Yes

SETTING UP YOUR AUDIO FILE

Most of your setup time will consist of getting the audio clip you want and saving it out in the right format. If you are using audio as a music loop under a whole site, you will want to make sure it is a clean loop and hopefully not a very annoying one. The last thing you want to do is drive people away from your site.

When you have chosen the clip you want to use, you need to convert it to the right file format. I have used a lot of different audio programs and found some easier to use than others, but in the end, they all need to export the audio in the same way. Most programs will be able to convert audio into at least one of the formats accepted by Flash. The Pro version of Apple's Quicktime 4 has the ability to take your files and convert them. Not many people know all of the features and abilities of Quicktime Pro. It is also one of the easiest programs to use. Of course, it does not have all the features of a sound editing program, but more often than not, it will get the job done. If you have a slower machine and/or not a lot of RAM, you should make your sound file a mono file to decrease the file size. The larger the file size of your movie, the more it will slow down Flash. One thing that you should try to do is get your file into the MP3 file format. Since you are allowed to import MP3s in Flash 5, you should take advantage and use them whenever you can. One drawback to Quicktime Pro is that you cannot export as an MP3 file. There are a few shareware programs that will let you convert files into MP3s. Here is a short list of programs you can use to create MP3 files: Musicmatch Jukebox for both Mac and PC, MPecker Drop Decoder for Mac, and Electronic Cosmo for PC.

> **If you bring in an audio clip at 48kHZ or higher, it will be converted to 44kHZ by Flash and this will affect the sound of your audio clip. This also holds true for clips that are imported below 11kHZ.**

IMPORTING YOUR AUDIO FILE

Let's go over how to import a sound file into Flash.

1. Open a new file.
2. Choose File -> Import.
3. Select and add the audio file you want and click Import. On a PC, you will just need to select the file and choose Open.

> **You will notice that your audio file is placed directly into the Library and not into the Timeline. (If you do not have a sound to import, use one that is supplied in Flash. Choose Libraries -> Sounds to see a list of sounds ready for use in Flash.)**

4. Select Frame 1.
5. Choose Window -> Panels -> Sound to open the Sound panel.
6. Choose your file from the Sound pull-down menu (Figure 4-1).

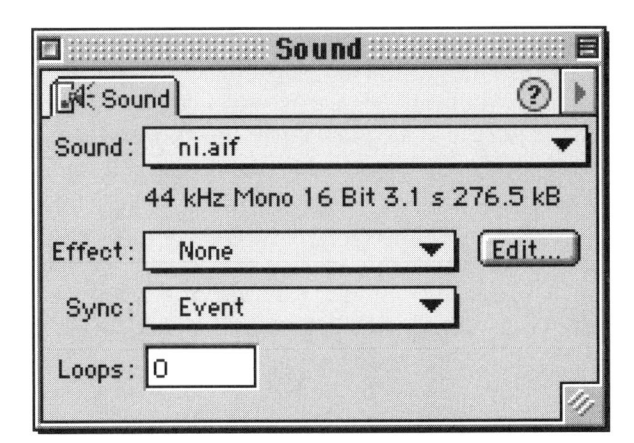

Figure 4-1   Sound panel with an audio clip selected.

7. Save this file so it can be used in later examples.

When you follow these instructions, your audio clip will use the default sound settings.

> **Note:** There is another way you can get a sound into the Timeline. Insert a keyframe (press F6) and drag the audio clip from the Library onto the Stage. The audio clip will appear in the keyframe you have highlighted. This file will use the default settings in the Sound panel.

CONTROLLING AUDIO

First, understand that using audio in Flash is not a perfect science. There are a lot of variables that will determine the playback of the audio for your project. Even though you cannot control some of these variables like a person's Internet connection or computer hardware, there are some things that you can control. You can make use of Flash's sound editing controls to control the volume or the start and end of your audio clip. You can choose between Event and Streaming sounds to optimize the user's experience. Let's jump right into learning how to use the sound editing controls.

UNDERSTANDING THE SOUND EDITING CONTROLS

We will have to become familiar with the Sound panel before we can move on to using the sound editing controls. You will need to use the file you created when we covered importing an audio file. The Sound panel gives you all the details about the sound you are using (Figure 4-1). If you look in the Sound panel under the Sound pull-down menu, you will see the selected clip's information. This information includes the compression, if it is stereo or mono, bit rate, length in seconds, and the file size in kilobytes. This information will help you later on when you are thinking about file size. You might realize that the clip is too long or maybe you will make it 8-bit to decrease the file size. As a rule of thumb, I have always tried to keep my audio clips under two seconds because anything over that just seems to be too long.

The next section of the Sound panel is the Effect menu. You will be able to choose from some effects that are built into Flash. These can change the volume or channel of the audio clip. For example, you can make the audio play out of the left or right channel, fade from left to right or right to left, or fade in or out. To get more precise, you might want to use the Envelope Handles to customize how quickly a clip fades. To do this, open the Edit Envelope window by clicking the Edit button located next to the Effect pull-down menu (Figure 4-2).

CHAPTER 4 • GETTING YOUR AUDIO IN SYNC

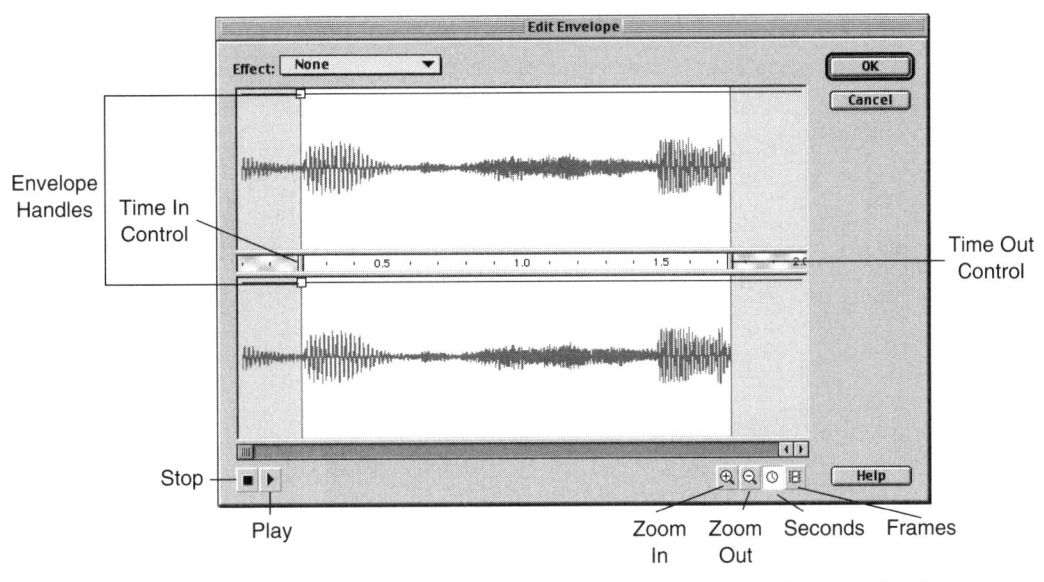

Figure 4-2 The Edit Envelope window, which is used to customize effects applied to audio clips.

This window offers the following controls: Time In/Out, Envelope Handles, and Envelope Line. These are ways to customize effects applied to your audio clips.

If we look back at the Sound panel, we will see the Sync menu. This menu allows us to choose the type of sound we want to use, either Event or Stream.

The last part of the Sound panel that we need to cover is the Loop menu, which is pretty obvious. Let's move ahead and go into more detail on all of these features.

Using the Time In/Out Controls

By using the Time In/Out controls, you will affect how much of a clip is exported with a movie. This is a little known feature that can be very helpful in fine-tuning audio clips. These controls can be found on the Timeline that is in between the two audio channels. They are little gray bars that you can drag up and down the Timeline. Since file size is so crucial on the Web, every little bit you save will make the experience better for your visitors by letting them download the file quicker. The Time In/Out features can also be used to remove unwanted sounds from your clip. By moving the Time Out bar a little bit, you can remove that annoying pop at the end of your audio clip.

1. Open a new file.
2. Choose Window -> Common Libraries -> Sounds.

3. Drag Visor Hum Loop from the Sounds Library onto the Stage.
4. Select Frame 1 and open the Sound panel if it is not open already.
5. Click the Edit button to open the Edit Envelope window.
6. Drag the Time Out bar to approximately .5 seconds.
7. Drag the Time In bar to approximately .1 seconds (Figure 4-3).
8. Click the Play button at the bottom of the window to hear the difference.

Not only are we saving file size by only using a section of the clip, we have found another use for the clip. Now the clip can be used as a rollover sound for a button. This brings up the possibility of using one audio clip for multiple sounds.

Understanding Envelope Handles and Envelope Lines

Envelope Handles and Lines are found in the Edit Envelope window. Envelope Handles are little hollow squares. With no effect selected, the handles are located at the top of the channel windows, above the Time In slider. They are on the Envelope Line that runs straight across the top of the channel windows. Using the handles, you have the ability to change the volume of your audio clip. To customize your own settings, you have to adjust the Envelope Lines with the Envelope Handles. This is a very intuitive feature because when the Envelope Handle is up, the volume is at its highest, and when it is all the way down, the volume is muted. You can look at the Envelope Handles as points of a line. When you want the line to be at an angle, you can add a point at the end of the line. Then you can drag the starting point down, causing the line to be sloped up. The following example will show how to use one of the built-in effects and how it looks.

1. Open a new file.
2. Choose Window -> Common Libraries -> Sounds to open the Sounds Library.

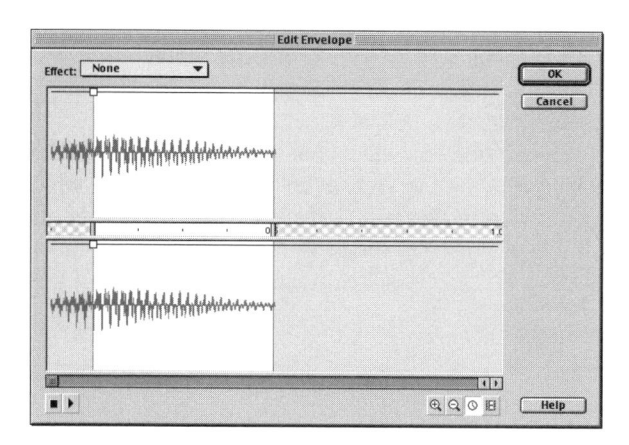

Figure 4-3   Time In/Out Handles used to change the length of a clip in the Edit Envelope.

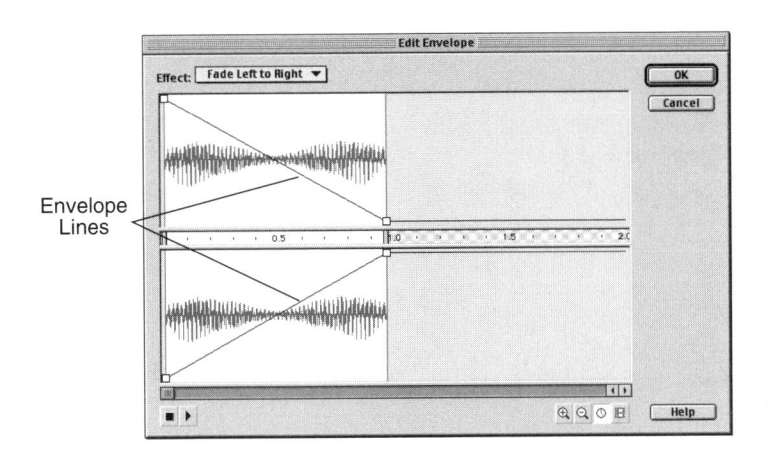

Figure 4-4 Fading a clip from left to right using the built-in effects.

3. Drag Visor Hum Loop from the Sounds Library onto the Stage.
4. Select Frame 1 and open the Sound panel.
5. Click Edit to open the Edit Envelope window.
6. Select Fade Left to Right from the Effect pull-down menu (Figure 4-4).

You will notice the effect that this has on the Envelope Handles and Envelope Lines. This is a great effect if your user has stereo sound coming out of their computer. You can have a lot of fun making noises that go from left to right.

Now let's experiment with customizing our own effects. To add a new Envelope Handle, just click in one of the audio channel windows and a new Envelope Handle will appear wherever you click. An almost identical handle will appear in the other channel's window. The new handle will be placed in the same place in the Timeline, but it will be placed on the Envelope Line where it is instead of adjusting the line for volume to match the one you just created (Figure 4-5). This way, you can manipulate the volume of the left and right channels separately.

Looping Audio Clips

The Looping feature in Flash works unlike others you have come across. What I mean by this is there is no way to set an audio file to infinitely loop. Basically, you have to set the loops to a number that is higher than you think the animation will need. This feature can also be used to allow you to set an audio clip to fade out after a certain number of loops.

1. Open a new file.
2. Use the Visor Hum Loop audio clip from the Sounds Library.
3. Open the Sound panel.

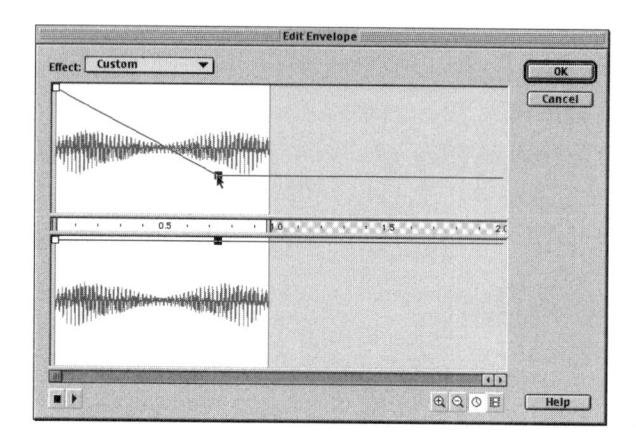

Figure 4-5   Adding new Envelope Handles to an audio clip.

4. Set the number of loops to 3.
5. Click Edit to open the Edit Envelope window.
6. You will see the waveform in the sound editing window is 3 times longer than it was before (Figure 4-6).
7. Adjust the envelope handles to make the sound fade out at the end of the third loop (Figure 4-7).

If you are using streaming sounds, you can have an audio clip fade out close to a specific frame. To locate where you are in the Timeline, use the Frames button, which changes the display of the audio clip from seconds to frames. The Frames button is located at the bottom of the Edit Envelope window next to the Help button. When you click this, you can choose a frame in the Timeline to which to add a fade. This is not perfect, like I mentioned before, but you should be able to get close. You should not try

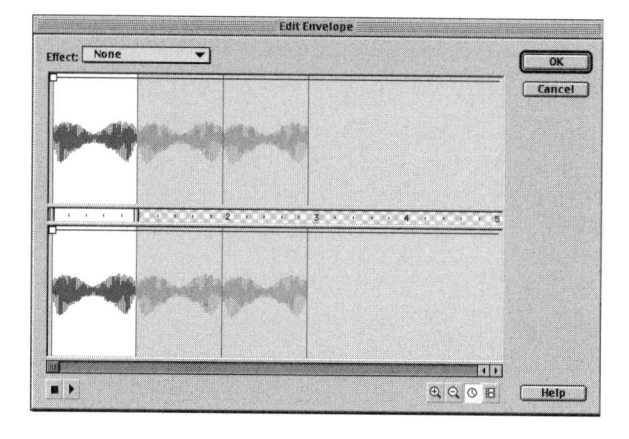

Figure 4-6   The Edit Envelope window showing an audio clip with the Loop option set to 3.

CHAPTER 4 • GETTING YOUR AUDIO IN SYNC   89

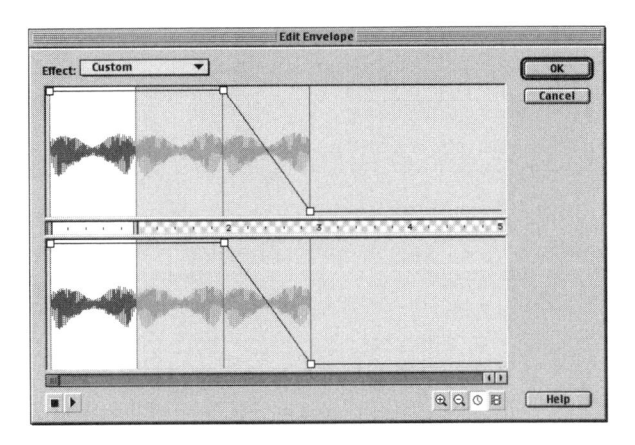

Figure 4-7 Fading out an audio clip in its third loop.

to hit a beat; you should always try to use a phase like "Visor Hum" to animate your graphics. This way, if you are not right on, it won't look bad. One thing you should also make sure of is that when you select the Loop feature with a streaming sound, that you have extended the audio layer in your movie's Timeline so that the clip can continue to play.

> **If you have a file that you want to loop under an animation and you set the audio clip to the Event Sync option, whether you choose 5 or 20 loops, the file's size will not change much at all. But, the same file set to the Streaming option changes in file size depending on the number of frames in your Timeline.**

EVENT SOUNDS

The Event Sound option is a way of synchronizing audio with specific events in your animation. This is very popular for using with buttons or as sound effects. For example, if you want to have a sound play when someone rolls over a button, you can place the sound in the Over state of the button. The following example shows you how to make a button and add sound to it.

1. Open a new file.
2. Create a new symbol by pressing Command + F8 (Control + F8 on a PC).
3. Select Button as the Behavior. This will take you into Symbol Editing mode.
4. Notice that the Timeline of a button is set up a little differently than the normal Timeline (Figure 4-8).

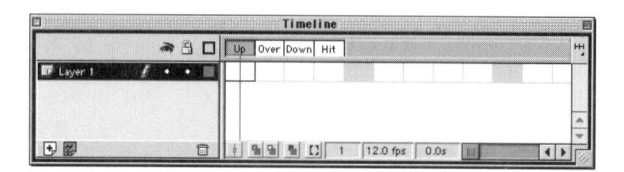

Figure 4-8 Timeline of a button in Symbol Editing mode.

5. To make it easier to understand the states of buttons, use the Text tool to make text for each state of the button. Type them in as "UP", "OVER", and "DOWN", and place each graphic in its own keyframe on the layer.
6. For the Hit state, you can just draw a box because it is not visible.

Note
The Hit state of a button is the area that makes the button active. For example, if you make a really small square as your Hit state, it will be hard for people to activate the button. On the other hand, if you make the Hit state very large, you will have problems with buttons overlapping and people getting to the wrong link. It is also best to use a solid image as your Hit state instead of text. If you use text as the Hit state, the button will turn on and off as you are rolling your mouse across the letters.

7. Create a new layer.
8. Add a keyframe (press F6) into the frame under the "OVER" label.
9. Place a sound into this keyframe. For this example, I have chosen the Smack audio clip (Figure 4-9).

Yes, it really is that simple to add sound to a button. Before you start using the Event Sound option, there are some pros and cons you should become familiar with. One big drawback to using the Event Sound option is that the audio clip has to download in its entirety to be able to play. If you are trying to sync the clip up with an event, it needs to either be small enough to download quickly or you will need to pre-load the audio clip. A quick way to pre-load an audio clip is to place the audio clip at the beginning of the Timeline. Then, set its volume all the way down by using the Event Handles. This way, the audio clip will play and load, but no sound will come out. So now

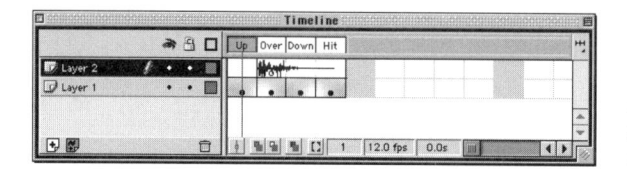

Figure 4-9 Timeline of a button with an audio clip in its Over state.

CHAPTER 4 · GETTING YOUR AUDIO IN SYNC 91

when you go to use this sound in another section, it will already be loaded. Another attribute of the Event Sound option is that it will play an entire clip whether the main movie is playing or stopped. This can be good and bad, depending on your use of the file. This example covers a way that you can stop an event sound in any frame that you want.

1. Open a new file.
2. Insert an audio clip in Frame 1.
3. Set the audio clip to loop so that it will play longer than you want (I have set the loop to 15 for this example).
4. Insert a keyframe in the Timeline, on the same layer as the audio clip, at a frame where you want the audio to stop.
5. Click to highlight the new keyframe.
6. Go to the Sound panel and set this keyframe up to use the same audio clip from the Sound pull-down menu.
7. Change the Sync option to Stop instead of Event (Figure 4-10).

STREAMING SOUNDS

The most popular use for the Streaming Audio option is synchronizing animation to a longer music clip. One downside to this type of audio is that Flash forces the animation to keep pace with the audio. Since audio cannot be slowed down, the animation will skip frames to keep up. On slower machines, this will be more noticeable as they will not be able to draw the graphics fast enough. Another disadvantage to streaming audio is that no matter how many loops you have the clip set for, it will stop when the playback head stops. The major advantage to streaming sound is that it can play after a little bit of it is loaded. The one thing that you have to be careful about is that the streaming file will not start right away. The streaming file will start playing when enough of the file is loaded.

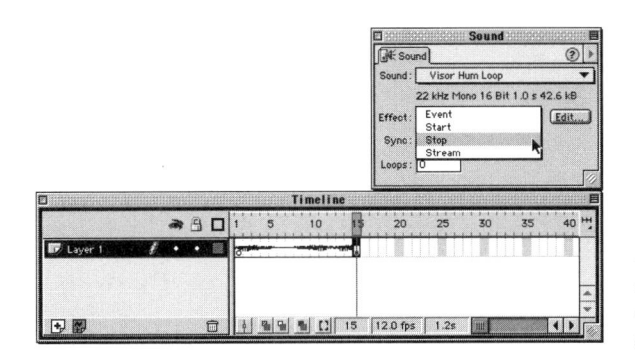

Figure 4-10   Sound panel with Stop being selected and Timeline showing the frame where the audio is stopped.

Flash uses an action called _soundbuftime to determine how much of an audio clip to pre-load before a movie starts. The default for this sound buffer is five seconds. ActionScript is the programming language used in Flash. Actions allow you to control objects, movie clips, and sounds. ActionScripts are covered in greater detail in Chapter 5.

1. Open a new file.
2. Import an audio clip.
3. Open the Sound panel.
4. Set the clip's Sync to Stream.
5. Set the Loop option to 10.
6. Extend the audio clip's layer in the main Timeline to Frame 100.
7. Add a new layer.
8. Click to highlight the first frame.
9. Choose Window -> Actions to open the Frame Actions window.
10. Select _soundbuftime from the Properties section of the Frame Actions windows.
11. Set the _soundbuftime expression equal to 3 (Figure 4-11).

This is a global property that affects all the streaming sounds in the movie, so you do not need to tell the movie where to add the buffer.

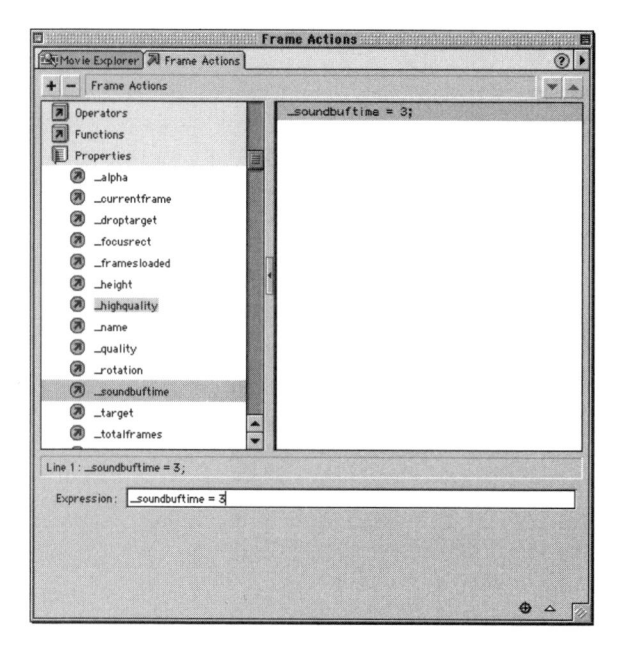

Figure 4-11   Frame Actions window showing how to set up the _soundbuftime action.

> If you set the buffer to a time that is too short, your audio will catch up with its buffer and stop until it loads a new buffer.

USING SHARED LIBRARIES FOR YOUR AUDIO FILES

Maybe you have a music loop or effect that you want to use across different movies. This is the perfect scenario to take advantage of the Shared Library feature that is new to Flash 5. This is a very simple feature to use and it will save your visitors minutes of download time. Yes that is right, you can have people waiting less for your site to download and still have the same multimedia impact as a larger site. By using the Shared Library feature, you will only need to download the file once and you can share it across multiple movie files. The following example will cover setting up a Library file and the main movie.

1. Open a new file.
2. Choose Window -> Common Libraries -> Sounds.
3. Choose Window -> Library to open the Library for the current movie.
4. Drag the Beam Scan audio clip from the Sound Library window into the Library window for the movie.
5. Control + click (right-click on a PC) on the Audio Clip icon in the Library.
6. Choose Linkage from the context menu. This will open the Symbol Linkage Properties window.
7. Select Export this symbol from the Linkage section of the Symbol Linkage Properties window.
8. Type in a name as the identifier of this audio clip. I have chosen "audio" for this example (Figure 4-12).
9. Choose File -> Export Movie and set the file format to Flash Player. For this example, I have named this file "shared.swf". Click Save when you are finished.

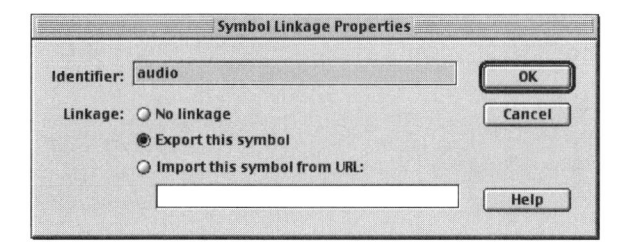

Figure 4-12 Symbol Linkage Properties window set to export or share a sound clip.

Note: The Identifier can be any phrase you want, as long as it does not include spaces. You should keep this name very simple so that it is easier to remember when you need to use it. This phrase is the way your main movie knows which clip to pull from the Library when you have multiple clips.

10. When the Export Flash Player window appears, accept the default settings by clicking OK to continue.
11. Choose File -> Save to save the movie file. To keep things easy, name the file "shared.fla" and click Save.
12. Close the shared.fla file.
13. Open a new file.
14. Choose File -> Open as Shared Library. Select shared.fla, the file you want to import, and click Open (OK on a PC). This will open the Library from the shared.fla movie.
15. Choose Window -> Library. This will open the Library file of the new movie.
16. Drag the audio clip from the shared Library into the new file's Library.
17. Close the shared.fla Library.
18. Control + click (right-click on a PC) on the Audio Clip icon in the new file's Library.
19. Choose Linkage from the context menu.
20. Check that the Symbol Linkage Properties window has the Identifier as "audio" and the Linkage section of the window is set to Import this symbol from URL "shared.swf". Click OK (Figure 4-13).

To test our Shared Library file, we will need to place the audio clip into the Timeline and save the main movie file. For this example to work, both the shared file and the main movie must be in the same location.

Now that we have mastered importing audio into our Flash movies, we will move on and learn about how to choose the right compression for our audio.

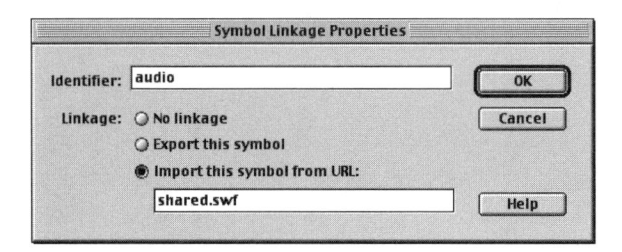

Figure 4-13 Symbol Linkage Properties window set to import a sound clip from an external file.

CHOOSING THE RIGHT COMPRESSION

This is really a trial-and-error thing. You cannot assume that what worked for one sound will work for another. Luckily, by double-clicking on a sound file in the Library, you can get the Sound Properties window. In this window, you can set the Export Settings of the audio clip. You will be able to choose from four Compression settings: Default, MP3, ADPCM, and Raw. This window will also show you the projected file size of your music clip. All you have to do is select which compression you wish to use and click the Test button. This Test button also lets you hear the audio clip with the selected compression. The following is a brief description of the four compression settings available in Flash.

> **Note:** By setting the Export Settings in this window, they will override the settings in the Export Flash Player window, unless you choose Default, which we will cover in Chapter 8.

Default—Uses the settings selected during export.

ADPCM (Advanced Differential Pulse Code Modulation)—This is best used for short sound effects and when you want to export a movie as a Flash 3 file. Even though it is hard to say what is the best compression, I have had good luck setting audio clips to 11kHZ and a bit rate of 3 (Figure 4-14).

Figure 4-14 Export Settings section of the Sound Properties window with ADPCM compression chosen.

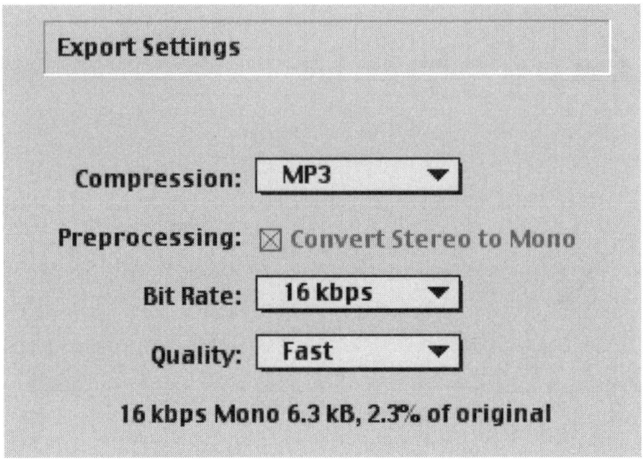

Figure 4-15 Export Settings section of the Sound Properties window with MP3 compression chosen.

MP3—This setting will compress your audio clip using the MP3 audio format. This setting will give you better quality audio and a smaller file size. The drawback to this setting is that it can only be used when you are exporting your file as Flash 4 or higher (Figure 4-15).

Raw—This setting is rarely used. The file size will be large and will cause the download of your movie to be too long. There are only two options you have to affect file size using this compression. One is the ability to change the clip from stereo to mono and the other is to change the sample rate (Figure 4-16).

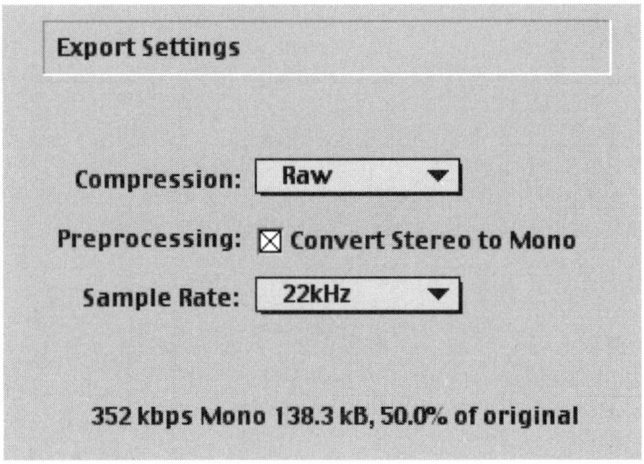

Figure 4-16 Export Settings section of the Sound Properties window with Raw compression chosen.

chapter 5

ALL YOU NEED TO KNOW ABOUT ACTIONSCRIPT

This chapter gives you a look into ActionScript and shows examples of some important scripts. There is no way that I could squeeze the 400-plus page book that comes with Flash 5 into this chapter, nor do I summarize it. I present ActionScript as I have learned it and how it works from my perspective and experience working with it. This approach should ease the learning of the programming language. While taking a look into ActionScript, I define the language and will give you the guidelines of ActionScript's syntax. The chapter wraps up with a few examples that you can apply to your projects to add life to them.

WHAT IS ACTIONSCRIPT?

ActionScript is the programming language in Flash that allows you to make interactive movies. This language has become more powerful in Flash 5 because it has adopted rules. Actually, it has come to look a lot like Javascript. This is because it is based on a document that is the standard for Javascript. This does not mean that you have to run out and learn Javascript, but if you know Javascript, you will be familiar with ActionScript. To learn more about the differences between ActionScript and Javascript, look at the section in the *ActionScript Reference Guide* that details the differences. In this chapter, I will break down all the examples line by line to let you know what is going on in each segment so you will understand why each line is necessary.

HOW DOES ACTIONSCRIPT WORK?

This is where things begin to get a little complicated. I have stripped out most of the programming jargon to make it easier to understand. When you are using Action-Script, you can control objects. Objects can be either graphics like movie clips or data. These scripts are placed in frames or attached to buttons or movie clips. These scripts are known as Frame Actions and Object Actions, respectively.

FRAME ACTIONS

Frame Actions are activated or run when the Playback Head enters a frame. The most common frame actions are those that control the playback of the movie. For example, the most common frame action would be the stop action that is needed to stop movies and movie clips from looping.

OBJECT ACTIONS

Object Actions work a little differently because they rely on handlers. Handlers activate a script that is placed in a button or movie clip. A handler requires an event to trigger its script. The handlers for buttons include on Press, Release, Release Outside, Key Press, Roll Over, Roll Out, Drag Over, and Drag Out. The handlers for movie clips include on Load, Enter Frame, Unload, Mouse down, Mouse up, Mouse move, Key down, Key up, and Data. I will go into more detail on these handlers as we use them throughout the chapter.

WRITING YOUR OWN ACTIONSCRIPTS

We are going to ease into this by creating some simple actions, then we will build up to more involved actions that will require much more explanation. Before we begin, I will cover some features of ActionScript that will be important for you to know to start programming. We will cover the Actions window, ActionScript syntax, targeting movies, and writing and using variables. After we understand the language, we will move on to the examples.

THE ACTIONSCRIPT WINDOW

The Actions window is where we will be doing all of our scripting (Figure 5-1). This was covered in Chapter 1, but I will cover it again here in more detail. All of our work in this chapter will be done in the Normal mode so that you will not have to worry as

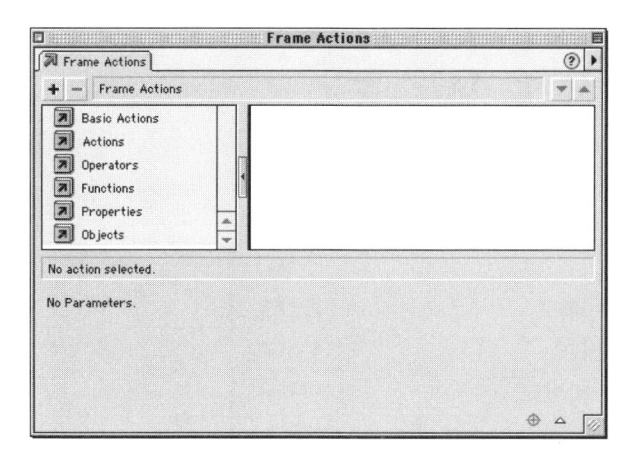

Figure 5-1   Actions window in Flash 5.

much about the syntax. This will let you concentrate on the actions that you want to complete.

The Colored Syntax feature is available while working in the ActionScript window. This will help you when you start to code because you will see certain tags highlighted. The Keywords and Predefined Identifiers will show up blue. The "Play" action is considered a Predefined Identifier, so it will show up blue in the Actions window.

> **Keywords are words that serve a particular function in ActionScript. These words cannot be used for anything else but their particular function. Here is the list of keywords: break, for, new, var, continue, function, return, void, delete, if, this, while, else, in, typeof, and with.**

The other color codes are green for Properties, magenta for Comments, and gray for Strings, which are contained within quotes.

When you look at the left section of the Actions window, you will see six square icons with arrows on them. These squares represent Basic Actions, Actions, Operators, Functions, Properties, and Objects.

Basic Actions

This one is very self-explanatory. These are your simple, everyday actions that are here just for quick access since they all appear in the Actions section (Figure 5-2).

Actions

This section holds all the actions that are available in Flash 5 (Figure 5-3).

You will notice that some actions have been deprecated since Flash 4. An action becomes deprecated when a language evolves and there is a better way to do that action. For example, the "with" action has replaced the "Tell Target" action:

Go To	Esc+go
Play	Esc+pl
Stop	Esc+st
Toggle High Quality	Esc+tq
Stop All Sounds	Esc+ss
Get URL	Esc+gu
FSCommand	Esc+fs
Load Movie	Esc+lm
Unload Movie	Esc+um
Tell Target	Esc+tt
If Frame Is Loaded	Esc+il
On Mouse Event	Esc+on

Figure 5-2   Basic Actions menu from the Actions window.

break	Esc+br
call	Esc+ca
comment	Esc+//
continue	Esc+co
delete	Esc+da
do while	Esc+do
duplicateMovieClip	Esc+dm
else	Esc+el
else if	Esc+ei
evaluate	Esc+ev
for	Esc+fr
for..in	Esc+fi
FSCommand	Esc+fs
function	Esc+fn
getURL	Esc+gu
goto	Esc+go
if	Esc+if
ifFrameLoaded	Esc+il
include	Esc+in
loadMovie	Esc+lm
loadVariables	Esc+lv
on	Esc+on
onClipEvent	Esc+oc
play	Esc+pl
print	Esc+pr
removeMovieClip	Esc+rm
return	Esc+rt
set variable	Esc+sv
setProperty	Esc+sp
startDrag	Esc+dr
stop	Esc+st
stopAllSounds	Esc+ss
stopDrag	Esc+sd
tellTarget	Esc+tt
toggleHighQuality	Esc+tq
trace	Esc+tr
unloadMovie	Esc+um
var	Esc+vr
while	Esc+wh
with	Esc+wt

Figure 5-3   Actions menu from the Actions window.

```
on (release) {
    with (_root.yourClip) {
        stop ();
    }
}
```

This action targets a movie clip called "yourClip" in the main Timeline of the movie and tells it to stop.

Operators

This section shows all the Operators available in Flash (Figure 5-4).

Operators are the symbols used to join variables, strings, and do calculations of numbers. For example, to set x equal to y, you would use this statement x == y. If you want to create a message by joining text, you would follow this code:

```
welcome = "Hello " + name + "." + " How are you?";
```

This script is setting the variable "welcome" equal to the expression (sentence) after the equals sign. The expression after the equals sign is a string that attaches the word "Hello" to a variable called "name" using the "+" operator. The variable "name"

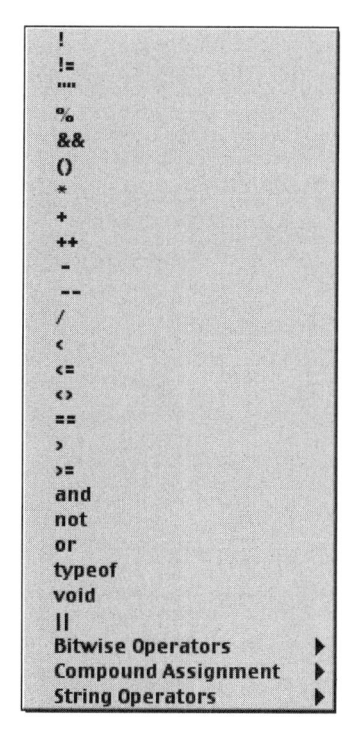

Figure 5-4 Operators menu from the Actions window.

would be a text field that the expression grabs the value "name" from. Then, the "name" variable is attached to a period "." followed by the sentence "How are you?" Again, these are all joined by the "+" operator.

Functions

This section shows all the functions available in Flash 5 (Figure 5-5).

To show you an example of a function, refer to the code below. I will add the "newline" function in this code to make the text break onto two lines. If you are familiar with HTML, this has the same effect as a line break tag "<BR>". It is also the same effect as pressing the Return key when you are typing:

```
welcome = "Hello " + name + "." + newline + "How are you?";
```

Properties

This section shows all the properties available in Flash 5 (Figure 5-6).

Properties are attributes of certain objects in Flash. For example, using the "xmouse" and "ymouse" properties will allow you to track the position of the mouse. An example of this is shown later in this chapter, in the "Change that Cursor" section.

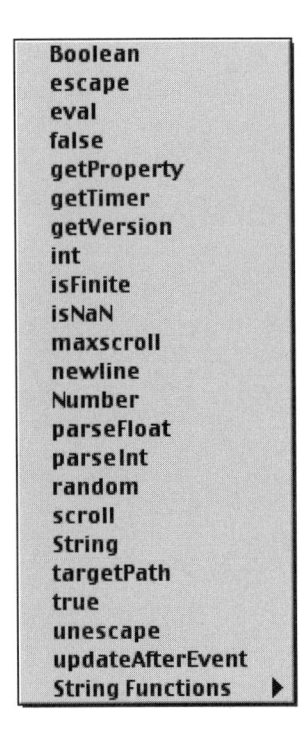

Figure 5-5   Functions menu from the Actions window.

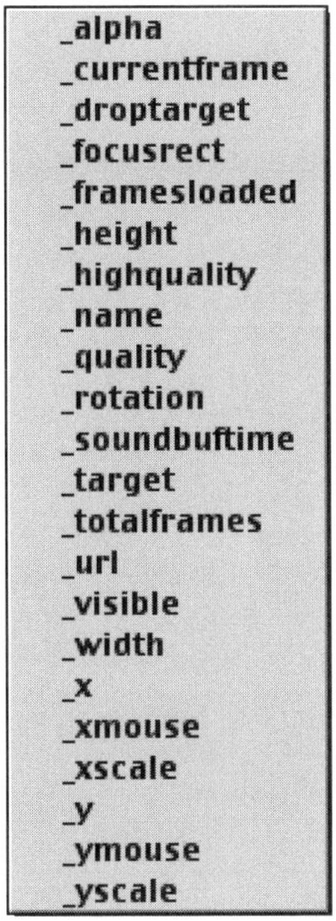

```
_alpha
_currentframe
_droptarget
_focusrect
_framesloaded
_height
_highquality
_name
_quality
_rotation
_soundbuftime
_target
_totalframes
_url
_visible
_width
_x
_xmouse
_xscale
_y
_ymouse
_yscale
```

Figure 5-6 Properties menu from the Actions window.

Objects

This section gives you a list of the predefined objects available in Flash 5 (Figure 5-7).

Each of these objects has a list of properties that you can alter or access. For example, you can tell a movie clip to stop playing by using the following code:

```
on (release) {
    yourClip.stop();
}
```

This action tells the movie clip "yourClip" to stop playing when the button this action is attached to is clicked. This action has the same result as the action in the first example.

ACTIONSCRIPT SYNTAX

Let's get into what comprises the ActionScript language. ActionScript has rules that have to be followed when you are creating code. If you use the Normal mode, you will not have to worry as much about this because the window will prompt you if you type

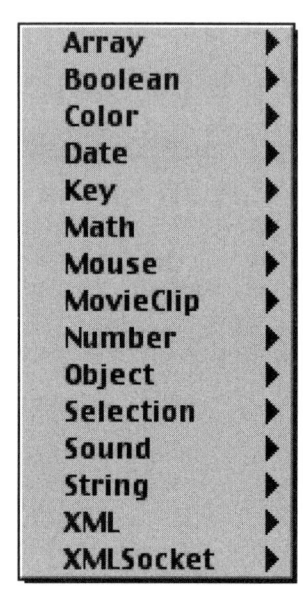

Figure 5-7 Objects menu from the Actions window.

something that is not correct. Flash 4 used the Slash syntax to target variables and movie clips. In Flash 5, you can use the new Dot syntax. The Dot syntax allows you to shorten your code by using the "_parent" alias. This will refer to the clip that holds the current clip or action. If you are building all of your links as absolutes, you will start them with "_root". I have picked up and am more comfortable with the new Dot syntax and I will show you why in the next few sections.

Targeting Movie Clips

This is probably one of the most important things to understand. You will have to think of the main Timeline as a folder that holds all of your elements. If you are trying to change the property of a movie clip, you will need to know where it resides. For example, if you have a movie clip on the Stage that is called "yourClip" and inside of this clip is another movie clip that is called "clip01", you will need to use the following to target the clip:

```
on (release) {
    tellTarget ("/yourClip/clip01") {
        play ();
    }
}
```

The Slash syntax has to use the "tellTarget" or "with" action to call the movie clip.

```
on (release) {
    _root.yourClip.clip01.play();
}
```

The Dot syntax is a much simpler and easier-to-use syntax that does not require extra code.

This was a simple example, but it should have helped you to understand how Flash is structured. It can get more complicated when you are trying to target movie clips from movies that are loaded into the main movie. You will just have to use the level that the movie is in to target it or any of its clips. For example, if you are targeting a clip that is in a movie in "level5," you will replace "_root" with "_level5".

Writing and Using Variables

When you start to make more complicated scripts, you will need to use variables. Variables can be looked at as boxes that hold information. Each box has a unique name that when it is called, it will show you its contents. A variable can be set by you, generated by an expression, or received from an external application. You can either set the variable equal to a literal statement or an expression. This is something you will have to be very careful of when you are using variables. This next example takes a name that a user inputs into a text field and places it into a sentence that appears in another text box.

1. Open a new file.
2. Open the Text Options panel.
3. Create an Input text field.
4. Set the text field to Single Line with a Border and Background and set Variable to "name".
5. Insert a new layer.
6. Create a button that says "Enter" on it (Figure 5-8).
7. Add a Go To action that makes the movie go to Frame 2 and stop.
8. Insert a new layer and call it "Actions".
9. Add a stop action in Frame 1.
10. Insert a new layer.
11. Go to Frame 2 and insert a keyframe in the new layer.
12. Create a Dynamic Text field.
13. Set the text field to Multiline, Word wrap, Selectable with Variable set to "welcome".
14. Go to the Actions layer in Frame 2.
15. Enter the following script into this frame.

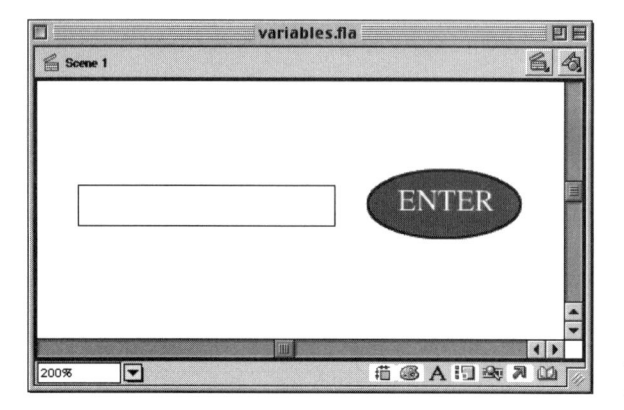

Figure 5-8 Text field and Enter button.

```
welcome="Hello" + name + "." + new line + "How are you?";
```
The "welcome" variable is set up to get the "name" variable from the first text field and add it into the expression that is created as its value.

> **Tip:** Make sure that you check the Expression box next to the value line. If you do not, you will not get the result that you expect. Actually, all that will happen is that Flash will print everything after the equals sign over into the "welcome" text field, including the quotes and plus signs.

16. Test your movie.

When you enter your name in the field and click the Enter button, the movie will jump to the second frame and display the text with your name in the sentence (Figure 5-9).

ACTIONSCRIPT DEBUGGER

This is a great feature that allows you to test and check all the properties and variables in your movie. You can use this to help fine-tune the variables in your movie. We are going to start with how you can use the debugger. Then we will move on to the features of the debugger: Properties, Variables, and Watch Lists. Let's take a closer look at how we can use the debugger.

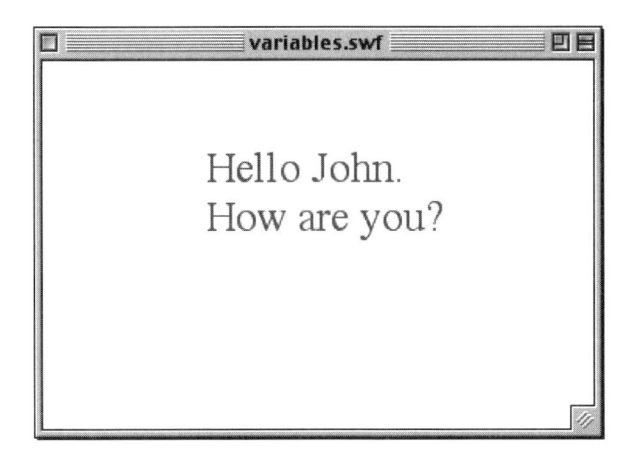

Figure 5-9 The result of the movie after the name has been entered and the Enter button has been clicked.

Local or Remote Debugging?

Yes, you can debug your movie remotely, which might raise concerns for people who do not want others seeing their variables or stealing the movie structure. First, we will cover debugging your movie locally.

1. Open the movie from the "Writing and Using Variables" example.
2. Choose Window -> Debugger.
3. Choose Control -> Debug movie.

This opens the movie into the special debugger Flash Player. You should notice that the display of the debugger changes from "Debugger is Inactive" to "Test Movie" (Figure 5-10).

Now I will show you how to set your movie up for remote debugging.

1. Open the movie from the "Writing and Using Variables" example.
2. Choose File -> Publish Settings.
3. Select the Debugging Permitted option in the Flash section of the Publish window.
4. Choose a password that you will remember because you will be prompted for it later.
5. Click the Publish button.
6. Save and close your file.
7. Choose Window -> Debugger.

8. Select Enable Remote Debugging from the pull-down menu in the Debugger window.
9. Leave Flash and open the SWF file you just published.
10. Choose Control -> Debugger from the Flash Player where the movie has opened.
11. Switch back to Flash and you will be prompted to enter your password before you can debug the movie.

Now that we know how to open the debugger, let me show you how to use it to your advantage.

Debugger Features

The debugger has three main features: the ability to see the properties of each movie, the variables in the movie, and a Watch List, where you can set up certain variables to be seen or watched. One thing that is important to understand is that all the changes made in the debugger will not be saved. It is merely a place for you to fine-tune what needs to change in the movie.

Properties List

The Properties List shows and allows you to edit all the properties in any movie clip in the movie (Figure 5-10). For example, you can change the transparency of the movie to 50% by changing the _alpha value to 50.

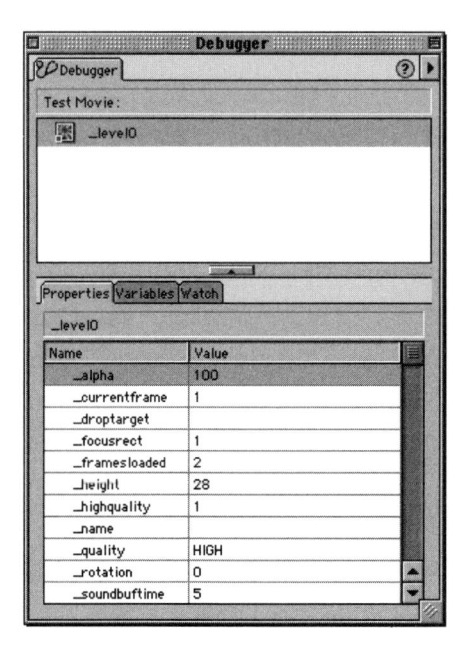

Figure 5-10   Debugger window while it is active.

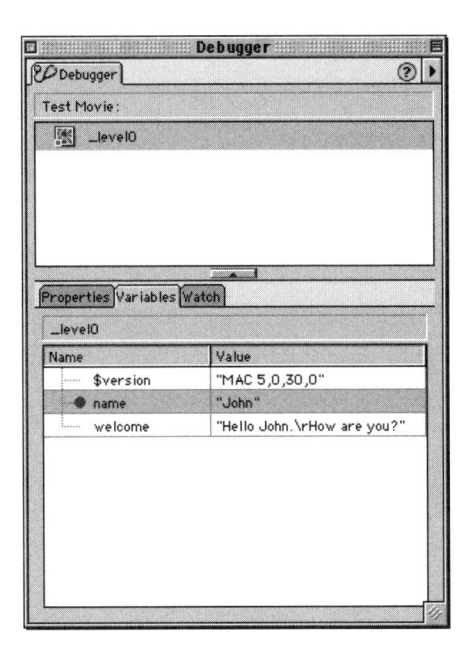

Figure 5-11 Debugger window showing the variables found in the main movie.

Variables List

The Variables List shows all the variables in the selected clip in the top window (Figure 5-11). In this file, nothing will show up until you run the little application. This is because there are no variables established until you input something into the Name field. Once you input your name, you will see the "name" and "welcome" variables show up in the window.

Watch List

This feature is great when you want to single out some variables that you want to watch as the movie plays. To add variables to the Watch List, highlight them in the Variables List and select Add Watch from the pull-down menu in the Debugger panel. This will highlight the variable in the Variables List by placing a blue dot next to the variable (Figure 5-11). If you select the Watch tab, you will see the variable you have selected appear in the Watch List (Figure 5-12).

SAMPLE ACTIONSCRIPTS

This section will put everything we have gone over in this chapter together to create some scripts you might use in your everyday projects. We are going to learn scripts that will put the date on your site and change the mouse cursor. Then we will create a

110   **CHAPTER 5 • ALL YOU NEED TO KNOW ABOUT ACTIONSCRIPT**

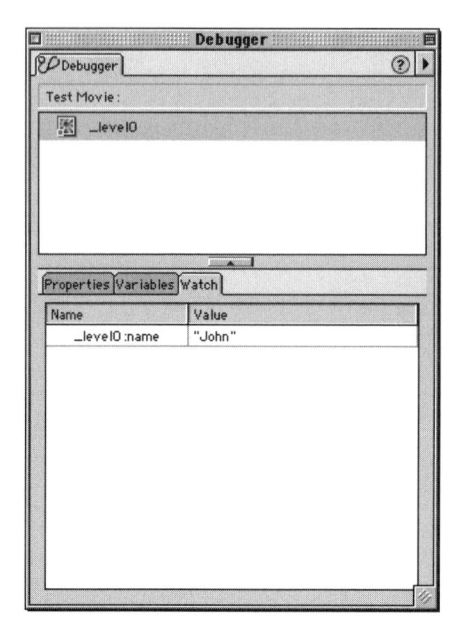

Figure 5-12   Debugger window showing the selected variable in the Watch List.

movie clip that we will use as a slider to control the volume of the audio in a site. The chapter wraps up with an email form that interacts with ASP (Active Server Pages). These sample scripts will prepare you for the scripting required in a site.

Date Script

This action gets the time from the user's computer. There are a couple ways that you can go about this. I will show you two ways to get the script to work.

1. Open a new file.
2. Choose Window -> Panel -> Text Options to open the Text Options window.
3. Create a text field on the Stage.
4. Select Dynamic Text and set variable to "time".
5. Insert a new layer call it "actions".
6. Select Frame 1 of the Actions layer.
7. Choose Window -> Actions to open the Actions window.
8. Set the variable "time" equal to "new Date" (Figure 5-13).
9. Test your movie (Figure 5-14).

This example will grab the time once and does not allow it to update because the movie doesn't loop. The quick fix to this is to add another frame to the movie by extending both frames to Frame 2. This will allow the movie to update the time with

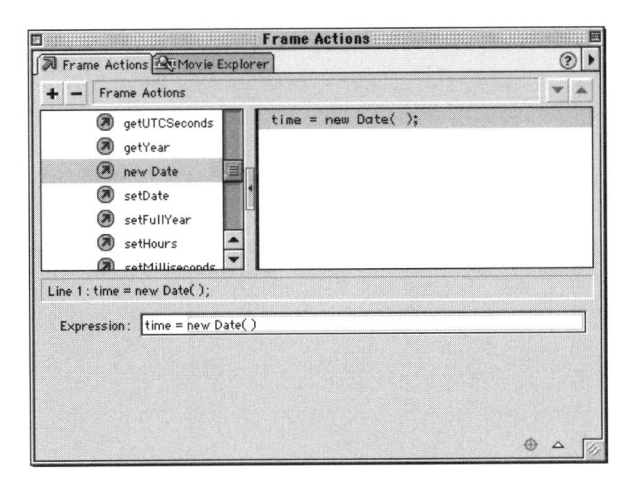

CHAPTER 5 • ALL YOU NEED TO KNOW ABOUT ACTIONSCRIPT 111

Figure 5-13 Actions window showing the variable "time" being set to "new Date".

each loop past the action. The best way to fix this is to create a movie clip with a text field in it. The next example will show you how to create the date and time in a movie clip. It will also give you a way to control how the time and date appear.

1. Open a new file.
2. Create a text field on the Stage.
3. Select Dynamic Text and set Variable to "time".
4. With the text field selected, choose Insert -> Convert to Symbol.
5. Select Movie Clip as the Behavior.
6. Attach the following script to the movie clip.

You do not need all the lines that start with double slashes ("//"). These are just comments to explain what the next lines in the code are doing. It is always a good habit to have comments in your code because this will help you and others to know what is going on when you look at the code.

7. Choose Control -> Test Movie to check that the movie is working properly (Figure 5-15).

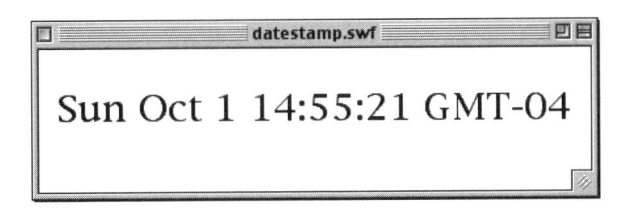

Figure 5-14 The result of this movie showing the time.

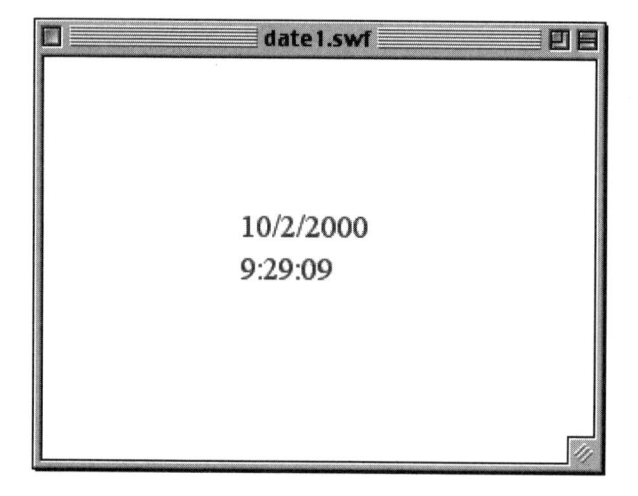

112 CHAPTER 5 · ALL YOU NEED TO KNOW ABOUT ACTIONSCRIPT

Figure 5-15 Date and time example.

```
onClipEvent (load) {
// Creates a new date object
  dateStamp = new Date();
}
onClipEvent (enterFrame) {
  hour = dateStamp.getHours();
  minutes = dateStamp.getMinutes();
  seconds = dateStamp.getSeconds();
  day = dateStamp.getDate();
  month = dateStamp.getMonth();
  year = dateStamp.getFullYear();
// Sets the month to the correct number because getMonth action retrieves January as 0 and December as 11
  month += 1
// Checks the hours to convert all of them from the 0-23 hour clock
  if (hour > 12) {
        hour -= 12;
  } else if (hour == 0) {
        hour = 12;
  }
// Checks to see if the minutes are in single digits If they are, a 0 gets added to the front
  if (length(minutes) == 1) {
        minutes = "0"+minutes;
  }
// Checks to see if the seconds are in single digits If they are, a 0 gets added to the front
  if (length(seconds) == 1) {
        seconds = "0"+seconds;
  }
// Joins all the date and time variables into one string that is broken into two lines
```

CHAPTER 5 • ALL YOU NEED TO KNOW ABOUT ACTIONSCRIPT

```
currenttime =
month+"/"+day+"/"+year+newline+hour+":"+minutes+":"+seconds;
// The next two actions basically reset the dateStamp variable so we
can update the time
  delete dateStamp;
  dateStamp = new Date();
}
```

This example is great because you will be able to use this movie clip in any project that you want. All you have to do is bring the movie clip into the next project and you won't even have to write any code.

Now that we have this date script down, let's move on to the next example, which will make use of the Mouse object and will show you how to control a movie clip.

Change that Cursor

Changing the cursor can add a great effect to your site. Some people choose to make small versions of their logos with little animations in them as the cursor. For this example, we are going to use the Biplane movie clip that comes with Flash.

1. Open a new file.
2. Choose Window -> Common Libraries -> Movie Clips.
3. Drag the Biplane movie clip just off the top left corner of the Stage.
4. Choose Window -> Panels -> Transform to open the Transform panel.
5. Scale the Biplane graphic to 20% in the Transform panel; make sure you have the Constrain box checked.
6. Choose Window -> Panels -> Instance to open the Instance panel if it is not open already.
7. Set the Instance name of the Biplane to "Plane".
8. Insert a new layer.
9. Choose Insert -> New Symbol, with the Behavior set to Movie Clip.
10. Go back to the main Timeline and drag the new Movie Clip symbol onto the Stage.
11. Click on the movie clip to highlight it.
12. Choose Windows -> Actions.
13. Set the actions to those in Figure 5-16.
14. Test your movie.

Your movie should show the plane following the cursor around the screen. This example uses the Mouse object to get the mouse location and to hide the mouse. This is a simple technique, but with the right graphics, it can add a unique touch to your site.

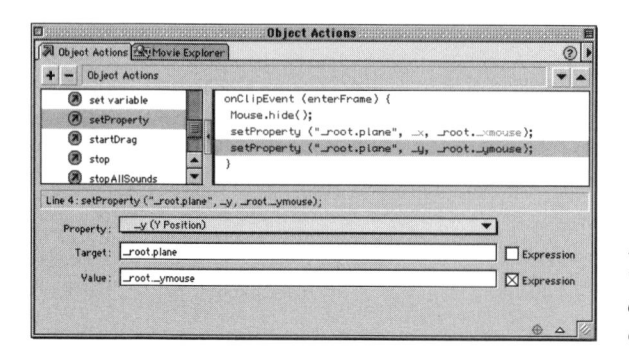

Figure 5-16 Actions window with code that hides the cursor and attaches the Biplane movie clip to the mouse position.

Control Your Volume

This is a great addition to any site or game. This will allow the user to control the volume of your audio without leaving the Web page. This example uses a series of movie clips and variables to create a sliding volume control.

1. Open a new file.
2. Choose Window -> Common Libraries -> Sounds.
3. Drag the Visor Hum audio clip into the Library of your movie.
4. Control + click (right-click on a PC) on the Visor Hum clip in the Library. Select Linkage from the menu.
5. Set the Identifier to "mySound" and set the Linkage to Export this symbol. This allows the clip to be accessed by ActionScript.
6. Create a graphic that represents an Audio icon (Figure 5-17).
7. Select the graphic on the Stage and choose Insert -> Convert to Symbol.
8. Set the Behavior to Movie Clip.
9. Choose Window -> Panels -> Instance if the Instance panel is not open already.
10. Set the Name of the movie clip to "slider".
11. Click on the "slider" movie clip.
12. Choose Window -> Actions.
13. Place the following scripts into the ActionScript window.

Just a reminder: You do not need to copy the comments into the window. Comments are the lines starting with //.

```
OnClipEvent (load) {
// Creates new sound object
_root.s = new Sound();
// Links the sound file from the library to the variable "s"
_root.s.attachSound("mySound");
```

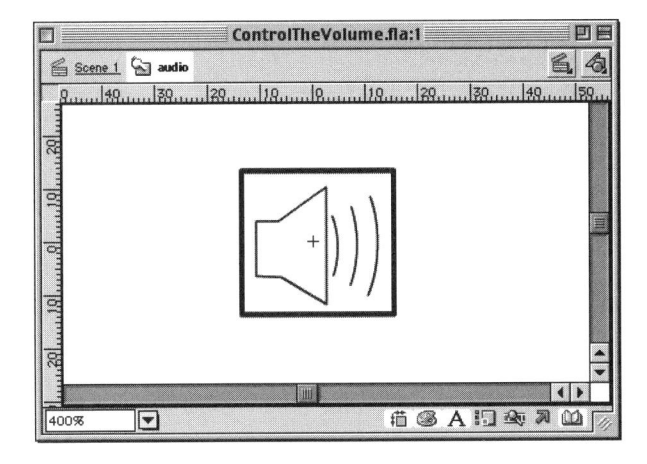

CHAPTER 5 • ALL YOU NEED TO KNOW ABOUT ACTIONSCRIPT

Figure 5-17 The Audio icon I used for this example.

```
// Starts playing the audio clip and sets it to loop 50 times
_root.s.start( 0 , 50);
}
onClipEvent (enterFrame) {
// Sets the volume on the slider to the actual volume of the audio clip
_root.volume = _root.s.getVolume();
}
```

14. Double-click on the "slider" movie in the Library to enter Symbol Editing mode for the Sound icon.
15. Select the Sound icon and choose Insert -> Convert to Symbol.
16. Set the Behavior of the symbol to Button.
17. Choose Window -> Panels -> Info if the Info panel is not open already.
18. Set the Y position of the button in the Info panel to 120 (Figure 5-18).
19. Choose Window -> Actions if the Actions window it is not open already.
20. With the button selected, place the following scripts to the ActionScript window:
    ```
    on (release) {
        _root.slider.play();
    }
    ```
21. Insert a layer and call it "actions".
22. Place stop actions in Frames 1 and 2.
23. Insert two new layers and place them under the Button layer; call one "knob" and the other "track".
24. Go to Frame 2 of the "track" layer and create something like I have in Figure 5-19.

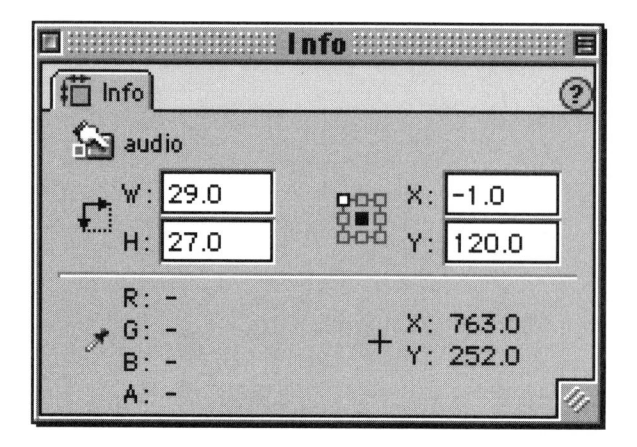

Figure 5-18 The Info panel with the Y position of the button set to 120.

25. Note how the line in the middle stops at the crosshair, or middle point of the movie clip. This is important for aesthetics because this is where we will have the knob stop.
26. Go to Frame 2 of the "knob" layer.
27. Create a square without an outline.

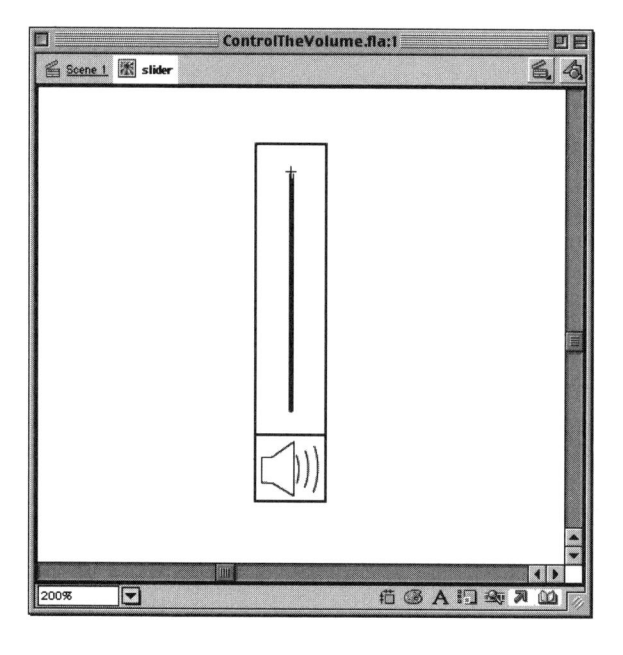

Figure 5-19 The "track" graphic created above the button in this example.

CHAPTER 5 • ALL YOU NEED TO KNOW ABOUT ACTIONSCRIPT

28. Select the square and choose Insert -> Convert to Symbol.
29. Set the Behavior of the new symbol to Movie Clip and set the Name to "knob".
30. Set "knob" Movie Clip X and Y positions to "0" in the Info panel.
31. Apply these actions to the "knob" movie clip:

    ```
    // When the movie enters the frame, it will set these actions in
    effect
    onClipEvent (enterFrame) {
    // Starts dragging the knob and keeps it constrained to up and down
    movement
        startDrag ("_root.slider.knob", true, 0, 0, 0, 100);
    // Sets the volume of the audio clip to 100 minus the slider's
    position
        _root.s.setVolume(100 - (_root.slider.knob._y));
    }
    // When the mouse button is pressed down, the following actions will
    be run
    onClipEvent (mouseDown) {
    // Stops the knob from being dragged
        _root.slider.knob.stopDrag();
    // Makes the slider movie go back to Frame 1
        _root.slider.gotoAndStop(1);
    }
    ```

32. Double-click on the "knob" movie clip to edit it.
33. Insert a new layer above the Knob graphic in the "knob" movie.
34. Create a text field that is a little smaller than the knob (Figure 5-20).
35. Set the text field to Dynamic Text, Single Line, with Variable set to "_root.volume". This will show the volume of the movie inside the knob as people slide it up and down.
36. Test your movie.

When you click on the Audio icon, the slider should pop up and the audio level should change when the slider is moved up and down. This example has made use of movie clip-to-movie clip interaction, creating and reading variables from multiple points, and Timelines. You will notice that the variables in this example are all placed in the root because of how easy it is to target them from any point of different movie clips. This example also makes use of the on Clip events that control how scripts are run. For example, the on Load handlers instantly run the scripts when the clip loads and only run these scripts once. The Enter Frame handler will run the scripts every time that a particular frame is entered, and the Mouse down handler will only run the scripts when the mouse is clicked.

This wraps up this example, so let's move on to email and ASP to see how Flash works with other applications.

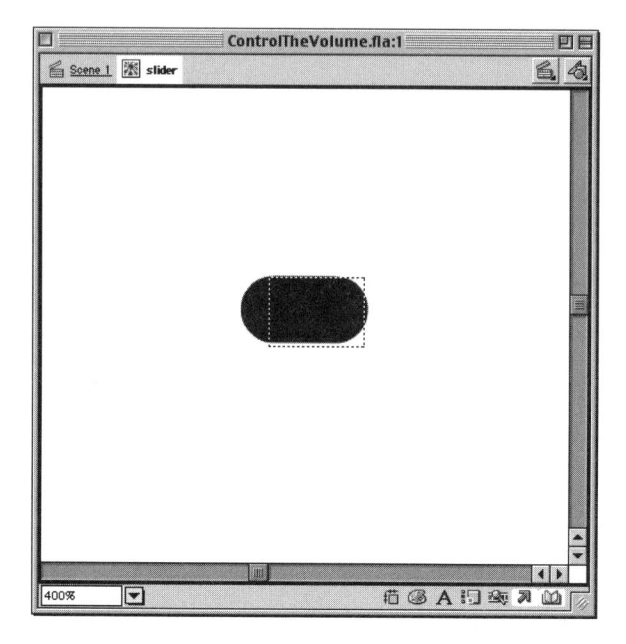

118   **CHAPTER 5 • ALL YOU NEED TO KNOW ABOUT ACTIONSCRIPT**

Figure 5-20   The Knob graphic with the text field placed on top of it.

Email and ASP

This example shows you how Flash deals with other applications. Actually, the easy part is setting up the Flash files the hard part is dealing with the other languages such as ASP or Perl. This particular example uses an ASP script to send email. ASP, for those of you who do not know, stands for Active Server Pages. It is a file type that links Flash to a server so that you can run server-side applications such as sending mail. I provide you with the ASP file you need at the end of this example, so you really do not need to know ASP at all to create this example.

1. Open a new file.
2. Create three text fields that are the same size and a fourth one that is the same width but much taller (Figure 5-21).
3. Select the first text field and set the Text Options panel to Input Text, Single Line, and Variable should be "to".
4. Select the second text field and set the Text Options panel to Input Text, Single Line, and Variable should be "from".
5. Select the third text field and set the Text Options panel to Input Text, Single Line, and Variable should be "subject".
6. Select the fourth text field and set the Text Options panel to Input Text, Multiline, Word wrap, and Variable should be "body".

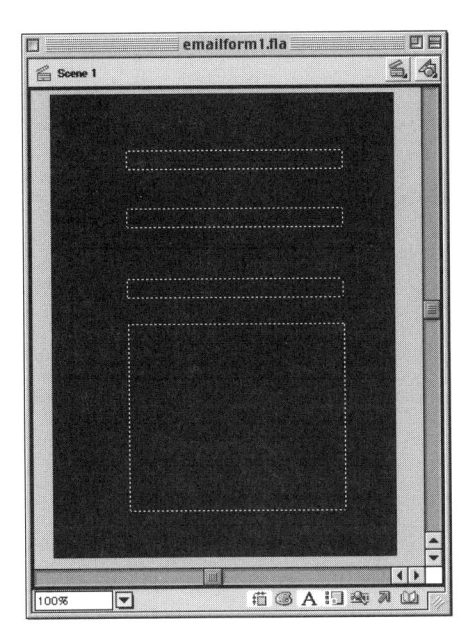

Figure 5-21 The email window with the text fields placed in their positions.

7. Insert a new layer and call it "field labels".
8. Create text next to the fields so that people will know which field is which, starting with the first field, "to".
9. Insert a new layer behind the text fields and call it "graphics".
10. Add any other graphics behind or around the fields to dress up the page how you want it (Figure 5-22).
11. Insert a new layer and call it "Send button".
12. Choose Window -> Common Libraries -> Buttons.
13. Drag "Pill button" onto the bottom of your Stage in the "Send button" layer.
14. Double-click the "Pill button" to enter Symbol Editing mode for the button.
15. Insert a new layer in the button and call it "send text".
16. Type "send" and center it over the Pill graphic.
17. Go back to the main Timeline.
18. Select the button.
19. Choose Window -> Actions.
20. Add the action from Figure 5-23 to the button.

This script assumes that you are placing the ASP file in the same directory as your Flash file. If you are not, you will need to type an absolute URL for the ASP file.

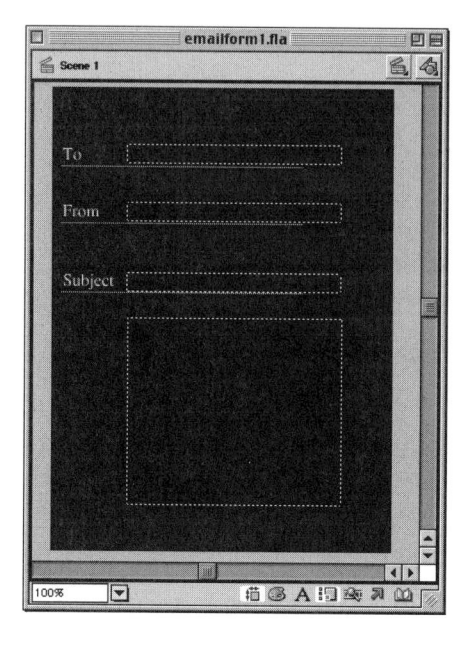

Figure 5-22 The email window with graphics and text fields set up.

21. Insert a new layer and call it "Actions".
22. Add stop actions in Frames 1 and 2.
23. Insert a new layer and call it "Thanks".
24. Create text in Frame 2 of this layer that says something like "Thank You! Your mail has been sent".
25. Save and export the Flash file as an HTML file.
26. Now we need to create the ASP file. All you have to do is copy this code into a file called "mail.asp".

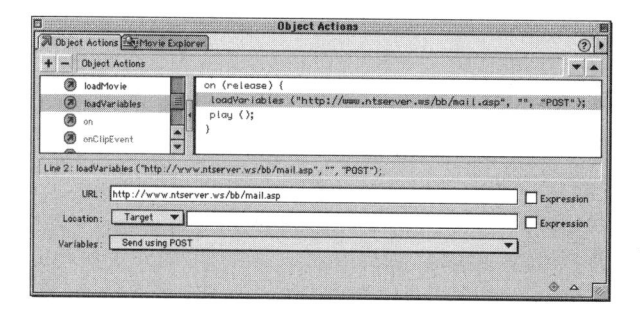

Figure 5-23 The Actions panel with the action that sends the variables from the Flash movie to the ASP file.

```
<%@ LANGUAGE=VBSCRIPT %>
<!—#include file="adovbs.inc"—>
<%
Dim objSendMail
Set objSendMail =
Server.CreateObject("CDONTS.NewMail")
        objSendMail.To = request.form("to")
        objSendMail.From = request.form("from")
        objSendMail.Subject = request.form("subject")
        objSendMail.Body =
request.form("body")
        objSendMail.Send
Set objCDOMail = Nothing
%>
```

27. Upload mail.asp, your Flash file, and your Flash file's HTML file to your NT server.

This is a very simple script that really has no bells and whistles, but it works and is easy to learn with. This example shows you how to pass variables to an external application. You will notice from Figure 5-23 that the load variable's action is set up with Location to Target and Variables to Send using POST. This is important for this to work with ASP. Some applications work better using Send using GET, but for this example, we do not need to use this.

chapter 6

FLASH YOUR WEB SITE

It's time to put all that you have learned in the previous chapters to work. We will be building a portfolio site using examples from the previous chapters. You can design your own site and follow along with these instructions. The example is designed to cover enough scenarios for you to build a site for a client or yourself. This chapter covers ways to streamline the site-building process, right through building the site and adding a splash page.

PRE-PRODUCTION TECHNIQUES AND HINTS

This section will help you organize your site before you begin to produce it. You will learn about movie dimensions and how they will affect the people who visit your site. Storyboarding your site is also covered and will help you to plan out the animation as well as the flow of the site. The last part of this section covers some hints to staying organized while building your site.

UNDERSTANDING MOVIE DIMENSIONS

One of the most important things to decide early on is the size of your Web page. By size, I mean the actual width and height in pixels, which is also referred to as the dimensions. Even though Flash is a vector-based program, if you let your movie scale with the size of the browser, you might not like the outcome. From experience, I have noticed the ill effects of letting the movie fill the screen. One of these ill effects is that bitmap images that are embedded get very pixilated. This is the same result you would get if you went into Photoshop and enlarged an image. Another side-effect is that the animation will not play as smoothly as it would if it were constrained to a smaller size. You can set the dimensions in the Movie Properties window (Figure 6-1). To open this window, choose Modify -> Movie or Command + M (Control + M on a PC).

Some other aspects you have to consider when selecting the dimensions of your movie are the limitations of the target audience. For example, are most of your clients or visitors working with their monitor resolution set to 640 x 480 or do they have their monitors set to 1024 x 768? This is more important than most developers realize. If you design a site that is 800 x 600 and someone views the site with a monitor set to 640 x 480, they will not be able to see the whole site without having to scroll. If your target audience is the group of people who have their monitors set to 640 x 480, I have had good luck using the default dimensions of 550 x 400. The reason you want to make the dimensions smaller than 640 x 480 is that you have to take into account the space the browser window takes. If you have already built a site and want a quick fix to make the dimensions smaller, you can set the dimensions for your movie in the HTML file. This is a little trickier because you have to make sure that you keep the correct aspect ratio. We will go into more depth on this topic in Chapter 8. Another reason why it is important to figure out the dimensions of your movie early on is because if you want to change the size of the movie when you are halfway through the project, it will take some time. You will need to make sure that you keep all of your graphics and layers together when you move them. It is almost guaranteed that you will have to move the elements in your site if you change the dimensions. The reason for this is that Flash scales the dimensions to the right and down. This means that all of your graphics will stay in the upper left-hand corner of the Stage if you increase the width and height of the Stage. This is not really what you would expect to happen. You would think that it would scale out evenly on all sides. With this in mind, let's make sure that we set our file dimensions up before we start working.

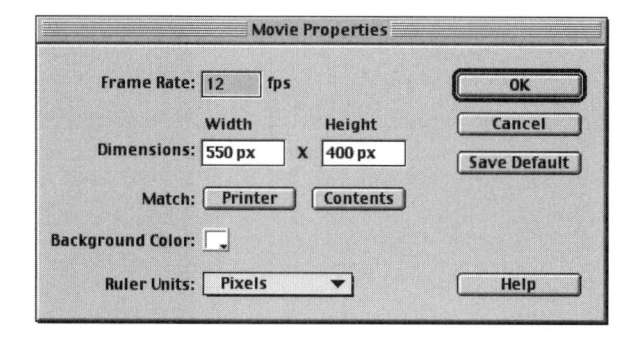

Figure 6-1 Movie Properties window.

STORYBOARDING

It is always a good idea to storyboard your site before you start working in Flash. This will mean less aggravation and changes later. You do not have to draw all the frames; you can use FreeHand or Illustrator to show screen shots of how you want things to look. This may seem like a waste of time, but if the client doesn't like the direction the site is going in, at least you won't waste all your time importing the artwork and animating the site. This is also for your benefit. By storyboarding and imagining how it will look, you might find a better way of animating the site. It will save you the time of tinkering around to see what looks best in Flash. The storyboarding phase is a good time to consider using only a few bitmap images or none at all. You would be surprised how much you can do with good vector clip art. This is a great time to finalize how many sections there will be in your site. You can also figure out the best way to create each section and how they will interact with each other. For example, will the sections have a transition between them or will they just click on and off?

ORGANIZING YOUR FILES

Now that you have completed your storyboard, it's time to build your site. Before you dive right into building your site, follow these steps. First, you should check to see that you have all the files in the correct formats. Make sure that when you are importing

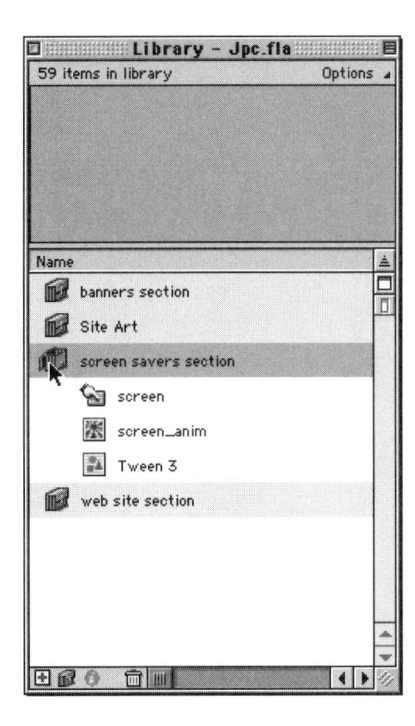

Figure 6-2   Library window showing the use of folders to organize your site.

graphics, each one that needs to be is on its own layer and that you are naming the layers so you can find them easier. As for the rest of the graphics, you might want to bring them in one section at a time. If you bring in all of your graphics at once, they could just get in the way when you are trying to work. Setting up folders in the Library will help you from having to dig through a cluttered mess as you are importing graphics and creating symbols. If the Library window is not open already, open it by choosing Window -> Library or Command + L (Control + L on a PC). In Figure 6-2 you will see a picture of the Library window. To create a new folder, click on the little Folder icon at the bottom of the Library window. You can also click on the Option menu at the top of the window and select New Folder. It is best to group images into folders. This will help you to find them quickly and easily. For example, you can create folders for the various sections of the site.

PREPARING YOUR FLASH MOVIE

Let's start at the bottom and build our way up. There are a few things we should set up before we start building a site.

1. Open a new file.
2. Open the Movie Properties window (Command + M or Control + M on a PC).

> **Note:** I have had good results using 15 fps. The higher you set this value, the faster your movie will want to play, but it will be limited by the machine it is playing on and the user's Internet connection. I would advise against using anything over 18 fps because it is just too much for some slower computers. The default of 12 fps is also as low as I would set the frame rate.

3. Set the Frame Rate (for this example, I used 15 fps).
4. Set the Dimensions (for this example, I used the default, 550 x 400).
5. Set the Background Color to dark blue (#000033).

It is always a good idea to set up a movie before you start working, especially when you are going to be working with files that are not going to use the default settings.

CREATING AN INTERFACE

This is the most important part of the site for many reasons. One main reason is when we have finished setting up the interface, we will have a shell that we can drop the elements into. The interface usually relies on background art such as bars or ovals for placement. For example, most sites on the Web have their navigation attached to a shape or placed inside of one. If you have created any of your navigation or background elements outside of Flash, you should import them. If you have any text elements, it is best to recreate them in Flash unless you have created your elements in FreeHand or Fireworks, which allow you to import text boxes as editable text in Flash. After you have imported your elements, create anything else you need to in Flash and arrange them so everything is in the place you had planned (Figure 6-3). Now that you have arranged your interface and design elements, you need to make your interface elements into buttons.

CREATING BUTTONS

This section will cover creating a button from text. If you are following along, you might want to mimic the site shown in Figure 6-3. It is possible to create your own site that looks different and has different links, but to keep the examples consistent, I will

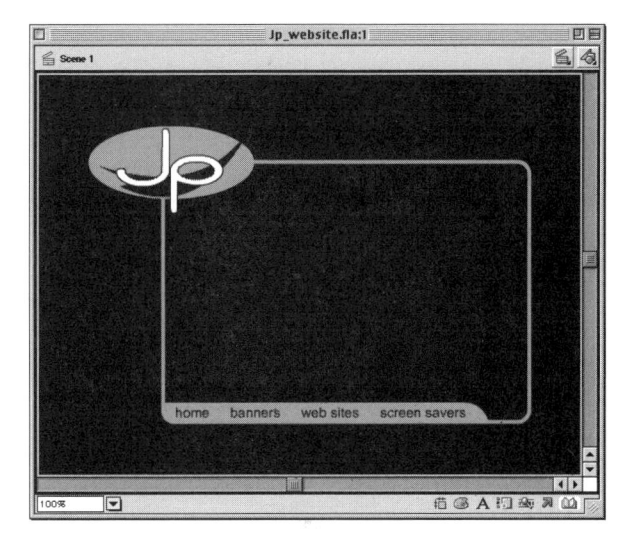

Figure 6-3   Picture of sample site's background elements in place.

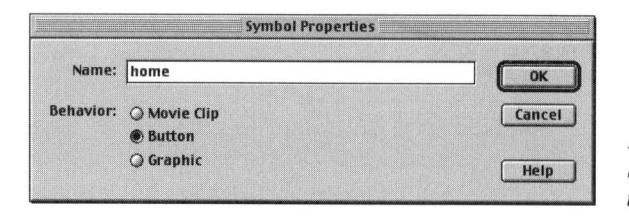

Figure 6-4 Setting up the Symbol Properties window for the "home" button.

be referring to the graphics and sections created for this site. I am going to create four buttons because the site has four sections: "home", "banners", "websites", and "screensavers". This example refers to the "home" button. When you have completed the first button, repeat the process for the rest of the buttons just substituting the correct name when needed.

1. Select the Text tool.
2. Create the text for the first button, "home".
3. Select the Arrow tool; this should select the "home" text.
4. Choose Insert -> Convert to Symbol (press F8). This will open the Symbol Properties window.
5. Enter the Name of the button so it will be easier to locate and edit in the Library.
6. Set the Behavior of the symbol to Button (Figure 6-4).
7. Click OK and the button will be placed in the Library.

We have just created our first button. The problem with this button is that all we created was the Up state of the button. Buttons consist of four states: Up, Over, Down, and Hit. Now we need to create the other states of the button. To do this, we need to enter the Symbol Editing mode for the button (Figure 6-5). There are a few ways to do this, but the best way is by double-clicking the symbol on the Stage. You will notice when you are in Symbol Editing mode that the Timeline and Stage have changed. The Timeline now has text above the frames showing the four states of a button. The Stage now has the Home Button icon at the upper left corner of the screen, next to Scene 1.

To make the button more interesting, we will make the Over state animated. To do this, we will be using a movie clip in its keyframe. It makes more sense to finish the other states of the button and return to the Over state when we have finished with the other states of the button.

1. Create a keyframe (press F6) in the Down state.
2. Select the "home" text in the Down state.
3. Change the color of the text so that it is distinguished from the Up state.
4. Create a keyframe (press F6) in the Hit state.
5. Draw a rectangle around the letters in the Hit state (Figure 6-6).

CHAPTER 6 • FLASH YOUR WEB SITE

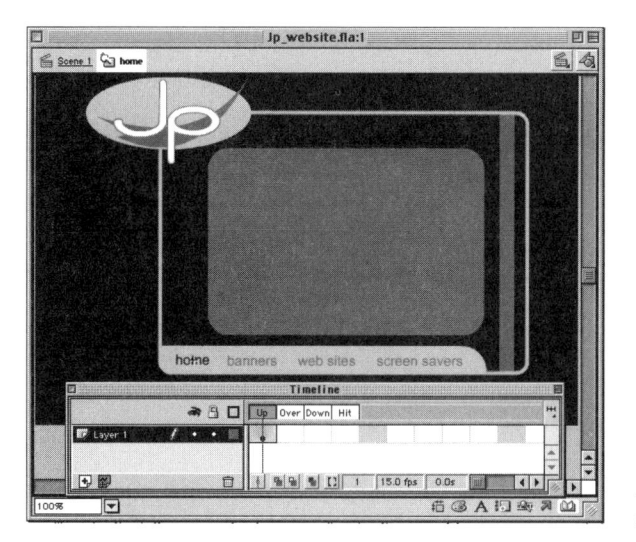

Figure 6-5 Symbol Editing mode for a button.

> **Note:** The best way to create the Hit state for text is to draw a rectangle around the text so that when people get close to the letters, it will activate the button. If you do not use a box as the Hit state, it will be hard for people to click on the button because they will be going on and off the button as their cursor moves over the letters. As a personal preference, I like to delete the text in the Hit state after I have created the rectangle.

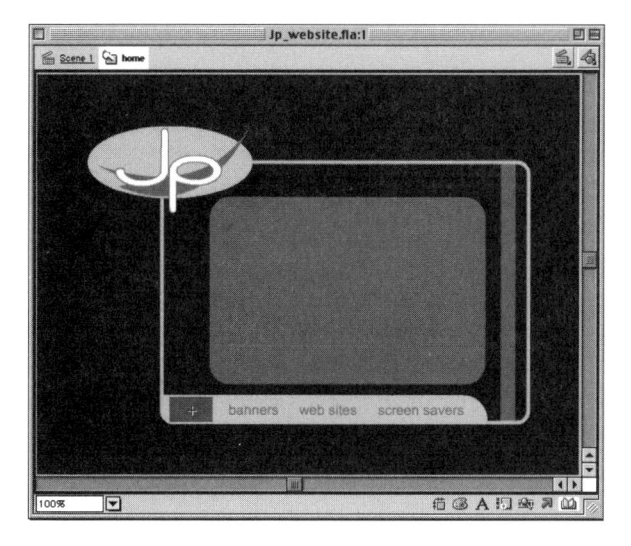

Figure 6-6 Hit state of the "home" button.

Now that we have finished the Down and Hit states of the button, it is time to get to the Over state.

USING MOVIE CLIPS TO ADD ANIMATION TO BUTTONS

This section shows how to add animation to a button using a movie clip in the Over state of the button. The movie clip will run using its own Timeline so that it will be able to animate even when the main Timeline is stationary. This also means that the movie clip will be able to continuously loop to keep drawing attention to the button. Since we have text as our button, I have decided to make the animation use outlines that pulse out from the letters.

1. Use the button from the previous example.
2. Insert a keyframe in the Over state of the button (press F6).
3. Convert the button text in the Over state into a symbol (press F8).
4. Name the clip and set the Behavior to Movie Clip.
5. Double-click the new movie clip symbol; this will send you to the Symbol Editing mode for the movie clip.

> **Note:** When you are editing a symbol inside a symbol, the screen will show you at the upper left-hand side which symbol you are editing, which symbol it is inside of, and what scene you are in. This is helpful because it lets you navigate easily back to the symbol that you started in.

6. Make outlines for the text.

> **Tip:** There is no setting to make outlines for text, so you have to break the text down into shapes and use the Line Fill tool to create outlines for the text. You do have control over the thickness of the outlines, and I suggest that you change the stroke to ".5" in the Stroke panel. I have also made the outline a lighter color so that they stand out a little better. Make sure that you select all the letters before you start to make the outlines. When you are using the Line Fill tool to make the outlines, make sure that you get the insides of the "o" and the "e" in the "home" button.

CHAPTER 6 • FLASH YOUR WEB SITE

Figure 6-7 "Home" text with outline highlighted.

7. Insert a new layer.
8. Move the new layer under the layer with the text in it.
9. Select the outlines (Figure 6-7).
10. Use Command + X (Control + X on a PC) to cut the outlines from this layer.
11. Select the new layer, then use Shift + Command + V (Shift + Control + V on a PC) to paste the outlines into the new layer in the same place.
12. Control + click (right-click on a PC) in the first keyframe of the outlines layer.
13. Select Create Motion Tween from the context menu.
14. Select Frame 10 in the outlines layer and insert a keyframe (press F6).
15. Select Frame 10 in the text layer and insert a frame (press F5).
16. Choose Window -> Panel -> Transform.
17. At the keyframe in Frame 10, change the Scale of the outlines to 150% using the Transform panel.

> **Tip:** If you want to make the animation look a little different, you can add an effect to the outlines in Frame 10. Choose Window -> Panels -> Effect to open the Effect panel. In this panel, select Alpha from the pull-down menu and set it to 0%. This will cause the outlines to fade out as they are growing. See Chapter 3 for a more in-depth look at changing the transparency of a symbol while animating.

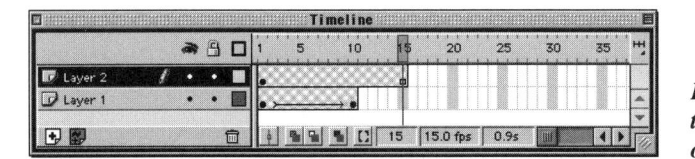

Figure 6-8 Timeline of the movie clip with the outlines animation.

If we were to look at our animation right now, it would just continually loop without any space in between the loop of the outlines flying out. What we can do to make this work a little better is add some frames to the layer with the solid letters. Let's add frames out to Frame 15 by selecting Frame 15 in the layer with the solid letters and pressing F5 (Figure 6-8). This will give us a little space in between the loops of the outlines.

After you have repeated this process for the other buttons, we need to move on to setting up sections for our navigation. First, we need to go to the main Timeline and make sure we have layers for each button. Make sure that you name them so you can keep track of the buttons when you need to edit them (Figure 6-9).

ESTABLISHING NAVIGATION

This section covers techniques for organizing your site, adding actions to buttons, and changing the behaviors of buttons. To keep things consistent, all the examples in this section will apply to the site that is being put together in this chapter. This section will detail ways to organize the site Timeline, add actions that will call sections of the movie, and change the behaviors of buttons. We will start by organizing our Timeline.

ORGANIZING THE TIMELINE

We are going to break up the main Timeline into sections, using labels and actions to mark each section.

1. Add two new layers to the top of the Timeline window.
2. Call one of the layers "actions" and the other "labels".

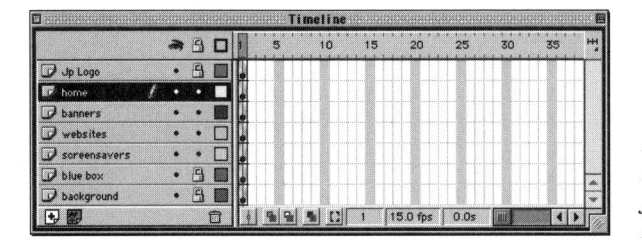

Figure 6-9 Timeline of the main movie set up with layers for all the buttons and separate elements.

CHAPTER 6 • FLASH YOUR WEB SITE

3. Go to Frame 40 and extend all the layers to this frame by highlighting all the layers in this frame and pressing F5.
4. Insert keyframes at Frames 10, 20, and 30 on the "labels" layer.
5. Choose Window -> Panels -> Frame to open the Frame panel.
6. Select Frame 1 of the "labels" layer.
7. Type "home" into the Label field of the Frame panel.
8. Repeat step 7 for the "banners", "websites", and "screensavers" sections by placing them in Frames 10, 20, and 30, respectively (Figure 6-10).

> **Note:** This example uses the names of the buttons for the names of the labels. You do not have to do this, but it makes life a lot easier. To add labels, double-click on a keyframe and select the Label tab in the Frame Properties window. Once you have typed in the names for all the sections, you will see them in the Timeline with little red flags next to them.

We have placed our labels to mark our sections, but when you play the animation, it will just play through all of the sections without stopping. To fix this, we have to add frame actions to stop the playback head when it tries to play through all of the sections.

1. Add keyframes on Frames 9, 19, 29, and 40 in the "actions" layer. These keyframes are the last frames of all the sections.
2. Choose Window -> Actions to open the Actions window.
3. Select Frame 9 of the "actions" layer.
4. Select the stop action, which is located under Basic Actions in the Actions window.
5. Repeat Step 4 for Frames 19, 29, and 40.

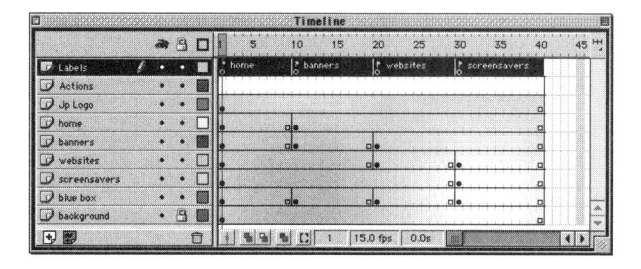

Figure 6-10 Timeline showing labels for the sections.

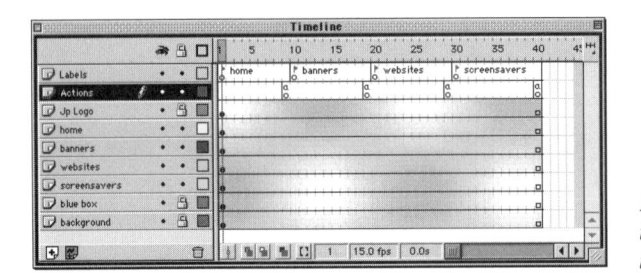

Figure 6-11 Timeline showing the stop actions applied to the end of sections.

Your Timeline should have four keyframes with an "a" above them in the "actions" layer (Figure 6-11).

It's time to put the buttons to use. We have completed our sections so that when we play back the movie it does not play straight through every section. Now we need to make our buttons access their sections so we can navigate between all the sections.

APPLYING BUTTON ACTIONS

To apply actions to buttons, you do not put the actions within the button symbol, but instead you apply the action to the instance of the symbol that is on the Stage.

1. Use the file from the previous examples.
2. Go to Frame 1.
3. Select the "home" graphic.
4. Choose Window -> Actions; this will open the Actions window.
5. Choose the "Go To" action, which is located under Basic Actions.

Note: Actions that are attached to instances of buttons automatically come up with "on Release" as the event that will trigger the action. "on Release" is the most often used state for actions that are applied to buttons. This gives the person who clicked the wrong button the chance to move their cursor and release outside the button and not get sent to the wrong link.

6. In the Actions window, set the Type pull-down menu to Frame Label and select the "home" label from the Frame pull-down menu (Figure 6-12).
7. Repeat these steps for the other buttons, making sure that each button goes to its appropriate label/section of the Timeline.

When you have finished these steps, we can move on to building the sections of the site.

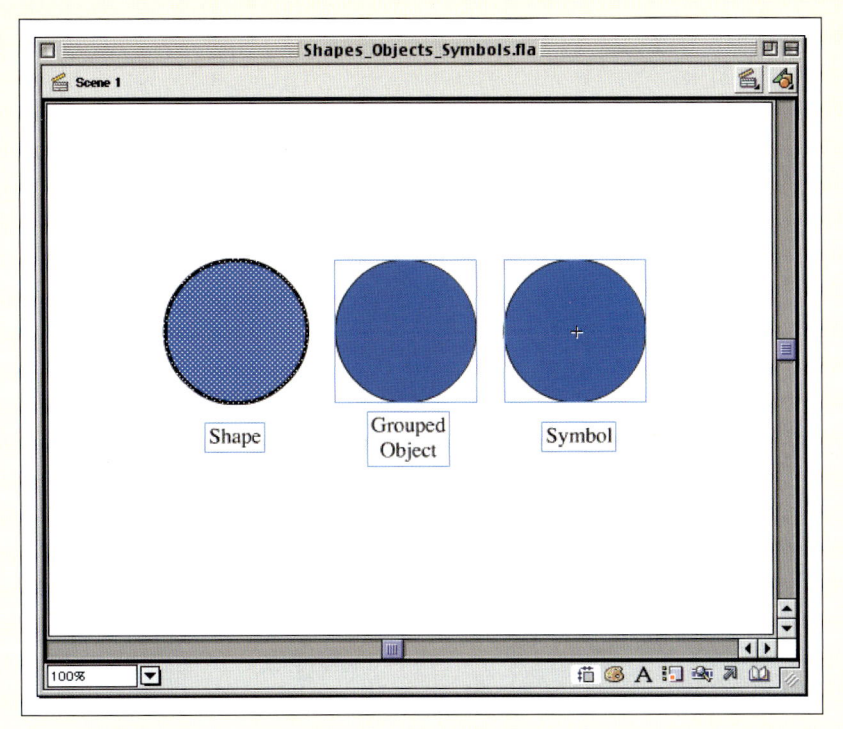

Color Figure 1
Three types of graphics found in Flash: Shape, Grouped Object, and Symbol.

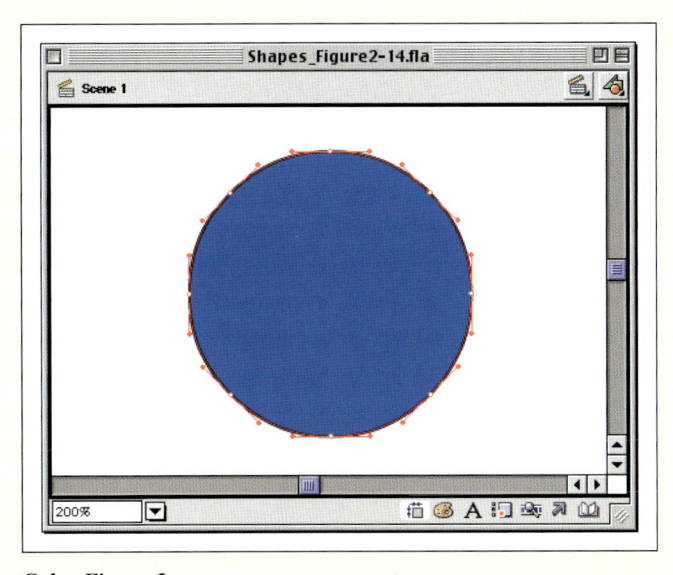

Color Figure 2
Editable points on a circle that has been selected by the Subselect tool.

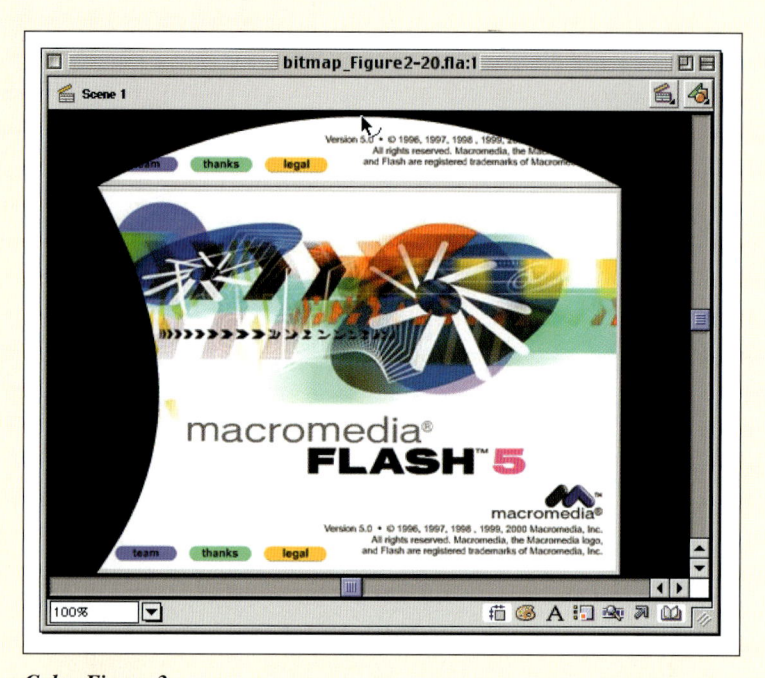

Color Figure 3
Bitmap image that has been broken down and manipulated using the Arrow tool. You will notice that the image repeats when the edge is pulled out.

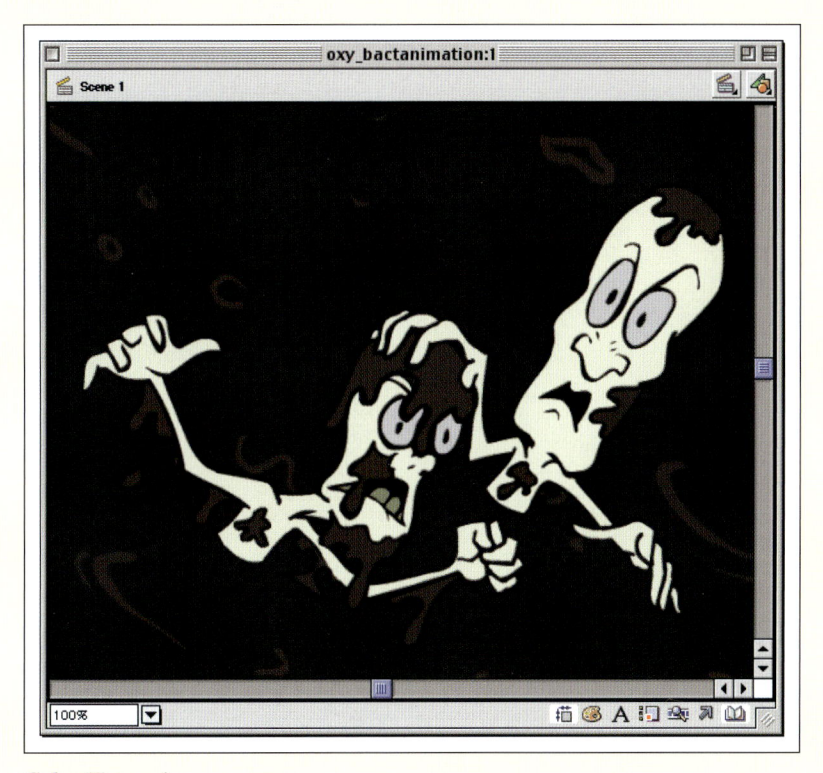

Color Figure 4
A frame of the bacteria animation that can be found on the Oxy Web site (http://www.oxyoxygen.com).
Visuals provided courtesy of Oxy® © 2000 SmithKline Beecham.

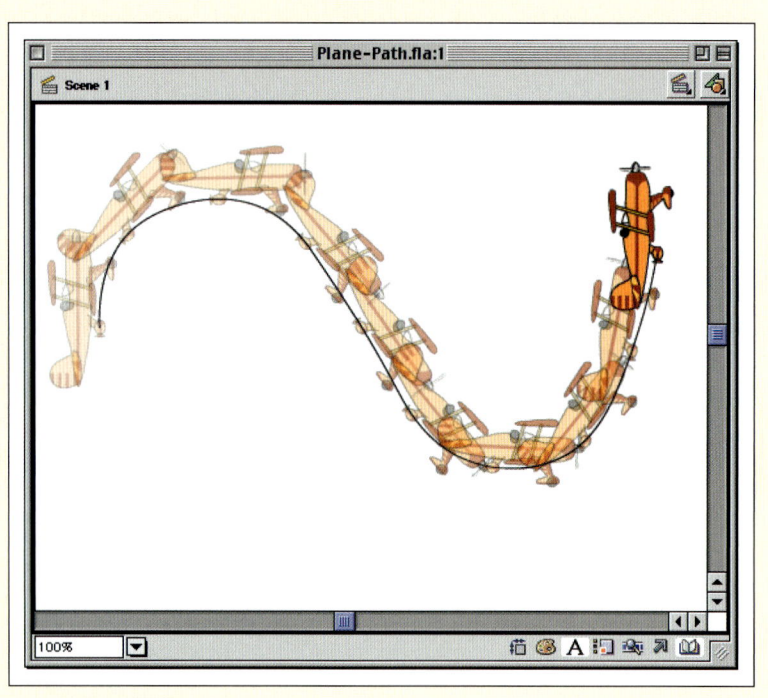

Color Figure 5
Frames of a Biplane following a path.

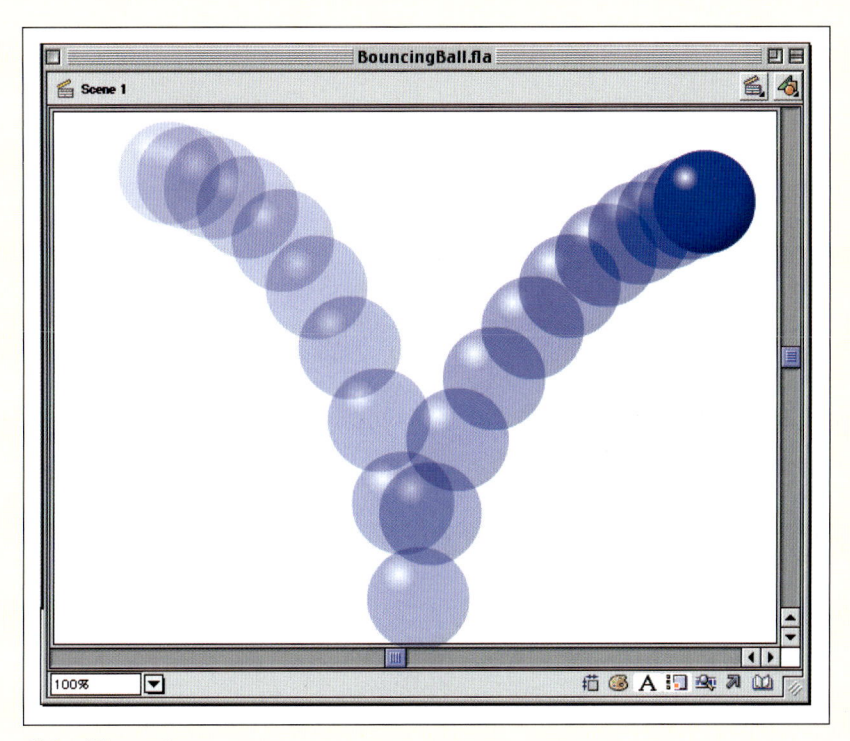

Color Figure 6
Frames of a ball bouncing. You will notice that the ball's position is closer together at the top of the arch.

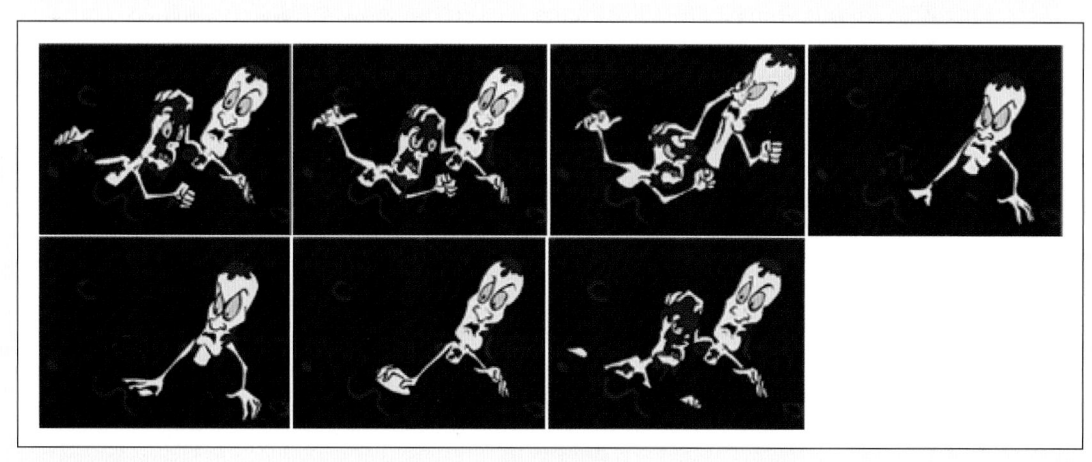

Color Figure 7
Another example from the Oxy animation, this time showing frames from the Frame-by-Frame animation of the bacteria being dunked by another bacteria.
Visuals provided courtesy of Oxy® © 2000 SmithKline Beecham.

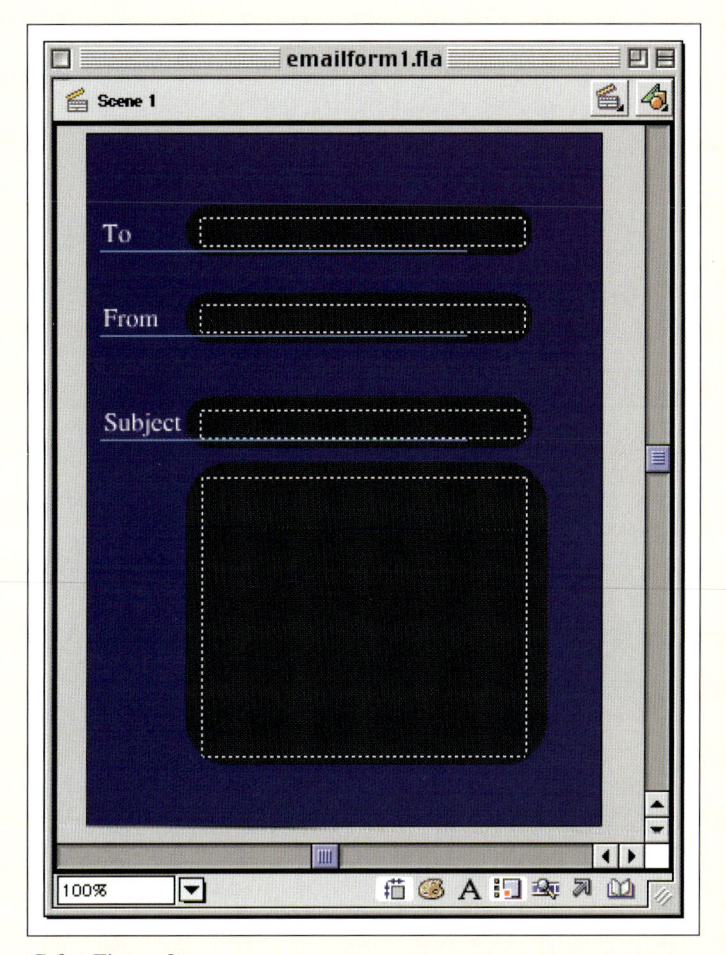

Color Figure 8
An email form created for use with Flash and another language, such as ASP or Perl.

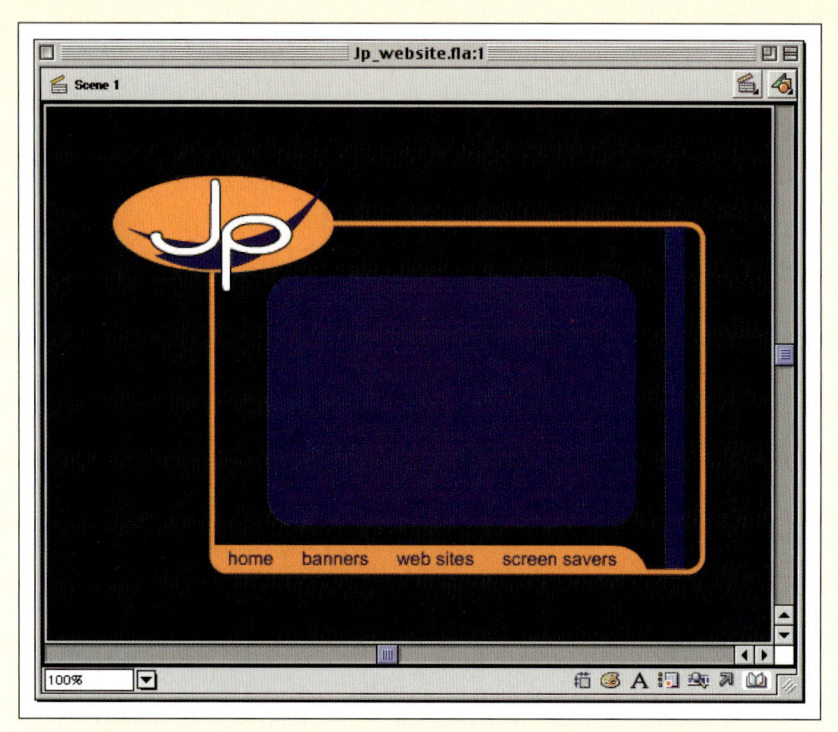

Color Figure 9
Screenshot of the JpGraphics.net site as it is being built.

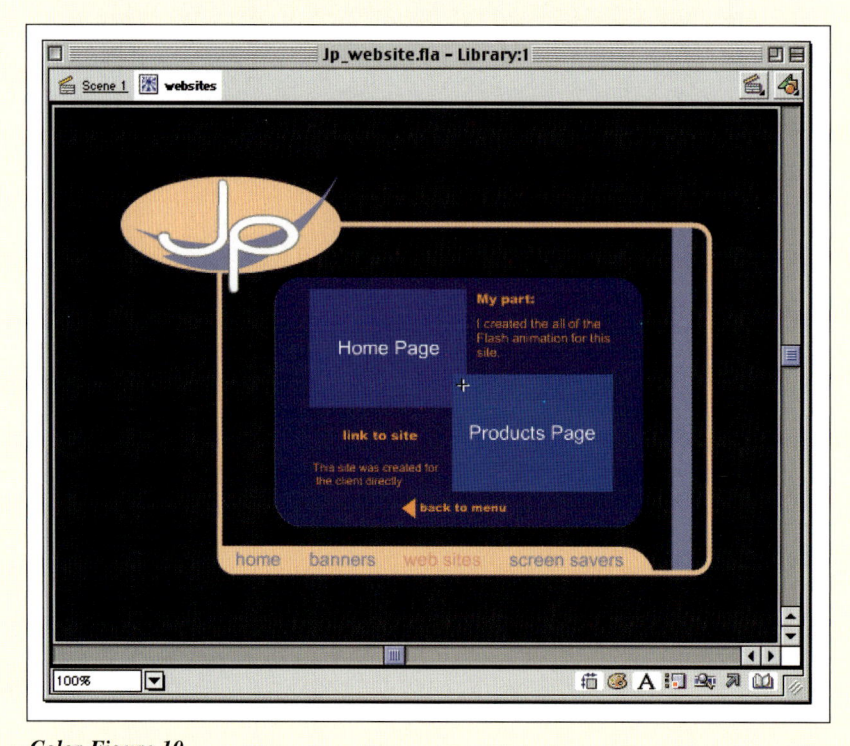

Color Figure 10
JpGraphics Web site section, showing how the template is set up so that you can easily update and add Web sites.

Color Figure 11
JRVisuals.com Web site, showing a mix of Flash and HTML to create a more interesting site.

Color Figure 13
Shapes created in Illustrator and imported into Flash to use in the ShapeMatch game.

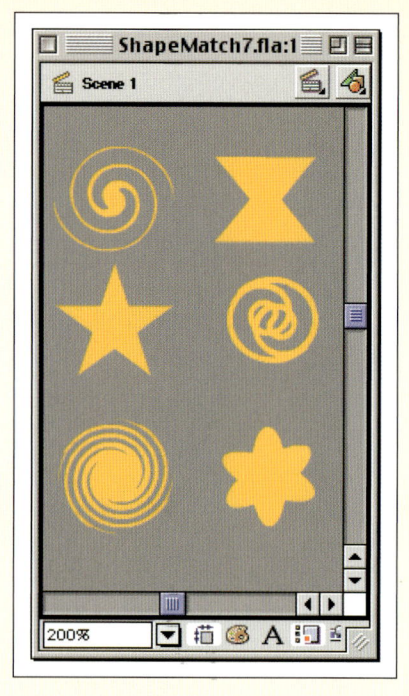

Color Figure 12
Screenshot of the ShapeMatch Game you will create when you follow the directions in Chapter 7.

Color Figure 14
ShapeMatch game's end screen is revealed when the player successfully matches all the tiles.

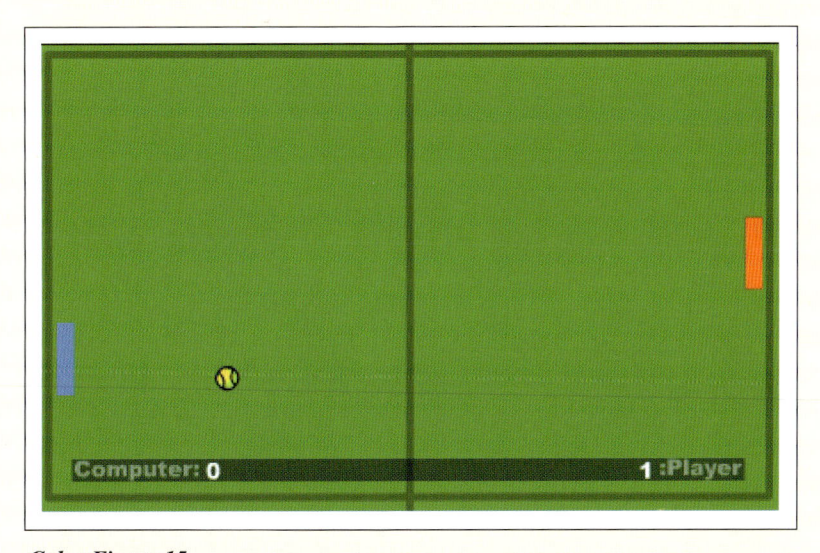

Color Figure 15
A screenshot of the Flash Tennis game that you will create when you follow the directions in Chapter 7.

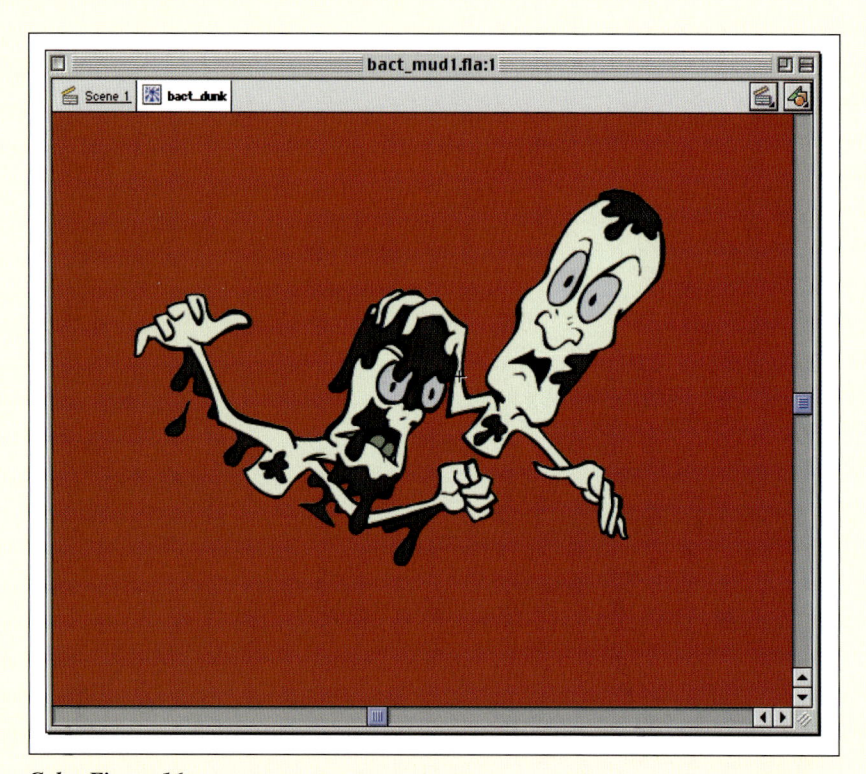

Color Figure 16

Color Figures 16, 17, and 18
Oxy bacteria images being optimized using the Optimize Curves feature. These figures show the starting point and different levels of optimization.
Visuals provided courtesy of Oxy® © 2000 SmithKline Beecham.

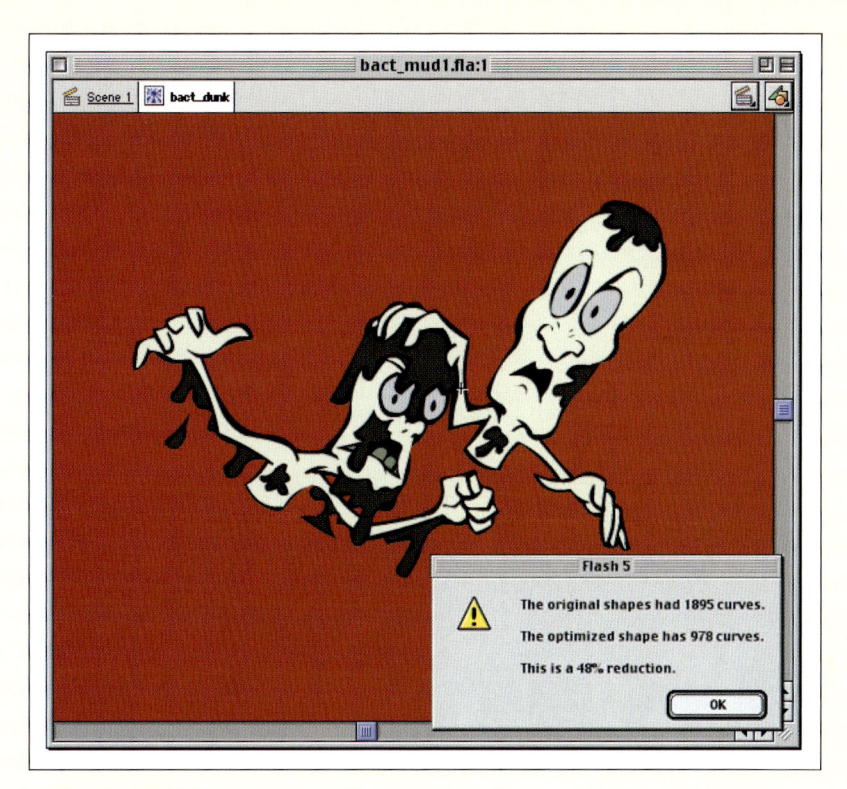

Color Figure 17

Color Figure 18

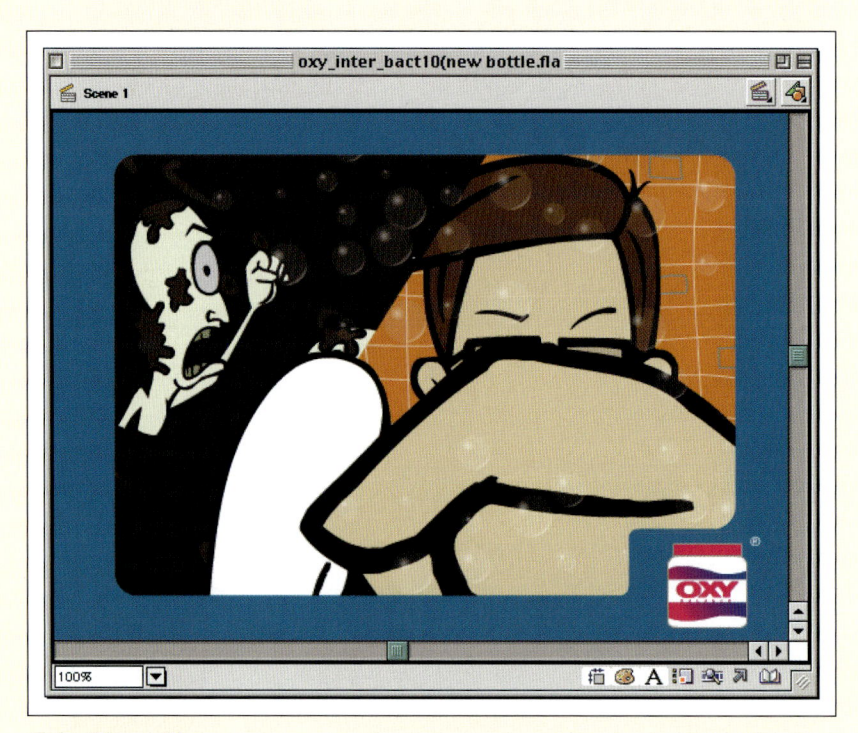

Color Figure 19
Scene from the Oxy Interstitial, showing the use of the mask feature in Flash.
Visuals provided courtesy of Oxy® © 2000 SmithKline Beecham.

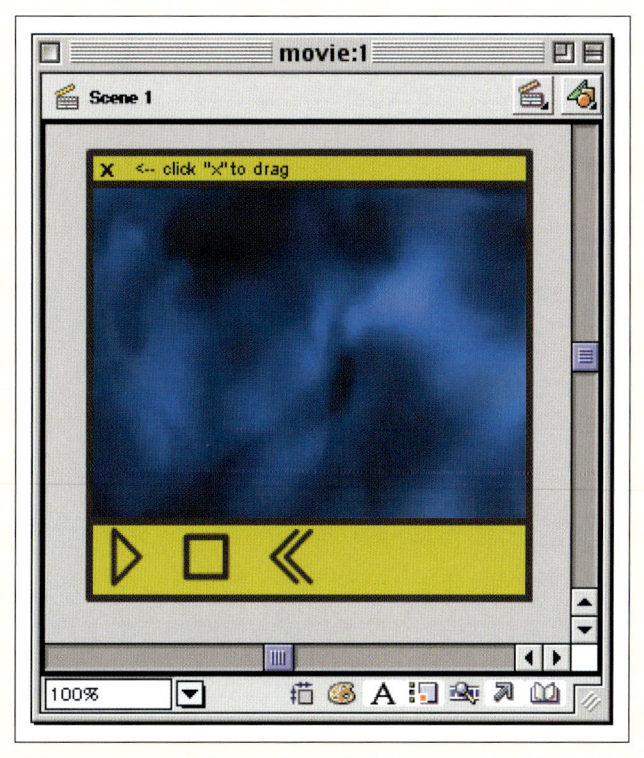

Color Figure 20
Window created to control a sequence of Bitmap images.

Color Figure 21
Mock e-commerce site, which is created in Chapter 10 to illustrate how use the drag feature in an e-commerce environment.

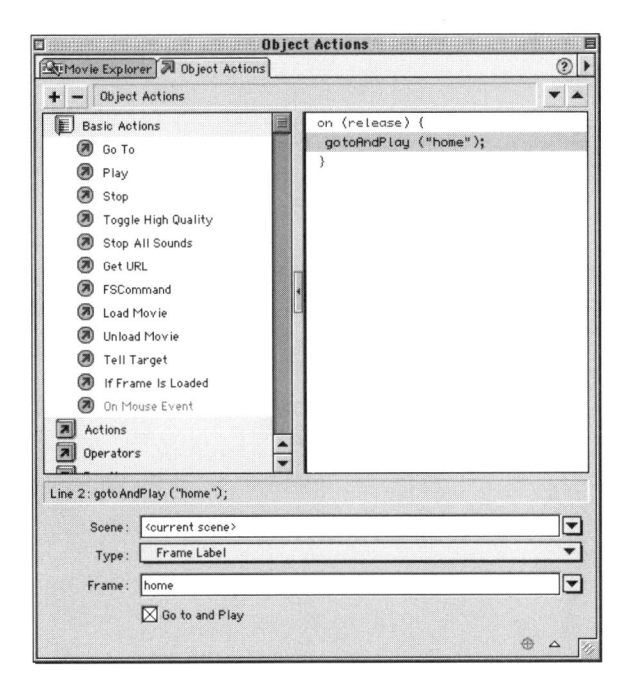

Figure 6-12   Actions window with "Go To" action selected and set up to go to a label called "home".

CHANGING THE BEHAVIORS OF BUTTONS

When you test the movie, you will notice that you do not have any way of knowing when you are in a particular section, and even worse, whether the button for that section is still active. Of course, once we put in all the copy and artwork for the sections, you will know what section you are in, but that still doesn't solve the problem of the buttons still being active in their sections. This section will cover how to change the behaviors of the buttons so they are not active while in their sections.

1. In each button's layer, place new keyframes under the button's label and the label for the section after it in the Timeline (Figure 6-13).
2. Go to Frame 1.

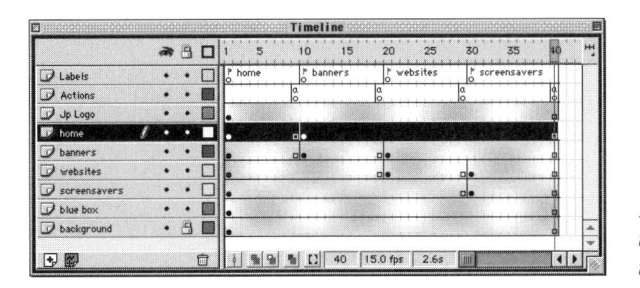

Figure 6-13   Timeline showing the new keyframes inserted into the button layers.

3. Select the "home" button on the Stage.
4. Choose Window -> Panels -> Instance.
5. In the Instance panel, change the Behavior to Graphic from the pull-down menu.
6. Go to Frame 10.

> **Note:** You will also want to change the Play mode to Single Frame. This pull-down menu is located under the Behavior menu in the Instance panel. To set which frame you want the button to show up as, type a "3" in the field next to the word "First". This means that you want your graphic's first frame to be Frame 3 and you only want a single frame displayed. Frame 3 of our button is the Down state; this is why I have chosen this to be the frame that is displayed.

7. Select the "banners" button on the Stage.
8. Change the Behavior to Graphic.
9. Go to Frame 20.
10. Select the "websites" button on the Stage.
11. Change the Behavior to Graphic.
12. Go to Frame 30.
13. Select the "screensavers" button on the Stage.
14. Change the Behavior to Graphic.

> **Warning:** When you are changing the Behavior of movie clips or buttons to Graphic, you will need to change the Play mode because by default it will make them loop. It is also important to know that when you change a symbol's behavior, it acts only like the behavior you are changing it to. For example, a button that has been changed to a graphic cannot act like a button and have a button action applied to it unless its Behavior is changed back to Button.

The reason for placing a keyframe in the section after each button's own section is so they keep their behaviors intact in other sections of the site. If these keyframes were not added in the next section, the buttons would still have the Behavior set to Graphic and would not function as buttons. This is an important point to remember: When you change the instance of a graphic in a keyframe, it will keep that instance until you add another keyframe and change it.

Now that we have nailed down our navigation, we need to add some content to our site.

ORGANIZING THE SECTIONS OF THE SITE

What I like to do to organize my sections is to make them into movie clips. Since the example I have been using for my site has a box in the middle, I will use this image as the background for my sections. The reason why I want to use the box as the background is that it will be my guideline for aligning the images and text. This way, all the sections will appear in the same place on the screen. By using movie clips, we will be able to duplicate the section and reuse it for the next one. This will save a lot of production time and help to keep a consistent look across the sections of the site.

USING MOVIE CLIPS FOR SECTIONS

The first section we will start with is the Home section. This is where we will want to store a brief introduction to our site and contact information. One thing to make sure of is that the box or shape you have selected as your movie clip is on its own layer. In this example, the layer for the movie clip is "blue box".

Home Page Section

In this section, we will be creating the home page of our site. This section is one of the most important because it is the first visitors will see. The following example will run through the steps that will build animations for the welcome text for the site. This whole section takes place in a movie clip, making it easier for us to work. The rest of the section will work the same way, using a movie clip to hold the section's graphics.

1. Use the file from the previous sections.
2. Select the box in the middle of the Stage.
3. Press F8 to convert the box into a symbol.
4. Name the symbol "home" and select Movie Clip as the Behavior.
5. Double-click on the new movie clip to enter Symbol Editing mode.
6. Create a new layer.
7. Call this layer "header".
8. Type in "Welcome to my site". This will be the header for our section.
9. Control + click (right-click on a PC) on Frame 1 of the "header" section.
10. Select Create Motion Tween.
11. Insert a keyframe on Frame 6 of the "header" layer.
12. Click and move Frame 1 to Frame 2.

13. Move the text in Frame 2 to the right.
14. Set the alpha of the text in Frame 2 to 0%.
15. Create a new layer.
16. Select the animation from the "header" layer.
17. Option-drag (Alt-drag on a PC) it to the new layer, but start it in Frame 3.
18. Drag this new layer under the "header" layer.
19. Extend this layer so that it can be seen in Frame 10 (press F5).
20. Rename the original header layer to "header trail".
21. Create a new layer.
22. Type in any text that you want to use for your site.
23. Animate the text by fading it using the Tint Color effect. Start the text fade in Frame 5 and make it go until Frame 10 (see Chapter 3 for more involved instructions).
24. Add two new layers.
25. Call one "actions" and the other "labels", just like we did earlier with the main Timeline.
26. In the first frame of the "labels" layer, add a label called "welcome".
27. Add a stop action in Frame 10 of the "actions" layer.

By adding the stop at the end of the animation, it will limit the movie clip to playing once instead of continually looping. Your Timeline for the "home" movie clip should look like the one in Figure 6-14.

SAVE TIME; REUSE ELEMENTS

To save time and keep a consistent look in your site, it is wise to reuse elements. This example will show you how to save some time by reusing the "home" movie clip that we built in the previous example.

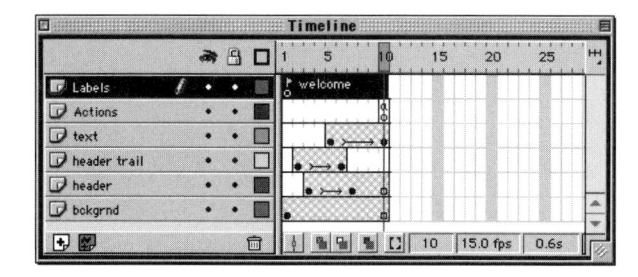

Figure 6-14 Timeline for the "home" movie clip.

Banners Section

The "banners" section makes use of the Home page movie clip so that we can save time and keep a consistent look across the site. This section will hold the buttons that will call out to HTML pages that hold the banner graphics that you want to show. Using an ActionScript, we will call out to pages that will load in new browser windows on top of our site, showing the different banners.

1. Use the file from the previous sections.
2. Open the Library window.
3. Select the "home" movie clip.
4. Select Duplicate from the Options menu of the Library window (Figure 6-15).
5. Name the new clip "banners".
6. In the main Timeline, insert a keyframe (press F6) under the "banners" label in the "blue box" layer.
7. Open the Instance panel.
8. Use the Swap Symbol button to change the "home" movie clip to the "banners" movie clip.

Figure 6-15   The Library window's pull-down menu.

9. Double-click on the "banners" movie clip on the Stage to enter Symbol Editing mode.
10. Change the label in the "labels" layer to read "banners" instead of "welcome".
11. Duplicate the symbol for "Welcome to my site" and rename the new graphic "banners header".
12. Change "banners header" to read "Banners".
13. Use the Swap Symbol button to change the "welcome" header to the new "Banners" header.

> **Note**: When swapping a graphic that is part of a tween, you only need to change the first frame. The last frame will automatically reflect the change.

Now we need to change the About Us/Contact graphic with a menu so that people can see the banners. We need to create buttons for each client we wish to highlight in this section. These buttons will open a new browser window with an HTML page displaying the banners for the respective clients.

1. Delete the "text" (About Us/Contact) layer.
2. Create three new layers.
3. Insert keyframes (press F6) in Frame 5 on the new layers.
4. Create three buttons in Frame 5, one on each of the new layers, and call the layers and buttons "client 1", "client 2", and "client 3".
5. Align the three buttons evenly in the window.
6. Animate the buttons using a 4-frame tint, starting them a frame apart (Figure 6-16).
7. Add a "Get URL" action to each button calling an HTML page that has the banners for that client on it (Figure 6-17).

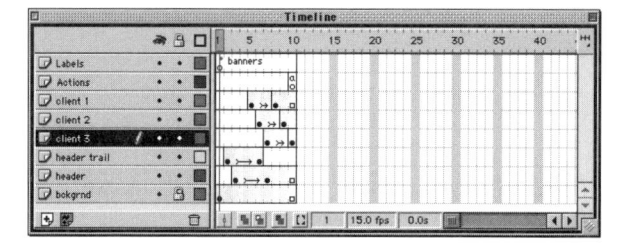

Figure 6-16 Timeline of the "banners" movie clip.

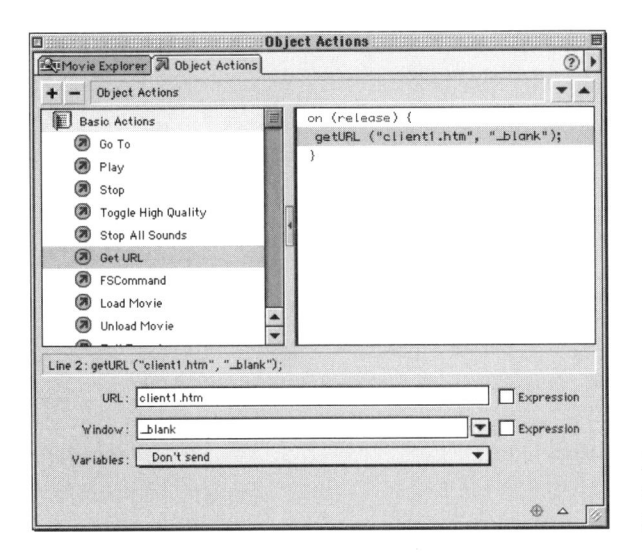

Figure 6-17   Object Actions window showing the "Get URL" action.

> **Note:** To make these buttons open HTML pages, we need to first create HTML pages for each client with banners on them. Then, we must use the "Get URL" action to call out a blank window with the HTML files. By choosing "_blank" as the Window Type, Flash will launch a new browser window with the HTML file selected. The only problem with this is we do not have any control over the window that is opened. In Chapter 10, there is an example on how to use Javascript to launch a window with certain specifications.

Web Sites Section

The next section of our site is the "websites" section. For this section, we will duplicate and use the "banners" movie clip. This section will be a little different than the "banners" section because we are not going to pop up an HTML window when the user clicks on a client. Instead, we will have some screen shots and descriptions of the sites that the user will be able to look at. Then they will be able to link to a site if they want. To keep a consistent look across this section, we are going to build a movie clip to be used as a template to showcase our Web sites. This movie clip will contain pictures of the site, a brief description, and a link to the site. Before we begin, let's set up the "websites" movie clip.

1. Use the file from the previous sections.
2. Open the Library window.
3. Select the "banners" movie clip.

4. Select Duplicate from the Options menu of the Library window.
5. Name the new clip "websites".
6. In the main Timeline, insert a keyframe (press F6) under the "websites" label in the "blue box" layer.
7. Use the Swap Symbol button from the Instance panel to change the "banners" movie clip to the "websites" movie clip.
8. In the main Timeline, highlight the "websites" movie clip.
9. Open the Instance panel and change the Name field to "websites". This field is located under the Behaviors pull-down menu.
10. Double-click on the "websites" movie clip on the Stage to enter Symbol Editing mode.
11. Change the label in the "labels" layer to read "websites" instead of "banners".
12. Duplicate the symbol for "banners header" and rename the new graphic "websites header".
13. Change "websites header" to "Web Sites".
14. Use the Swap Symbol button to change the "banners" header to the new "websites" header.
15. Extend all the layers except the "header trail" layer out to Frame 30.
16. Insert labels called "1", "2", and "3" to represent the three clients on Frames 15, 20, and 25.
17. Add stop actions on Frames 19, 24, and 30 (Figure 6-18).

Now that we have set up our section, we can start putting together our first Movie Clip template. The best way to build the clip is to start laying out the graphics and text on a layer above the "websites" section. Once we finish this, we can make it a Movie Clip symbol. By having the file as a symbol, all we need to do is duplicate it and rename it for each of the following client sections. I suggest that you make your screen shots into symbols so you can just use the Replace Symbol feature. It would also help to have the screen shots close to the same size so they will fit the same in the Movie Clip template.

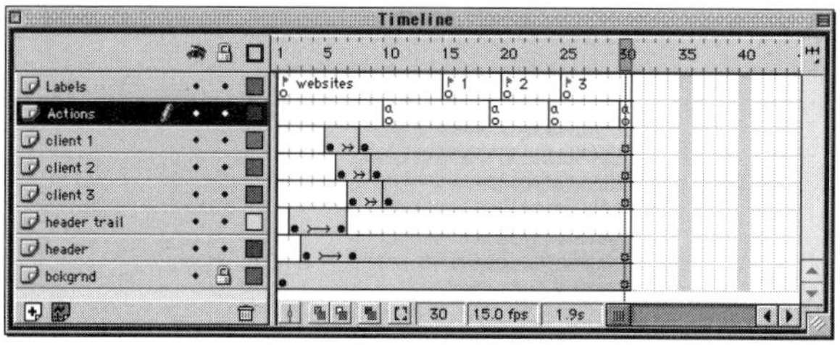

Figure 6-18 Timeline of the "websites" movie clip showing the layout of the "websites" section.

CHAPTER 6 • FLASH YOUR WEB SITE

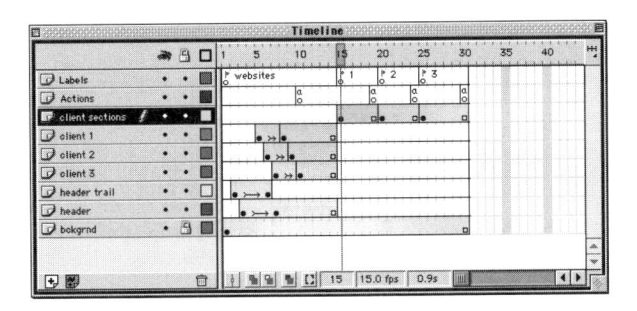

Figure 6-19 Timeline of the "websites" section.

1. Use the file from the previous sections.
2. Go into the Symbol Editing mode of the "websites" movie.
3. Insert a new layer and name it "client sections".
4. Insert a keyframe in the new layer under the label "1" in this movie clip.
5. Make sure that all the graphics in the other layers except the background layer are not viewable after the 14th frame (Figure 6-19).
6. Lay out your graphics and text for the first client's section on the "client sections" layer.
7. Add a "Back" button under your graphics in the "blue box" on this layer. This button can be any graphic you want.
8. Add a "Go To" action to this button that sends the "websites" movie clip back to Frame 10 (Figure 6-20).

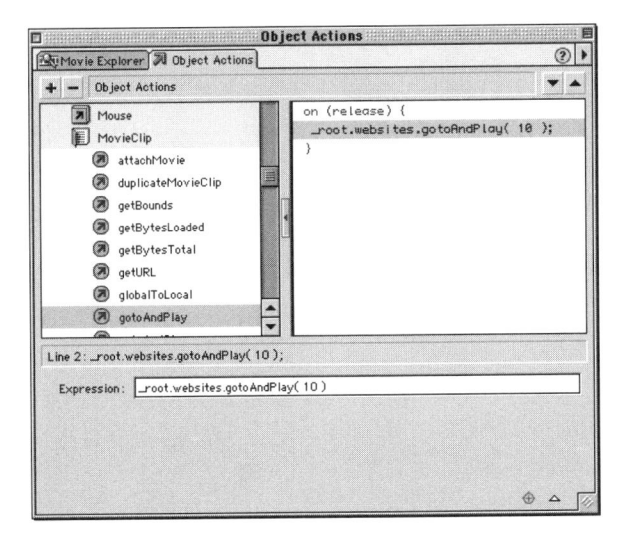

Figure 6-20 Actions window with the "Go To" action of the "Back" button.

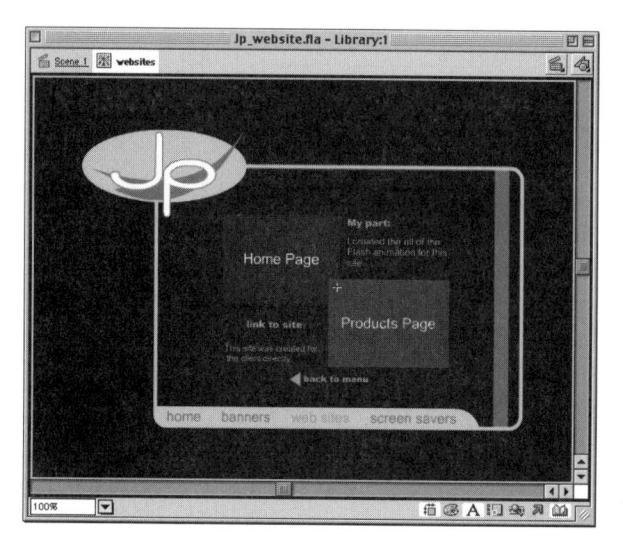

Figure 6-21 Web site template created for the "sections" movie clip.

9. Make the template into a symbol (Figure 6-21).
10. Duplicate the template clip from "client 1" and rename it for the other clients.
11. Swap the clients' graphics and adjust the text for each client's page.
12. Once you have finished this, then you can place the clients' movies under their respective labels.
13. Go to the clients' buttons in Frame 10.
14. Add "Go To" actions to them that makes the movie jump to their respective sections when clicked. For example, "client 1" when clicked, will go to "label 1" in this movie clip.

Screen Savers Section

The "screensavers" section can be done just like the "websites" section. All we have to do is follow the instructions from the "websites" section except we want to replace "websites" with "screensavers" wherever it needs to be. We also need to duplicate one of the Movie Clip templates for the "websites" clients and replace the graphics with the "screensavers" graphics and text.

> **Warning:** Make sure that you look closely at all the ActionScripts because some might make references to the "websites" movie and they will need to make references to the "screensavers" movie.

CHAPTER 6 • FLASH YOUR WEB SITE   145

PRINTING FROM FLASH

This section will cover the Print feature that was added late to Flash 4. It was just an upgrade to the plug-in that allows you to program your files to print Flash files. Since this example is a portfolio site, I was thinking we should add a link that will print a resume or one sheet to the "welcome" section. This section is broken down into two sections, the first covering how to set up the file you want to print and the second covering how to set up your main Timeline to print this secondary file.

SETTING UP A PRINTABLE DOCUMENT

To allow Flash to print your resume or one sheet, you must first convert it to a Flash file. The best way to do this is to redo your resume in FreeHand or Illustrator. Once you have your file recreated in one of these programs, you can import it into Flash.

1. Open a new Flash file.
2. Add two new layers and call them "labels" and "actions".
3. Insert a keyframe in Frame 3 of the "actions" layer.
4. In this new keyframe, add the action from Figure 6-22.

Note: The action from Figure 6-22 is an "If" statement that checks to see if the total frames loaded equal the total number of frames in the movie. If they are equal, then the action is called to tell the "home" movie clip of the main movie to go to and play the "loaded" label. If they are not equal, then the action calls the "Go To" action, which causes a loop to keep playing the "If" statement until the frames loaded equal the total frames.

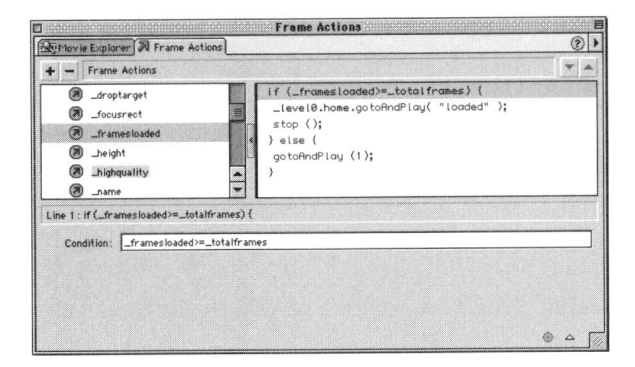

Figure 6-22   The "If frame is loaded" action for the resume Flash movie.

5. Import the resume or one sheet that you created in FreeHand or Illustrator.
6. Choose Modify -> Movie and set the dimensions of the file by selecting the Match to contents button. This will size the movie to that of the imported file.

> **Note:** This movie does not have to be the same dimensions as our main movie. Actually, this is the best way to make Flash print a document that is a different size than the main movie. If you tried to print something from the main movie that was larger than the Stage, the item would get clipped to the dimensions of the Stage.

7. Drag the resume keyframe to Frame 7 so that Frame 7 is the only frame in which the resume is visible.
8. Insert a keyframe in Frame 7 of the "labels" layer.
9. Add the label "#p" in this new keyframe.

> **Note:** The "#p" in the "labels" layer tells Flash that this is a printable frame. When Flash calls to print this movie, it will only print what is visible in the frames designated to be printed by "#p".

10. Insert a blank keyframe (press F7) in Frame 8 of the "resume" layer.
11. Draw a solid box in Frame 8 that is the size of the resume.
12. Insert a keyframe in Frame 8 of the "labels" layer.
13. Add a label called "#b" in this new keyframe.

> **Note:** The "#b" in the "Labels" layer tells Flash that this frame designates the print area. The combination of the "#b" and the box drawn in Frame 8 is telling Flash what you want the print area to be so that is doesn't try to print either too much or too little.

14. The last step is to export the movie file. Choose File -> Export Movie, save the file as "res.swf", and then click OK from the Export Flash Player window. Chapter 8 covers this topic in greater detail, but for this example, the default settings are fine.

This completes our resume file; now we need to work on our main movie.

MAKING A MOVIE PRINT

We have completed the resume movie; now we need to complete the setup by finishing the main movie. The reason why we created a separate file to print was mainly because we do not want everyone to have to download this file if they are not going to use it. Another reason was that we needed the dimensions of the file to be different from the main movie.

1. Open the main site file if it isn't already open.
2. Open the "home" movie clip in Symbol Editing mode.
3. Insert a new keyframe on Frame 11 of the "labels" layer.
4. Create a label for this keyframe and call it "print".
5. Open the "welcome text" symbol into Symbol Editing mode.
6. Create a button that says "click here to print my resume".
7. Place this button into the "welcome text" symbol.
8. Set up an action for this button to "Go To and play" the "print" label (Figure 6-23).
9. Go back to the "home" movie clip.
10. Insert a keyframe on the "labels" layer at Frame 15.
11. Create a label for the new keyframe called "loaded".
12. Insert a keyframe on the "actions" layer at Frame 20.
13. Add a "Go To" action to the new keyframe. This will send the "home" movie clip to Frame 10 (Figure 6-24).
14. Insert a keyframe in the "actions" layer right under the "print" label.
15. In this keyframe, add a "Load movie" action that will load our resume file ("res.swf") into level 5 (Figure 6-25).

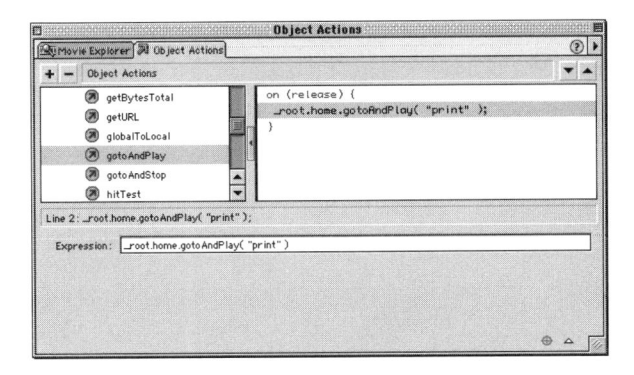

Figure 6-23 The action for the "print" button calling to the "home" movie clip and telling it to go to the "print" label.

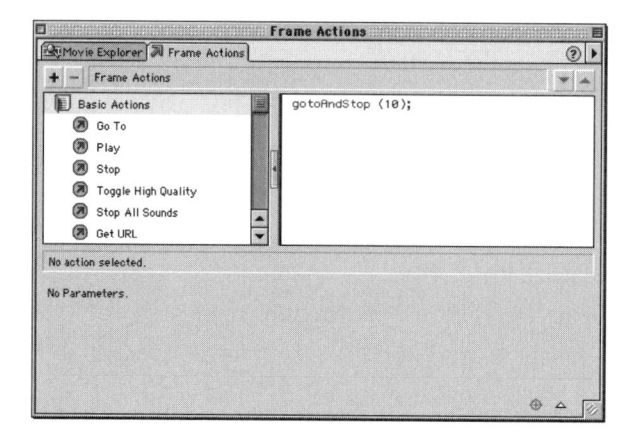

Figure 6-24 "Go To" action that sends the movie to Frame 10.

> **Warning:** If the resume movie is not loaded when you start printing, it will not print correctly or it may not print at all. This is why we added the script to the resume file that checks to see if it is loaded. When this file is loaded, it will tell our main clip.

16. Add a new layer to our "home" movie clip and call it "prepare".
17. Insert a keyframe in the "prepare" layer under the "print" label.
18. Add a graphic into the new keyframe that says "Preparing to Print".
19. Add a blank keyframe (press F7) in the "prepare" layer under the loaded label (this is to stop the new graphic from being seen when we do not want it to be).
20. Insert a keyframe in the "actions" layer under the "loaded" label.

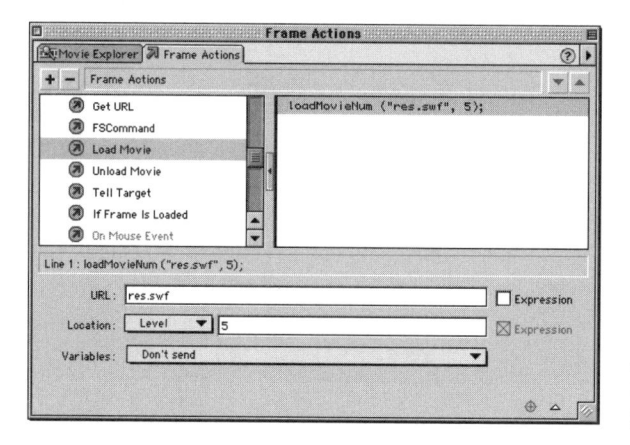

Figure 6-25 Action that loads the resume movie into level 5, above the main movie.

CHAPTER 6 · FLASH YOUR WEB SITE

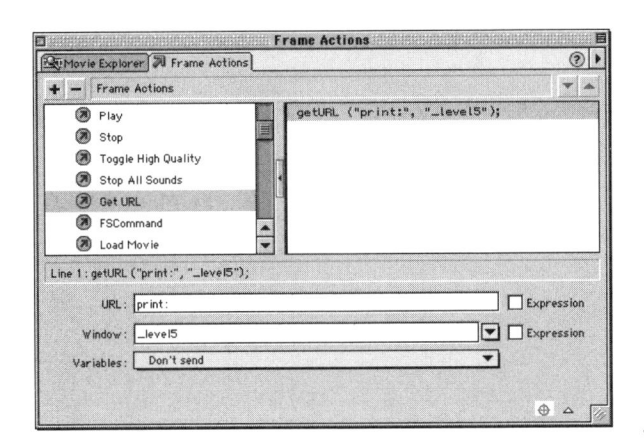

Figure 6-26 Action that tells the movie to print the resume file.

> **Note:** It is important to note that the "print" action calls "level 5". This is where we have loaded the "res.swf" file. If you do not call the right level, the movie will not print anything.

21. Add the action from Figure 6-26 to the new keyframe.
22. Add a graphic in the "prepare" layer, under the "loaded" label.
23. The graphic should say "Printing Resume". This is just to fill the space instead of having a blank screen while people are waiting for the resume to print.

This completes the set up of our main movie. Your Timeline for the "home" movie clip should look like the one in Figure 6-27. It is important to note that the "print" feature only works with the players that are Version 4.0.20 and higher. Since this site includes features specific to Flash 5, I did not incorporate a detection script. For more information about detecting Flash plug-ins, see Chapter 8.

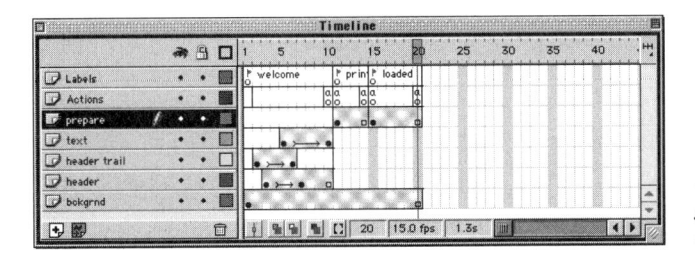

Figure 6-27 Timeline for the "home" movie clip.

TROUBLESHOOTING YOUR SITE

When you are building a site, the last thing you want to do is have links that are not functioning. The first thing you need to do is check on your ActionScript if links are not working. Some things to look for are incorrect names or incorrect syntax.

The printing function should also be checked, but it will not work until the site is playing in a Web browser. The best way to see how your site is going to look is to place it on the Web and troubleshoot while it is on a staging server.

With the site on a staging server, you will see how the site will react when you actually make it live on the Web. The most important problem to look for is buttons not working correctly. If your buttons are not working correctly, double-check your code to make sure that you are calling the right frames, labels, movie clips, or HTML files. This is the biggest mistake and the easiest one to overlook when you are putting a site together.

The next thing to check is to see that all of your animations are working the way that you wanted them to when you created them. If objects are not scaling, fading, or moving correctly, you should double-check your tweening settings. If an item is not scaling most of the time, the Tween scaling checkbox may not be checked. If items are not moving or fading correctly, they might not be the same objects at the beginning and end of the animation. For example, you might have been moving a symbol across the Stage and then broken the symbol apart for one reason or another in the ending keyframe. This would cause the animation to not work correctly. These are the areas that should be looked at when you are troubleshooting your site.

BRINGING YOUR HTML SITE TO LIFE

There are a few ways that you can make an HTML site look better without converting the whole site to Flash. You could add a menu bar in Flash or you could add some animation to draw attention to certain items. Building a menu bar in Flash for your HTML site is easier than you think. Flash will embed into your HTML page like a regular graphic, but it just has a lot more code. For more information on how to embed Flash into an HTML page, go to Chapter 8. The menu bar just has to consist of buttons that will use the "Get URL" action to call HTML pages. Just make sure that you embed the correct names of the HTML files into your menu bar. You cannot use an "<A HREF>" tag around your Flash file like you would a graphic. You can try using Flash animations like people use animated Gifs. The Flash animations will be much cleaner and cooler-looking than animated Gifs. Their file size will also be a lot smaller than animated Gifs. A great use of this is in the site for JR Visuals (www.jrvisuals.com). This site uses a

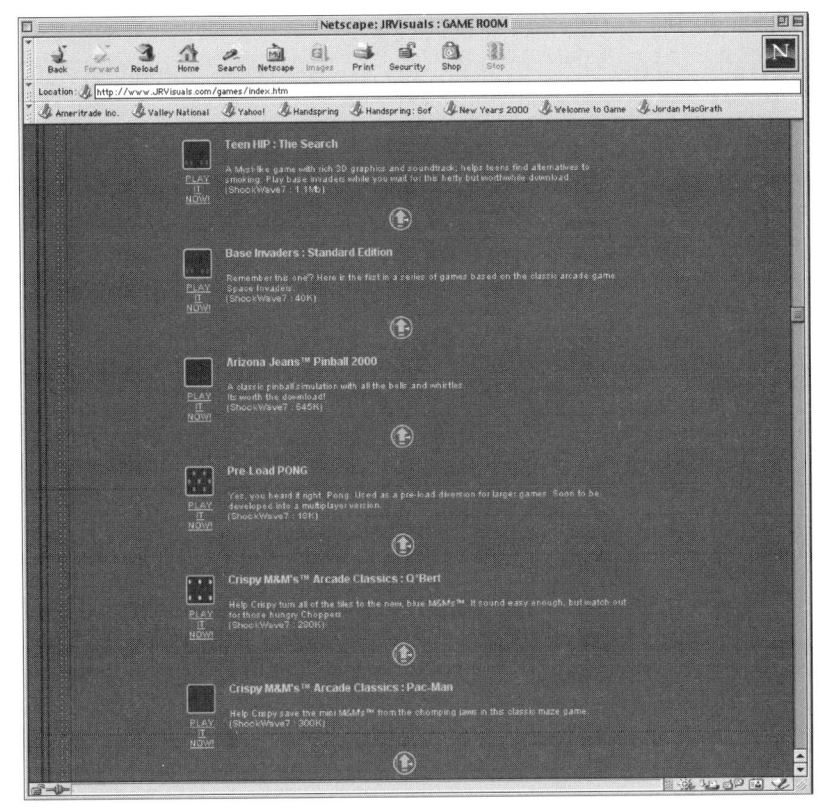

Figure 6-28   Screen shot of JR Visuals' Game Room section.

great combination of Flash animations as buttons and decorations. It makes the whole site easier to look at than a standard, flat HTML page (Figure 6-28). Look at the Game Room section of this site where the sites creator, Jose Rodriguez, uses a combination of Flash buttons to line the side of the page as links to the games. These buttons add some life to a page where there would normally not be any.

ADDING A SPLASH SCREEN TO YOUR SITE

Splash screens can be a simple logo animation, like the one found at www.get togethergames.com, right up to a more complex splash screen that builds the Home page of the site. They are very simple to make, but should be light in file size so the person watching does not have to wait a long time just to see the splash screen. If the animation is long, you should put a Skip button in the animation so that visitors can skip right to the site, especially when they are returning to the site multiple times. It is a good idea to put the Skip button in the HTML just below the animation, just in case the person does not have Flash and the detection method you have used does not work. See Chapter 8 for more details about plug-in detection.

When you are building a whole site in Flash, it is good to use another scene for the splash screen. It will help you keep everything in order. For example, if we were to add a splash screen to the site we just created, we could simply add a new scene. Then we would need to go into the "Inspectors" window for the scenes and move the new scene in front of the current scene. The reason why we need to move the new scene to the top or in front of the old scene is that Flash always plays the first scene in the list. The great thing about splash screens is you can use them in conjunction with loading screens to keep people entertained while your site is loading. They are also a great way to get a message across about what your site has to offer. They can be like a commercial, or preview, of what the site has to offer.

chapter 7

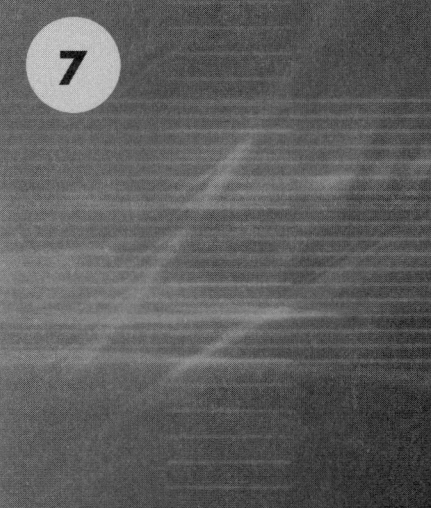

CREATING GAMES

This chapter will show you how to go about building games using Flash. There are some things that you have to understand about building games before you can start. The game-building process takes a lot of planning and preparation before you can start coding the game. Once you have designed and built the game graphically, then you can apply your code. The coding process can sometimes take a lot of trial and error before you perfect the game. This chapter will guide you through the production of two games. The first one is *ShapeMatch*, a classic memory game. The second one is *Flash Tennis*, a game in which a player plays against a computer.

SHAPEMATCH

For those of you not familiar with memory games, let me explain how *ShapeMatch* works. The board is built with tiles that the player clicks on to see what shape is behind them. The player turns over two tiles to see if they match. If there is a match, the tiles disappear; if there is no match, the tiles flip back to their starting state. The object is to match all the shapes with the fewest number of clicks.

As with every game, this one poses a unique set of challenges. You have to first figure out the functionality that you want in the game before you can even start building the graphics. You need to know how many tiles you are going to use for your game. In this example, I used 12 tiles, which means there are six different shapes for the tiles since there are two tiles per shape. One of the big challenges is deciding how to make the tiles appear in different positions every time the game is played. For this, I have some scripts that use the random number action that help position the tiles on the Stage.

CREATING THE GRAPHICS

Before we start creating the graphics for the game, let's make sure that we know what we have to create. We will need to make a board or background for the game. Well, we do not need to do it, it just makes the game look better. The 12 tiles and 6 shapes need to be created, of course, because without these, we really wouldn't have a game. The game will also need a text field that we will use to keep track of the score. This text field should have text next to it that says something like "number of tries". We will also need a background image to place behind the tiles so that when they are all removed, the player will see a message or image.

Figure 7-1 gives you a peek at what I have created for this game. This also will serve as a reference throughout the process to see where items get placed.

We have our work cut out for us, so let's start creating. This section has been broken up to ease the inclusion of the graphics.

1. Open a new file.
2. Choose Modify -> Movie to open the Movie Properties window.
3. Set the movie Dimensions to 185px x 300px and the Background Color to light gray.

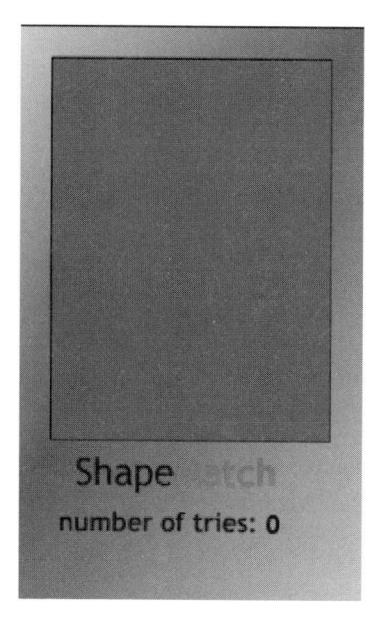

Figure 7-1 ShapeMatch game screen.

Background

1. Choose the Rectangle tool with no stroke.
2. Create a rectangle the whole size of the movie.
3. I applied a gradient that goes from light gray to dark gray and back to light gray to my rectangle. The gradient starts at the top left corner and goes to the bottom right corner (Figure 7-2).

Score Board

1. Insert a new layer and call it "number of tries".
2. Create text that says "number of tries" on this new layer.
3. Create a text field next to the "number of tries" text (Figure 7-3).
4. Choose Window -> Panels -> Text Options to open the Text Options panel if it is not open already.
5. Set the properties of the text field you have created to Dynamic Text, Single Line, and set the Variable to "totalclicked".
6. Group the text and the text field.
7. Choose Window -> Panels -> Align to open the Align panel if it is not open already.

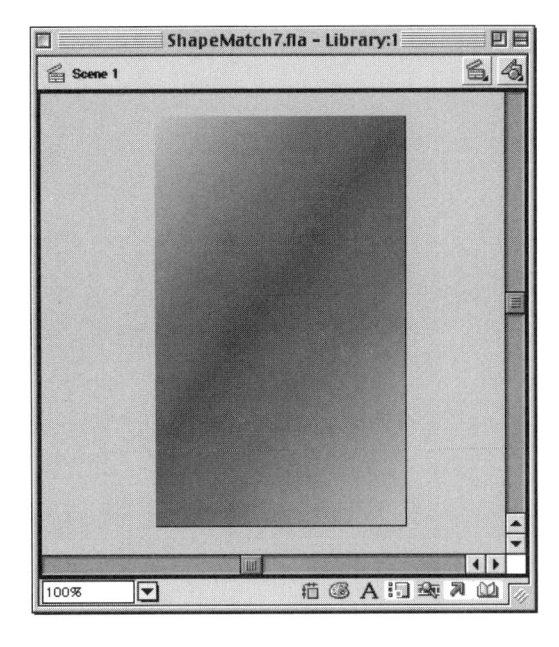

Figure 7-2   The background image with the gradient applied to it.

8. Horizontally center the grouped text to the Stage, then move it to the lower part of the window (Figure 7-1).

Reset Button

1. Insert a new layer called "reset".
2. Choose the Rectangle tool with no stroke.
3. Click the Round Rectangle Radius button in the Options section of the Toolbar and set the Corner Radius to 25.
4. Create a small pill shape using this setting on the new layer (Figure 7-4).
5. With that shape selected, choose Insert -> Convert to Symbol.
6. Set the Behavior to Button.
7. Double-click on the new button to enter Symbol Editing mode.
8. Insert a new layer that is above the pill shape.
9. Create text that says "Reset" and place it over the pill shape.
10. Insert a keyframe in the Over state of the text layer.
11. Change the color of the "Reset" text in this layer to something that will stand out, like a bright orange or green.
12. Insert a frame (press F5) in the Down state so that the text will be visible in this layer.
13. Go to the pill shape's layer and insert a frame (press F5) in the Hit state. This will extend the graphic through all states of the button.
14. Go back to the main Timeline and place the "Reset" button in the lower right corner (Figure 7-1).

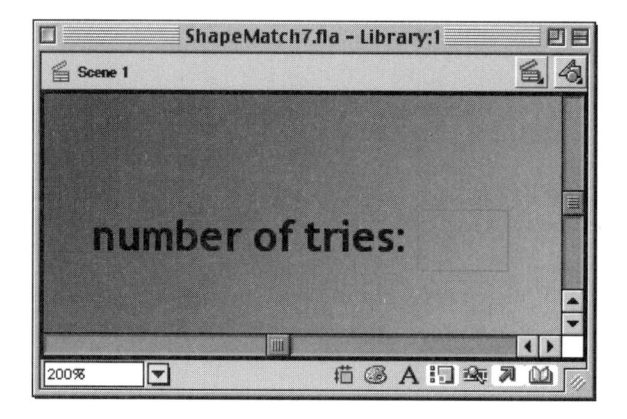

Figure 7-3 Text field lined up next to the "number of tries" text.

CHAPTER 7 • CREATING GAMES

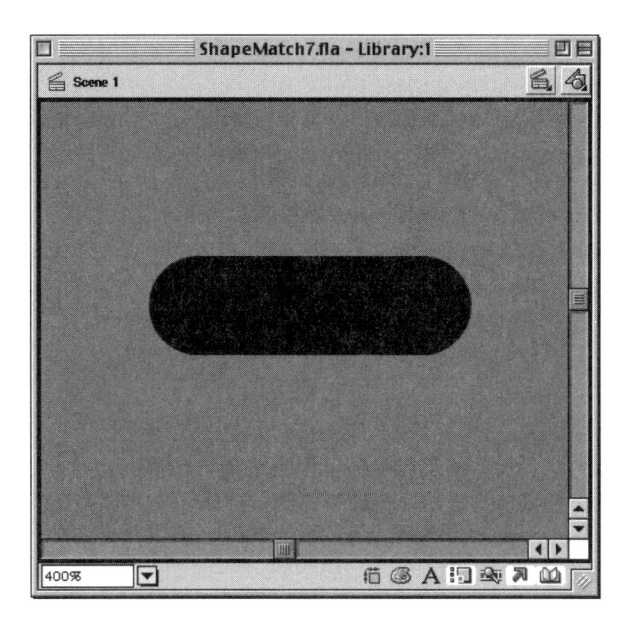

Figure 7-4 Pill shape created when using the Rectangle tool with the Corner Radius set to 25.

ShapeMatch Graphic

1. Insert a new layer called "ShapeMatch".
2. Create text that says "ShapeMatch".
3. Horizontally center this text above the text field and the "number of tries" text (Figure 7-1).

Grid

1. Insert a new layer and call it "Grid".
2. Choose the Rectangle tool with the stroke set to a dark gray and no color selected for the fill.

> **Tip:** Make sure that you set the Corner Radius option back to 0. If you don't, you will have a hard time trying to make a rectangle.

3. Create a rectangle that has a width of 150 and a height of 200.

> **Note:** When you are trying to make a shape a particular size, you are better off drawing a rectangle, then manipulating the dimensions. You can do this by selecting the shape and using the Info panel to alter the width and height of the shape. All you have to do is just type the dimensions into their respective fields.

4. Using the Info panel, set the Y coordinate of "Grid" to 116.
5. To set the X coordinate, horizontally align "Grid" to the page. (The X coordinate should wind up being 92.5 (Figure 7-5).

Tiles

Now it is time to create our tiles. We will start with the six images. I created mine in Illustrator; you can create yours in any program you are comfortable with. Figure 7-6 shows the images I used in this example.

You can use letters or numbers if you do not want to spend the time to create graphics right now. We will set up the files so that you can easily swap the images that appear with new ones.

1. When you have finished creating or importing your shapes, convert them individually to symbols. Then, remove the shapes from the Stage because we will not need them right away.
2. Insert a new layer behind the "Grid" layer and call it "tiles".
3. Choose the Rectangle tool with the stroke set to a dark gray at 1.5 pixels and the fill set to a light blue.

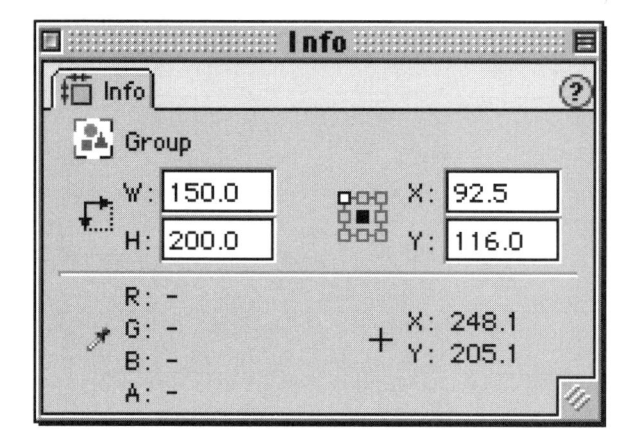

Figure 7-5 The Info panel when the "Grid" graphic is selected.

CHAPTER 7 • CREATING GAMES

Figure 7-6   Images used in the ShapeMatch game.

4. Create a square that has a width and height of 50.
5. Choose Insert -> Convert to Symbol and set the Behavior to Graphic.
6. Select the square and choose Insert -> Convert to Symbol again.
7. This time, set the Behavior to Movie Clip. The reason for this is that we need the tiles to be movie clips to work with them and it will save file size to have the square that will be used 12 times be the same symbol.
8. Double-click the square to enter Symbol Editing mode for the movie clip.
9. Go to Frame 30 and insert a frame (press F5) so that it extends the square's layer.
10. Insert a new layer above the square's layer and call it "shape".
11. Insert a keyframe in Frame 2 of the "shape" layer.
12. Drag a Shape graphic from the library into this new keyframe.
13. Make sure that the shape fits within the 50 x 50 dimensions of the square (Figure 7-7).
14. Insert a new keyframe (press F6) in Frames 10, 15, 25, 27, and 30 of the "shape" layer.
15. Select the shape in Frame 15.
16. Choose Window -> Panels -> Effect to open the Effect panel if it is not open already.
17. Select Alpha from the menu and set it to "0"; repeat this step for the shape in Frame 30.

Figure 7-7 The Shape symbol placed above the square.

18. Select the shape graphic in Frame 10.
19. Choose Window -> Panels -> Frame to open the Frame panel if it is not open already.
20. Select Motion from the Tweening menu; repeat this step for the graphic in Frame 27.
21. Insert a new layer in front of the "shape" layer and call it "button".
22. Copy the square from Frame 1 of the square's layer and paste it in place in the first frame of this new layer.
23. Select the new square.
24. Choose Insert -> Convert to Symbol and set the Behavior to Button.
25. Double-click this new button to enter Symbol Editing mode.
26. Drag the keyframe for the graphic to the Hit state so that nothing is visible in the Up, Over, and Down states.
27. Go back to the movie clip Timeline by clicking the Movie Clip icon or name at the top left corner of the Stage window.
28. Insert a blank keyframe (press F7) in Frame 2 of the "button" layer so that it is only visible in the first frame of the movie clip.
29. Insert a new layer and call it "actions".
30. Insert keyframes in Frames 15 and 30.
31. Add stop actions to Frames 1 and 30.

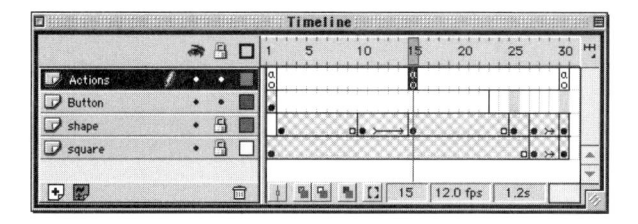

Figure 7-8 Timeline of the movie clip and how it should look at this point.

32. In Frame 15, add the "Go To" action, that goes to Frame 1 and stops (Figure 7-8).
33. Since there are only six images, we only need to make five more movie clips like the one we just made. To make the 12 tiles, we will just use two instances of each of the six movie clips. Open the Library and duplicate the "tile" movie clip.
34. Double-click the new movie clip to enter Symbol Editing mode.
35. Select the shape in Frame 2 of the "shape" layer.
36. Choose Window -> Panels -> Instance to open the Instance panel if it is not open already.
37. Swap the shape with one you have not used already.
38. You will need to repeat the previous step for Frames 10, 25, and 27, using the same shape you chose for Frame 2.
39. Repeat Steps 33- 38 for the last four shapes.

You Win!

1. Go back to the main Timeline.
2. Insert a new layer behind the "tiles" layer and call it "you win".
3. Draw an oval on this layer.
4. Create text that says "you win!" (Figure 7-9).

This completes the creating graphics section; now we need to add the code and wrap the game up.

ADDING THE CODE

This is the most difficult part of the game. It takes a lot of thought as to what is going to happen when the tiles get clicked, and even before we get to that point, how the tiles are going to be arranged. We are going to start by getting the positions of the tiles and setting up the tiles with instance names that we can call on to arrange them. Another item we should change is the appearance of the Reset button. It should only appear when all the tiles have been matched. The last thing that we need to cover is the scoring and how it will work. Every time someone either makes a match or fails to make a match, it will count as a try. Let's jump right into setting up our buttons.

Figure 7-9 "you win!" layer with congratulatory text.

1. Go to the main Timeline.
2. Select the movie clip from the "tiles" layer.
3. Choose Window -> Panels -> Instance to open the Instance panel if it is not open already.
4. Set the name of the clip to "tile1".
5. Command + D (Control + D on a PC) to duplicate this clip on the Stage.
6. Set the name of the clip to "tile2".
7. Drag one of the other five movie clips onto the Stage into the "tiles" layer.
8. Repeat Steps 4 -7 until you have all 12 tiles on Stage. Make sure to add one to the number after "tile" for each tile you name. The last tile should be "tile12".
9. Move all the tiles off the Stage into the work area on the side (Figure 7-10).
10. Take "tile1" and drag it to the upper right-hand corner of the grid (box) we created earlier.
11. Open the Info panel and check that the X coordinate is 42.4 and the Y coordinate is 41.0.
12. Write this down because we will be using this a little later.
13. Move the tile back off the Stage.
14. Double-click on "tile1" to enter Symbol Editing mode for the movie clip.

CHAPTER 7 • CREATING GAMES   163

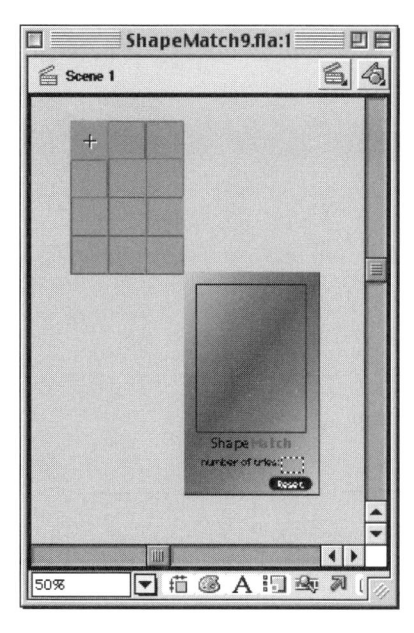

Figure 7-10   The 12 tiles placed off the Stage in the work area.

15. Select the button in Frame 1 of the "buttons" layer.
16. Add the following action to the button:
    ```
    on (release) {
        letter = "a";
    }
    #include "tileScript.as"
    ```

> **Note:** This action sets the letter variable to "a". The reason we are setting the letter variable to "a" is so we can differentiate which clips are grouped together. For example, "tile1" and "2" are set to "a", "tile3" and "4" are set to "b", etc. Since we have six groups, the last letter should be "f". It also uses an include action to call a script, called "tileScript.as", that is kept outside of Flash. The reason for this is that each tile uses the same code, so instead of editing the code in each clip every time you want to update it, you can just change the code in the external file.

17. Repeat Steps 14 - 16 for the last eleven tiles. Make sure that you read the Note for more detailed instructions.
18. Go back to the main Timeline.

19. Select Frame 1 and add the following code:

```
// First click or not
on (release) {
    if (_root.times == "1") {
        if (_root.clicked == letter) {
// There is a match
            this.gotoAndPlay(25);
            tellTarget (eval("_root.who")) {
                gotoAndPlay (25);
            }
            _root.times = "0";
            _root.totalclicked += 1;
            _root.matched +=1;
    if (_root.matched == 6){
    setProperty ("_root.reset", _visible, "1");
    }
        } else {
// There is no match
            tellTarget (eval("_root.who")) {
                gotoAndPlay (2);
            }
            this.gotoAndPlay(2);
            _root.times = "0";
            _root.totalclicked = _root.totalclicked + 1;
        }
    } else {
// If this is the first click
        _root.clicked = letter;
        _root.times = "1";
        _root.who = this;
        this.gotoAndStop(2);
    }
}
```

20. When you are done copying this code over to your file, choose Export as file.
21. Save the file as "tileScript.as" and then delete the code from Frame 1.

I know this code looks very complicated, but it really is not that bad. This code can be broken down into four parts right where I have placed the comments. Remember, this code is called into the buttons that are located in the tiles.

The first section of the code checks to see if this is the first tile clicked or not. If this is not the first tile clicked, then it checks to see if there is a match or not by checking the letter variables against each other.

If there is a match, it runs the code after the "There is a match" comment. This code tells the current tile (this) to go to and play Frame 25. Then it tells the first movie that was clicked to also go to Frame 25 and play. Next, the movie sets a few variables that help the movie keep track of what is going on. For example, the times variable lets us keep track of whether or not this is the first click or not. If the variable is "0", then it is

CHAPTER 7 • CREATING GAMES

the first click; if it is "1", then it is the second click. The reason this section is setting it to "0" is because there has been a match, so we get set back to our first click. The totalclicked variable sets our "number of tries" field to itself plus 1, keeping score for how many times someone matched and did not match tiles. The matched variable allows us to know when all the tiles have been matched and there are none left. When there are no tiles left, we set the visibility of the Reset button to 1, making it visible and allowing the player to reset the game.

If there is no match found, this section sets the time variable back to one and adds one to the totalclicked score. It also sets the current movie back to its first frame, and it sets the first movie clicked to its first frame.

If this is the first click of the movie, after a match or miss, the last section will be run. It will set the variables so that the next tile clicked will know which tile has been clicked and will allow it to see if there is a match.

This completes the tile code. Let's start with the code in the main Timeline.

1. Go to the main Timeline if you are not there already.
2. Select the Reset button from the "reset" layer.
3. Choose Insert -> Convert to Symbol.
4. Select Movie Clip as the Behavior.
5. In the Instance panel, set the Name of the movie clip to Reset.

> **Note:** We need to nest the button into a movie clip so that we can control its visibility using ActionScript.

6. Insert two layers, one called "actions" and the other "labels".
7. In the first frame, add the following actions:

```
// Makes the Reset button invisible
setProperty ("_root.reset", _visible, "0");
// Sets up some variables
totalclicked = 0;
tiles = 12;
total = tiles;
list = 1;
count = 1;
// Sets up 12 variables equal to their value (i.e., tilelist1=1)
while (list<=tiles) {
   set ("tilelist" add list, list);
list += 1;
     }
```

As the comments state, the first action sets visibility of the "reset" movie clip, which holds the Reset button to 0. Then, we set up the variables that keep track of the number of clicks and the total number of tiles that we are using. The last section makes a list of 12 variables equal to the numbers 1 - 12.

8. Insert a keyframe (press F6) in the second frame of the "actions" layer.
9. Add the following actions into the new keyframe:
   ```
   While (count<=tiles) {
   // Generates a random # between 1-12, then adds 1
   randomNum = random(total) + 1 ;
   // Generates variables called movie+ a number one for each clip just like before with the tilelist
   set ("movie" add count, eval("tilelist" add randomNum));
   // Changes numbers of the tilelist variables so that number selected will not be used again
   list = randomNum;
   while (list<total) {
   set ("tilelist" add list, eval("tilelist" add (list+1)));
   list += 1;
   }
   // Sets up the variables for the next pass
   total -= 1;
   count += 1;
   }
   ```

   If you are copying the comments into your code, make sure that these lines, starting with "//", are placed all on one line. Some of them above are wrapped around onto two lines.

   These actions take the list of variables generated in Frame 1 and set the number they are equal to to a random number between 1 - 12. But the unique feature of this is that it will only use a number once, so there are no duplicates.

10. Insert a keyframe into Frame 3 of the "actions" layer.
11. Add these actions into the new keyframe:
    ```
    // y coordinate of the top left corner
    ypos = 41.0;
    // x = 1 and y = 1 to refer to the top left corner of the grid
    x = 1;
    y = 1;
    next = 1;
    // Loops until all the tiles in the 4th row of the grid have been filled
    while (y<=4) {
    // x coordinate of the top left corner
    xpos = 42.4;
    // Loops until all the tiles in the 3rd column of the grid have been filled
    while (x<=3) {
    setProperty ("tile" add eval("movie" add next), _x, xpos);
    setProperty ("tile" add eval("movie" add next), _y, ypos);
    ```

CHAPTER 7 · CREATING GAMES

```
// Sets the x position to the next slot in the column
// Since all the tiles are 50 pixels, their center points are 50
pixels apart
xpos += 50;
// Advances the variable so that the movie will place the next clip
in the 2 slot of the column
x += 1;
// Advances the variable so that the movie will call the next movie
when this variable is called
next += 1;
}
// Sets the y position to the next slot in the row
ypos += 50;
// Sets the variable back to 1 so that the movie can fill the grid
starting at the first column
x = 1;
// Advances the variable so that the movie can start filling the
next row
y += 1;
}
```

These actions take the variables from Frame 2 and use them to assign the tiles to positions in the grid.

12. Insert a keyframe into Frame 4.
13. Add a stop action into Frame 4 of the movie.
14. Insert a keyframe into Frame 5.
15. Add these actions to Frame 5 of the movie:

```
next = 1;
while (next <= tiles) {
   tellTarget ("tile"add next) {
      gotoAndStop (1);
   }
   next += 1;
}
_root.matched = 0;
gotoAndPlay (1);
```

These actions reset the movie clips back to their first frame, basically resetting the movie so the game can be played again.

16. Insert a keyframe in Frame 5 of the "labels" layer.
17. Call the label in this layer "reset".
18. Move the "you win" graphic from the "picture" layer into Frame 4.
19. Test your movie.

This completes adding actions to our movie. Now, all you have to do is make sure that the external file is in the same directory as the main movie file when you export your movie.

FLASH TENNIS

This game is based on classic arcade games. It pits the player against the computer with nothing but two paddles and a ball. This means that this game is less dependent on graphics, but requires more thought with the scripting. This example makes use of the new Smart Clip feature for the ball and the walls. This new feature allows you to edit some of the features directly in the clip. The ball in this movie carries the bulk of the code in it. This is because when you think about it, the ball is basically the whole game.

CREATING THE GRAPHICS

There are only a few graphics in this movie, but enough to warrant this section. Like any other game, it is important to nail down the functionality of the game before you begin designing. There are some features you will need to take into consideration such as the score bar. This game is unique in the respect that it has two score windows, one for the computer and the other for the player. I have provided a screen shot of the game to give you an idea of how the graphics need to be put together while you are building the game (Figure 7-11). I have broken this section down into smaller sections to help you understand which part of the movie you are building.

1. Open a new file.
2. Choose Modify -> Movie.
3. Set the movie Dimensions to 400 × 250.

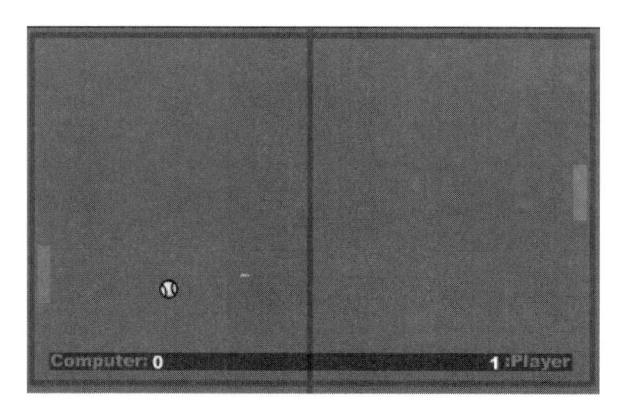

Figure 7-11 Finished Flash Tennis game.

Walls

1. Choose the Rectangle tool with no stroke.
2. Draw a rectangle larger than the width of the movie (Figure 7-12).
3. With the rectangle selected, Choose Insert -> Convert to Symbol.
4. Choose Movie Clip as the Behavior.
5. Choose Window -> Library to open the Library window if it is not open already.
6. Select the Rectangle movie clip in the Library.
7. Choose Define Clip Parameters from the Options menu in the Library; this opens the Define Clip Parameters window.
8. Click on the plus sign (+) under the Parameters section to add a variable. Set the Name of the variable to pWallType, set the Value to none, and leave the Type set to default, and click OK. This makes the clip a Smart Clip.
9. Select the movie clip on the Stage.
10. Choose Window -> Panels -> Clip Parameters if the Clip Parameters window is not open already.
11. Double-click on the "defaultValue" text in the Value column and change it to "top" (Figure 7-13).
12. Drag the Movie Clip symbol out of the Library onto the Stage and place it along the bottom.
13. Set the Value of this clip to "bottom".
14. Drag the Movie Clip symbol out of the Library onto the Stage and place it along the right side of the clip.

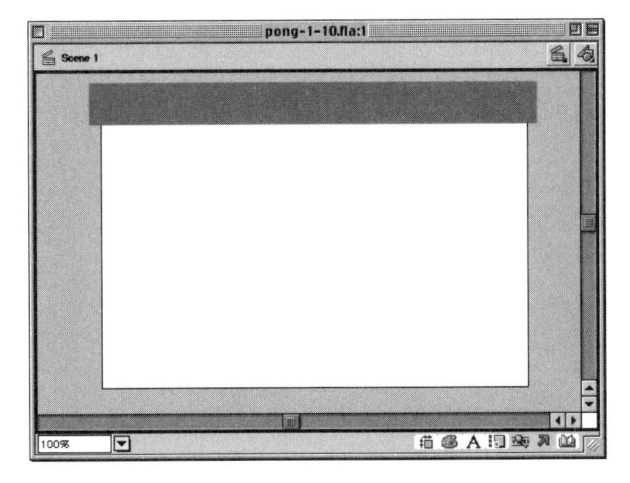

Figure 7-12 Top wall of the movie.

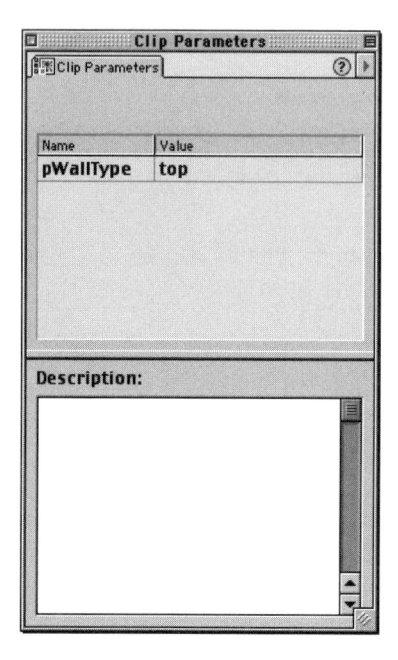

Figure 7-13 Clip Parameters window, where you set the value of a Smart Clip.

15. Resize the movie clip so that it is not more than a quarter of the way into the clips at the top and bottom.
16. Set the Value of this clip to "right".
17. Choose Edit -> Duplicate to duplicate this clip.
18. Move the clip to the left side (Figure 7-14).
19. Set the Value of this clip to "left".

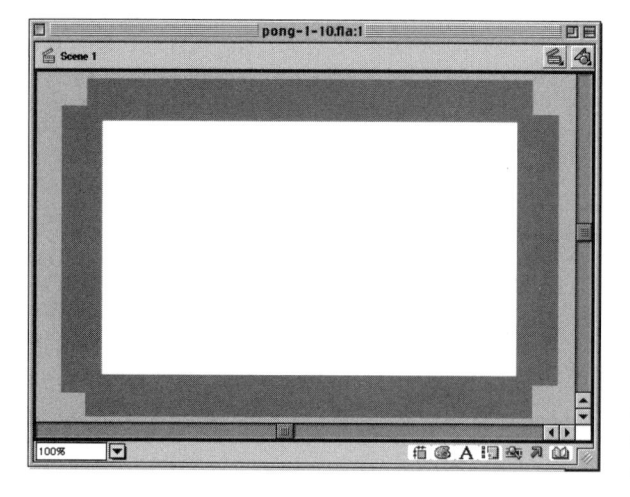

Figure 7-14 Walls of the movie added to help detection of the ball's position.

Background

1. Insert a new layer and name it "background".
2. Choose the Rectangle tool with no stroke.
3. Draw a box, about 20 pixels on each side, larger than the size of the movie dimensions.
4. Choose the Rectangle tool with a stroke set to 3 pixels and no fill color.
5. Draw a box within the larger rectangle, resembling the lines on a court.
6. Choose the Line tool, with the stroke set to 3 pixels, and draw a mid-court line (Figure 7-15).

Score Bar

1. Insert a new layer and call it "Score boxes".
2. Choose the Rectangle tool with no stroke.
3. Draw a rectangle that is about 360 pixels across and 20 pixels tall.
4. With the rectangle selected, choose Insert -> Convert to Symbol.
5. Select Movie Clip as the Behavior.
6. Double-click on the Rectangle movie clip to enter Symbol Editing mode.
7. Insert a layer and call it "text".
8. Use the Text tool and type two separate words, "Computer:" and ":Player".
9. Place the words on the bar at opposite ends: "Computer:" on the left side and ":Player" on the right side (Figure 7-16).
10. Go back to the main Timeline.

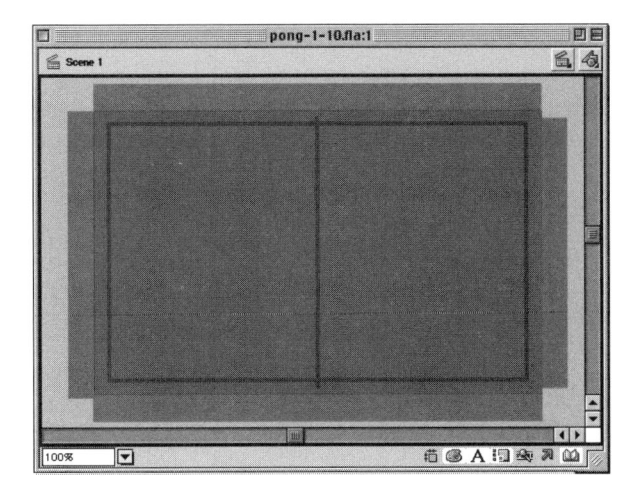

Figure 7-15 Background graphic that gives the game the look of a tennis court.

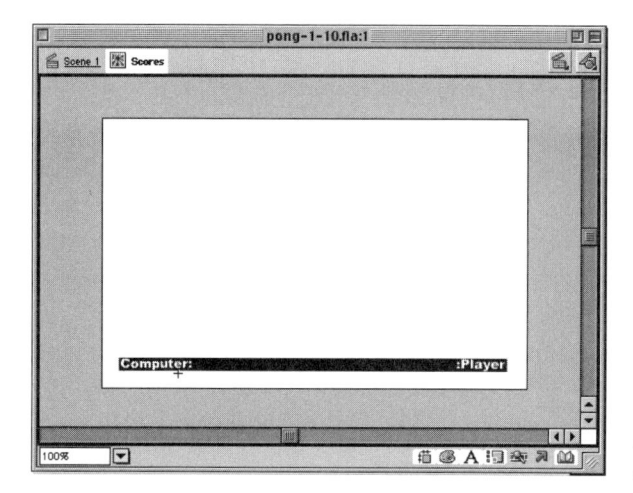

Figure 7-16 Score bar created with the text for the player and the computer.

11. Choose Window -> Panels -> Effect to open the Effect panel if it is not open already.
12. Select the score bar.
13. Choose the Alpha effect and set it to 50%.
14. Insert a new layer.
15. Create text fields and place them next to the "Computer:" and ":Player" text (Figure 7-17).
16. Choose Window -> Panels -> Text Options if the Text Options panel is not open already.

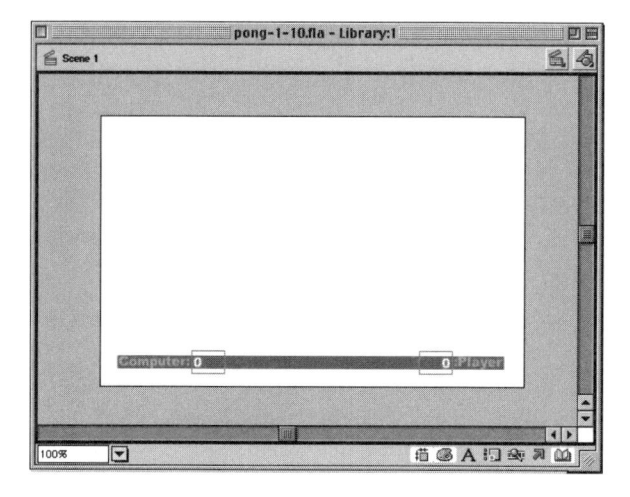

Figure 7-17 Text fields that will keep the score for the game.

CHAPTER 7 • CREATING GAMES

17. Set the options of the text fields to Dynamic Text and Single Line.
18. Set the variables of the text fields to "playerScore" and "computerScore", respectively.

Ball

1. Insert a new layer and call it "Ball layer".
2. Choose the Oval tool.
3. While holding the Shift key, draw a circle on the Stage.
4. With the circle selected, choose Insert -> Convert to Symbol.
5. Choose Movie Clip as the Behavior for the ball.
6. Double-click on the ball to enter Symbol Editing mode.
7. Create some lines on the ball and add a gradient to it to make the ball more realistic (Figure 7-18).
8. Select the ball and choose Insert -> Convert to Symbol; this way, we can manipulate the ball without worrying about file size.
9. Choose Graphic for the Behavior.
10. Insert keyframes in Frames 8, 12, and 15 on the "graphics" layer in the ball's movie clip.
11. Choose Window -> Panels -> Info to open the Info panel if it is not open already.
12. Set the ball's size in Frame 1 to about 50 pixels.
13. Set the ball's size in Frames 8 and 15 to about 12 pixels.
14. Set the ball's size in Frame 12 to about 24 pixels.

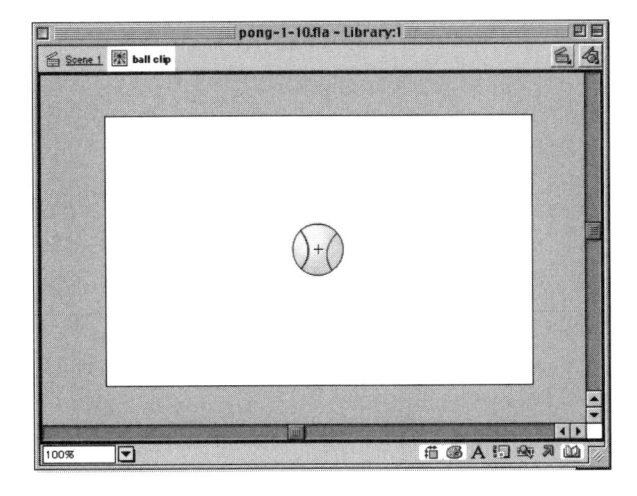

Figure 7-18 The Ball graphic with the lines and gradient added.

15. Choose Window -> Panels -> Frame to open the Frame panel if it is not open already.
16. Set Frames 1, 8, 12 to Motion Tween; this will give the ball a bounce effect, like it has been dropped onto the court.
17. Insert two layers, one called "labels" and the other called "actions".
18. Set a label in Frame 1 of the "labels" layer and call it "dropIN".
19. Insert a keyframe into Frame 15 of the "labels" layer.
20. Add a label to this keyframe and call it "HOLD".
21. Insert a keyframe into Frame 15 of the "actions" layer.
22. Add a stop action to this keyframe.
23. Insert a new layer, under the "labels" and "actions" layers, and call it "sounds".
24. Insert keyframes in Frames 8 and 15 on the "sounds" layer.
25. Choose Window -> Common Libraries -> Sounds.
26. Drag Keyboard Type Sngl onto the Stage while the keyframe in Frame 8 of the "sounds" layer is highlighted.
27. Also apply this sound to the keyframe in Frame 15.
28. Go out to the main Timeline.
29. Set the instance Name of the Ball movie clip to "ball" in the Instance panel.

Paddles

1. Insert a layer and call it "Player paddle".
2. Choose the Rectangle tool with no stroke.
3. Draw a small rectangle that is about 9 pixels by 39 pixels (Figure 7-19).
4. With the rectangle selected, choose Insert -> Convert to Symbol.
5. Choose Movie Clip as the Behavior.
6. Set the instance Name of the Player Paddle movie clip to "player" in the Instance panel.
7. Insert a new layer and call it "Computer paddle".
8. Drag the "Player" movie clip out of the Library and out onto the Stage.
9. Choose Window -> Panels -> Effect if the Effect panel is not open already.
10. Select the movie clip, choose Tint, and tint the clip blue.
11. Set the instance Name of the movie clip to "computer".

This finishes the graphics for this section. Now we need to get to the code. We have used a combination of movie clips and Smart Clips in this game to make it easier to code and change the code.

CHAPTER 7 • CREATING GAMES

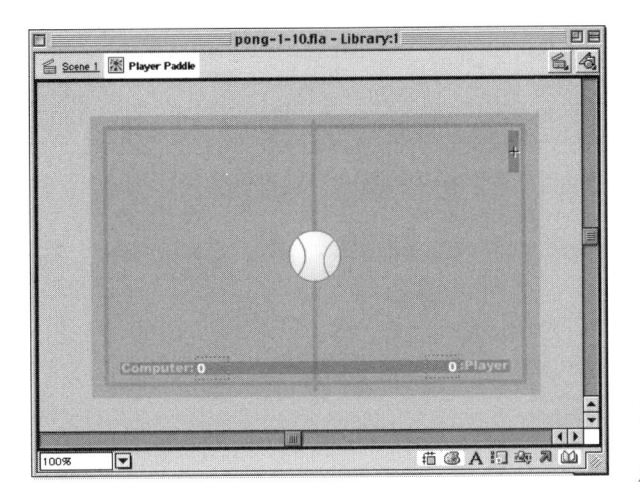

Figure 7-19   The rectangle we will be using as the player's paddle.

ADDING THE CODE

There are a few small scripts scattered throughout the game, but the bulk of the code is contained in the ball. The major difference between this game and *ShapeMatch* is that there is no code in the main Timeline of this game. This example starts with the code for the player and computer paddles, then it adds the code into the ball to complete the game.

Player Paddle

1. Make sure you are in the main Timeline of the game.
2. Select the player's paddle.
3. Choose Window -> Actions to open the Actions window if it is not open already.
4. Add the following code:
   ```
   onClipEvent (mouseMove) {
       _y = _root._ymouse;
   }
   ```

This code sets the "y" position of the player's paddle to the "y" position of the mouse. This action is activated every time the mouse is moved so that the paddle will always respond to the player's movements.

Computer Paddle

1. Select the "Computer paddle" movie clip.
2. Add the following code to the "Computer paddle" movie clip:

```
// Set up initial variables
        onClipEvent (load) {
            this.moveSpeed = 5;
        }
// ------------------------------------------------------------
        onClipEvent (enterFrame) {
            if ((_root.ball._y>_y) and (_root.ball._x<150)) {
                _y += 6;
            }
            if ((_root.ball._y<_y) and (_root.ball._x<150)) {
                _y -= 6;
            }
        }
```

This code starts by loading a variable that represents the speed of the ball. This happens as soon as this clip is loaded, which means that it will only happen once. The next set of actions happen when this frame is entered. These actions check the position of the ball. If the ball is within 150 pixels of the paddle, it will start to track towards the ball. If you want to make the computer's paddle move faster, increase the "y" variables that are set to either plus or minus 6. This will allow the paddle to cover more pixels.

Ball

1. Choose Window -> Library to open the Library window if it is not open already.
2. Select the Ball movie clip in the Library.
3. Choose Define Clip Parameters from the Options menu in the Library window.
4. Set up three parameters in this window:
   - Set rotateMultiplier to 4.
   - Set accelerationX to 5.
   - Set accelerationY to 2 (Figure 7-20).
8. Select the "Ball" movie clip on the Stage.
9. Add the following code to the Ball movie clip.

```
// Set up initial variables
        onClipEvent (load) {
// Set default directions
            this.directionX = +1;
            this.directionY = +1;
// Record starting location for reset
            this.orrigX = _x;
            this.orrigY = _y;
            this.orrigAccelX = this.accelerationX;
            this.orrigAccelY = this.accelerationY;
            this.orrigDirX = this.directionX;
            this.orrigDirY = this.directionY;
// Set default acceleration
// These are set via Clip Properties for ease of game tweaking.
```

CHAPTER 7 • CREATING GAMES

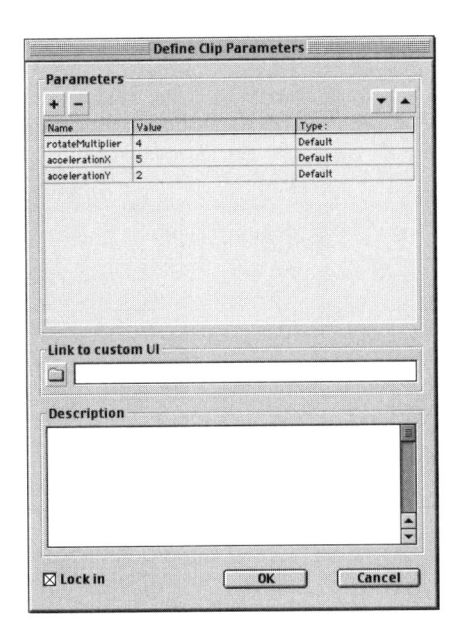

Figure 7-20 The Define Clip Parameters window, where the parameters are set to turn a movie clip into a smart clip.

```
// X=horizontal Y=vertical
// - The direction will be used to define if the
// ball is moving in a positive or negative direction.
// - The acceleration will be used to move the ball
// in the direction it is going.
// Set up the Sound object for the ball
        ballSounds = new Sound();
        ballSounds.attachSound("ballHit_1");
// Set up functions used
// -----------------------------------------------------------
// This function is called to reset the ball in position,
// generally after a score is made
        function resetBall () {
                _x=this.orrigX;
                _y=this.orrigY;
                this.accelerationX = this.orrigAccelX;
                this.accelerationY = this.orrigAccelY;
                this.directionY = this.orrigDirY;
                this.directionX = this.directionX * -1;
                gotoAndPlay ("dropIN");
            }
        }
// -----------------------------------------------------------
        onClipEvent (enterFrame) {
```

```
// Move the ball in the horizontal and vertical directions
            _x = _x+(this.directionX*this.accelerationX);
            _y = _y+(this.directionY*this.accelerationY);
// Spin the ball in the direction in which it is moving
_rotation =
           _rotation+(this.directionX*(rotateMultiplier*this.accel-
erationX));
// Check to see if the ball is hitting either of the left/right
walls
            if (_root.ball, hitTest(_root.wall_LEFT)) {
                    this.directionX = this.directionX*-1;
// Play Hit sound
                    ballSounds.attachSound("ballHit_1");
                    ballSounds.start();
// Score for the right player
        _root.playerScore = String (Number( _root.playerScore )+1)
// Reset the ball
                    resetBall ();
              }
if (_root.ball, hitTest(_root.wall_RIGHT)) {
                    this.directionX = this.directionX*-1;
// Play Hit sound
                    ballSounds.attachSound("ballHit_1");
                    ballSounds.start();
// Score for the left player
                    _root.computerScore = String (Number( _root.com-
puterScore )+1)
// Reset the ball
                    resetBall ();
              }
// Check to see if the ball is hitting either of the top/bottom
walls.
            if ((_root.ball, hitTest(_root.wall_TOP)) or
(_root.ball, hitTest(_root.wall_BOTTOM))) {
                    this.directionY = this.directionY*-1;
// Play Hit sound
                    ballSounds.attachSound("ballHit_2");
                    ballSounds.start();
// Bounce it back
        _x = _x+(this.directionX*this.accelerationX);
        _y = _y+(this.directionY*this.accelerationY);
              }
//-------------------------------------------------------------
// Check to see if the ball is hitting the player's paddle
// -------------------------------------------------------------
if ((_root.ball, hitTest(_root.player)) or (_root.ball,
hitTest(_root.player))) {
                    this.directionX = this.directionX*-1;
// Play Hit sound
                    ballSounds.attachSound("ballHit_1");
                    ballSounds.start();
```

CHAPTER 7 • CREATING GAMES

```
// Bounce it back
        _x = _x+(this.directionX*this.accelerationX);
        _y = _y+(this.directionY*this.accelerationY);
// Speed up the ball's horizontal(x) movement
        if (this.accelerationX<=10) {
            this.accelerationX = this.accelerationX+1;}
// If the ball hits the paddle at a good angle, speed up
// the ball's vertical(Y) movement... otherwise slow it down.
        if ((this.accelerationY<=15) and
(_root.player._y<this._y)) {
        if (this.directionY>0) {
            this.accelerationY = this.accelerationY+1;
                } else {
                this.accelerationY = this.accelerationY-1;
// Make sure we're not slipping into negative numbers
        if (this.accelerationY<=-1) {
            this.accelerationY = 0;
            }
        } else {
            if (this.directionY>0) {
                this.accelerationY = this.accelerationY-1;
// Make sure we're not slipping into negative numbers
        if (this.accelerationY<=-1) {
            this.accelerationY = 0;
            }
        } else {
            this.accelerationY = this.accelerationY+1;
        }
    }
  }
//-------------------------------------------------------------
// Check to see if the ball is hitting the computer's paddle
// -------------------------------------------------------------
if ((_root.ball, hitTest(_root.computer)) or (_root.ball,
        hitTest(_root.computer))) {
                    this.directionX = this.directionX*-1;
// Play Hit sound
                    ballSounds.attachSound("ballHit_1");
                    ballSounds.start();
// Bounce it back
        _x = _x+(this.directionX*this.accelerationX);
        _y = _y+(this.directionY*this.accelerationY);
// Speed up the ball's horizontal(x) movement
        if (this.accelerationX<=10) {
            this.accelerationX = this.accelerationX+1;
        }
// If the ball hits the paddle at a good angle, speed up
// the ball's vertical(Y) movement... otherwise slow it down.
if ((this.accelerationY<=15) and (_root.player._y<this._y)) {
        if (this.directionY>0) {
            this.accelerationY = this.accelerationY+1;
```

```
            } else {
                this.accelerationY = this.accelerationY-1;
// Make sure we're not slipping into negative numbers
            if (this.accelerationY<=-1) {
                this.accelerationY = 0;
                }
            }
        } else {
            if (this.directionY>0) {
                this.accelerationY = this.accelerationY-1;
// Make sure we're not slipping into negative numbers
            if (this.accelerationY<=-1) {
                this.accelerationY = 0;
                }
            } else {
                this.accelerationY = this.accelerationY+1;
            }
        }
    }
}
```

This might look very intimidating, but it is all broken down into sections. Actually, all you have to do is copy this code over to the movie clip and the movie will work. I will go over this code section by section so that you will have a better understanding of what is going on.

The first group of code sets up some variables so that the rest of the code can work. This code is very well-commented to clue you in on what is going on in the early sections. The next section sets up a function that can be called at any point throughout the movie. This function is only called when the ball needs to be set or reset. It will place the ball back onto the court and set it into motion. Next we have a group of actions that control the movement and rotation of the ball. The next actions check to see if the ball is hitting either the right or left wall. If either wall is hit, the score is awarded and the ball is reset. The next actions check to see if the top or bottom wall is being hit. If the wall is being hit, the ball is redirected and a sound is made. Checking to see if the player's paddle hit the ball is the work of the next group of code. This code does a lot of things like speeding the ball up when it hits the paddle, deflecting the ball at a realistic angle, and playing a sound. The last group of code checks to see if the ball hit the computer's paddle. This code works the same as the player's paddle code in that it redirects the ball, adds a sound on contact, and speeds the ball up when it hits the paddle. This wraps up the code for the game.

Test your movie and happy gaming!

chapter 8

EXPORTING YOUR FILES FROM FLASH

The main purpose of this chapter is to teach you how to export your files from Flash and how to place them on the Web once they are exported. Since Flash is a design program, you also have the ability to use it for other purposes such as video and print. This is why we have topics such as exporting movies and images, how to use the Publish feature in Flash, using Dreamweaver to make your HTML and detection code, and understanding the HTML behind your Flash file. There is also a section on the new "Macromedia Flash Deployment Kit." This chapter contains examples that show a few ways to get the same result, so you can choose which works best for you. There are examples that are for people who don't know a thing about HTML code. These examples allow you to place a Flash movie on the Web without even seeing any HTML or Javascript code. There are also examples which are purely for HTML junkies. These examples cover what each section of the code is doing and the Javascript that allows you to detect if the user has the correct Flash plug-in. First, we will cover the file types you can export.

EXPORTING MOVIES

When you are done creating your movie in Flash, you will need to figure out how you are going to export the file. This is all determined by how you want to display your final product. If you are making a video, you will want to use Quicktime, Windows AVI, or one of the file sequences or standard files. Maybe you are making a demo that is going to be placed onto a CD-ROM. For this, you will want to export as Macintosh and Windows Projector files. Most people, I am sure, will want to export their files to be placed on the Web. These people will be using the Flash Player (SWF) file. To see a list of what other file formats you can export from Flash, look at Table 8-1.

Table 8-1 Movie File Formats That Flash Can Export

File Type	Platform	Description
Flash Player	Mac, PC	SWF file type, used for Web
Generator Template	Mac, PC	SWT file type, used with Flash Generator
FutureSplash	Mac, PC	SPL file type, older file type (not used too often)
Windows AVI	PC	AVI file type, PC movie file
Quicktime 4 movie	Mac, PC	MOV file type, cross-platform movie file
Quicktime for video	Mac	MOV file type, video file
Animated GIF	Mac, PC	GIF file type, used for Web
WAV	PC	WAV file type, audio file format for the PC
EMF Sequence	PC	Enhanced Metafile
WMF Sequence	PC	Windows Metafile
EPS 3.0 Sequence	Mac, PC	EPS files
Adobe Illustrator Sequence	Mac, PC	Sequence of Illustrator 6.0 and earlier files
DXF Sequence	Mac, PC	AutoCAD DXF file type
BMP Sequence	PC	PC bitmap files
JPEG Sequence	Mac, PC	JPG file type
GIF Sequence	Mac, PC	GIF files
PICT Sequence	Mac	Macintosh PICT file type
PNG Sequence	Mac, PC	PNG files

ABOUT THE SWF FILE FORMAT

The SWF format is the way you will want to export your movie if you are going to place it on the Web. There are different types of SWF files you can make. You can export your movie in five different versions: Flash 1, 2, 3, 4, and 5. Understanding the differences between these versions will help you to make a better and more accessible Web site. I would suggest that you never use Versions 1 and 2, unless you are designing for Web TV. At the time of publication, Web TV only had the capability of viewing Version 1 on standard systems and Version 2 on higher-end systems. That leaves us with Versions 3, 4, and 5 for regular Web users. The main differences between these versions are found in the ActionScripting and audio types. If you used features that are unique to Flash 5, you will not be able to export the file as a Flash 3 or 4 file type.

CHAPTER 8 • EXPORTING YOUR FILES FROM FLASH

If you are not sure which features are unique to Flash 5, you can try to export as a Version 3 or 4 file and Flash will tell you what parts of the movie utilize features that are not part of Flash 3 or 4.

This all might seem a bit complicated, and you may choose to just use the newest technology available by using only Flash 5. As far as I am concerned, it is a good decision to try and push the envelope and use Flash 5 for all it is worth. But you might have clients who feel otherwise. These people are concerned with the number of people able to view their Web site. This is a valid argument on their part, but users can just download the new player to view the site, or you can make a version of the site that is totally created using still images and HTML. To get back to the point, you would want to use Flash 3 or 4 if you are worried that most of your viewers will not download the new Flash Player.

Once you have decided on which version of Flash you are going to use for your movie, you can export the file.

1. Choose File -> Export Movie.
2. Select Flash Player as the File Type.
3. Name the file and save it. This will bring up the Export Flash Player window (Figure 8-1).
4. Choose the settings you want and click OK.

The following is a breakdown of the options available in the Export Flash Player window.

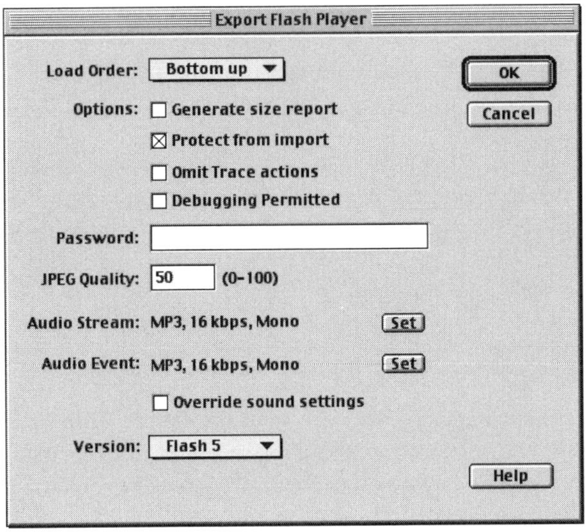

Figure 8-1 Export Flash Player window.

Load Order

The first menu is Load Order. This controls the way the layers in the first frame will load. The choices in the pull-down menu are Bottom up (default) and Top down. In most cases, it makes more sense to load your movie from the bottom up.

Generate size report

When you check Generate size report, Flash will export a text file that shows the details of what the file size is of each frame, what symbols the movie contains, what the file size is of each symbol, and which fonts and characters are used. This is very helpful if you are trying to make the file size smaller. It will help you pinpoint the trouble areas and allow you to make changes. Chapter 9 discusses the size report and ways to shrink the file size of your movie.

Protect from import

Protect from import is a box that I always check when I am exporting my files. This will not allow people who get a copy of your SWF file to import it into Flash. This way, they cannot steal your graphics or techniques.

Omit Trace actions

Omit Trace actions only needs to be checked if you have added trace actions to your movie.

Debugging Permitted

This allows the Debugging feature to be used. If you are planning to allow people to debug the file remotely, then you will need to make sure that this item is checked.

Password Field

This field is used when you have selected Protect from import and/or Debugging Permitted. You do not have to enter a password, but if you do, it will allow you to block everyone except those that you give the password to from importing the file into Flash or using the Debugger on your file.

JPEG Quality

This can be set anywhere from 0 - 100, with the default being 50. The JPEG Quality setting sets the compression level of all the imported bitmaps that you have in your movie. I never touch this setting because I like to set each graphic individually and it does not affect these images.

Audio Stream and Event

The Audio Stream and Event settings set the compression for all the audio clips that you are using as streaming clips or event-triggered audio. Your options in the menu are: MP3, ADPCM, RAW, or Disable. I like to set my clips individually; just like the graphics, each one compresses differently.

Override sound settings

This check box allows you to override the individual settings for the audio clips and use the settings created in the Audio Stream and Event menus. This is used mainly if you are presenting a movie locally on your machine and you want the audio to sound better for the presentation.

Version

This was covered earlier in the chapter. You can choose the version of Flash for your export.

FLASH FOR VIDEO

There are a few file formats you can choose from to export your movie for video. These formats are: Quicktime Movie (Mac), Windows AVI (PC), and PICT (Mac) or BMP (PC) sequence. Before you try to make your movie into one of these file formats, you need to make sure that your dimensions and frame rate are video-friendly.

Having previously worked with video, I can tell you there is a world of difference between the Web and video. One of the major issues you will have is with the colors. This can be fixed with programs like Adobe After Effects, which has filters that will lower the saturation level of the movie. Getting back to the dimensions of your movie, more than likely you will want them to be 720 x 540. This is a tricky situation because it all depends on what type of system you are using to get your file to tape. There is also the title safety issue that you have to worry about. This is roughly 20% of the file, making title safety 576 x 432 on a 720 x 540 pixel file. Frame rate is the next problem area. Video works at 30 fps, and most Flash files will be between 12-18. I suggest that all the movie files or sequences that you make should be imported into After Effects or a similar program to clean up and make them video-ready.

This example shows you how to export a Quicktime movie. If you are working on a PC, you will need to export as an AVI file. To do this, follow the same steps, except select Windows AVI as your format.

Exporting Quicktime Movies

Follow these steps to export your movie into either a Quicktime video file on a Mac or an AVI file on a PC. Remember when working on a PC to select Windows AVI as your format when exporting.

CHAPTER 8 • EXPORTING YOUR FILES FROM FLASH

1. Choose File -> Export Movie.
2. Select Quicktime Video as your Format.
3. Name the file and click Save. This will bring up the Export Quicktime window shown in Figure 8-2 (Export Windows AVI on a PC).

> **Note**: We will need to change a few of the default settings in the Export Quicktime window. First, we will need to make sure that the Dimensions are set up to the standard we have chosen, like what we discussed earlier in this section. The Format should be set to 24-bit color. As for the Compressor, the Animation setting is perfect for going to video. For the PC, you will want to use No compression because animation compression is not available. The Quality slider will need to be moved all the way to the right. If you are using audio, select the highest level for the Sound Format, which is 44kHz, 16-Bit Stereo.

4. Choose the settings you want and click OK.

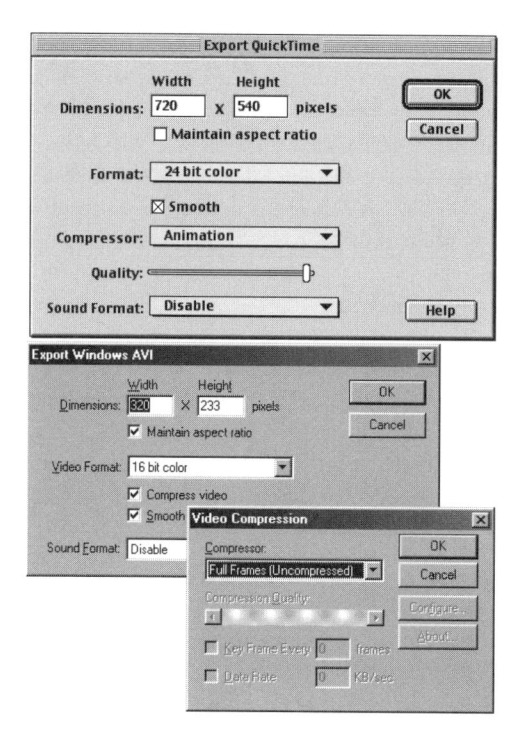

Figure 8-2 Export Quicktime, Export Windows AVI, and Video Compression windows.

EXPORTING A SINGLE FRAME

Sometimes you will only need to export one frame of a movie for one reason or another. Maybe you want to show some of the frames to a client without them having to watch the whole movie, or you need to grab some frames of a site for a print ad. You could also use the Export feature to export an image into another program to edit it. There are a couple of ways to export images from your movie file. You can export the image in a file format that best suits your needs and take a screen shot of the file, or you can copy and paste a frame into either Illustrator or Photoshop. Before I get into more detail about exporting files from Flash, I will give you a table with the formats that Flash can export (Table 8-2).

Table 8-2   Image File Formats that Flash Can Export

File Type	Platform
Flash Player	Mac, PC
Generator Template	Mac, PC
FutureSplash Player	Mac, PC
Enhanced Metafile	PC
Window Metafile	PC
EPS 3.0	Mac, PC
Adobe Illustrator	Mac, PC
AutoCAD DXF	Mac, PC
Bitmap	PC
JPEG	Mac, PC
GIF	Mac, PC
PICT	Mac
PNG	Mac, PC

To export your file from Flash into one of the file formats from Table 8-2, choose File -> Export Image. When you choose the file format you want, you will get a window that prompts you with settings for that particular format. If you are using the file for a print ad, I would suggest using the PICT, EPS, Illustrator, or BMP file format. I have had the best success using the PICT file format because it keeps the color the best. For a PC, I would use the EPS file format to get the best colors. If you are exporting the file to be edited in Illustrator or FreeHand, you will want to use the EPS or Illustrator file format.

If you need to export a few frames to show the stages of an animation, there are a couple of ways to do this. One way to grab a frame is to select the frame and copy all the layers. Then, paste the layers into Photoshop or another image-editing program. You have to make sure that you unlock all the layers that you want to copy over to the other program. A good feature of this method is that you can copy over only a few layers or a single layer to another program at a high resolution. Another way to get frame grabs of an animation is to take a snapshot on a Mac or use the Print Screen key on a PC to grab a frame then paste the image into an image-editing program.

PUBLISHING YOUR MOVIE

This section covers a couple of ways that you can create an HTML file for your movie. You can use the Publish feature that is built into Flash, or you can use Macromedia Dreamweaver. These programs will write the code for you, so you do not even need to know HTML to put your movie on the Web. One important feature that both of these methods offer is the ability to write the necessary code to detect the Flash plug-in. When creating a Web site, it is very important to be able to detect the plug-in and have a backup plan for those people without the plug-in. The Publish feature will show a still image of your choice, while Dreamweaver allows you to send people to another HMTL page if they do not have the Flash plug-in.

USING THE PUBLISH FEATURE

Flash has moved away from having to use an external application to create HTML files for your movie. This makes it a lot easier to put your files on the Web. All you have to do is set the Publish settings up how you want and click Publish. If you choose File -> Publish Settings, you will see the available formats you can choose from when using the Publish feature (Figure 8-3). The types of files listed in this window are those that can be used on the Web, with the exception of the Macintosh and Windows Projectors.

When you check an item in the list, you will see a tab appear along the top of the window for that item. If you select HMTL and click on the tab, you will see a list of options appear (Figure 8-4).

This section breaks down each menu in this window to help you make your HTML file with ease.

Template

This is the most important menu of the section. The templates found here can be manipulated, or you can create your own if you want. If you are creating your own template, it is easier if you have an HTML editor like BBedit for the Mac or Homesite

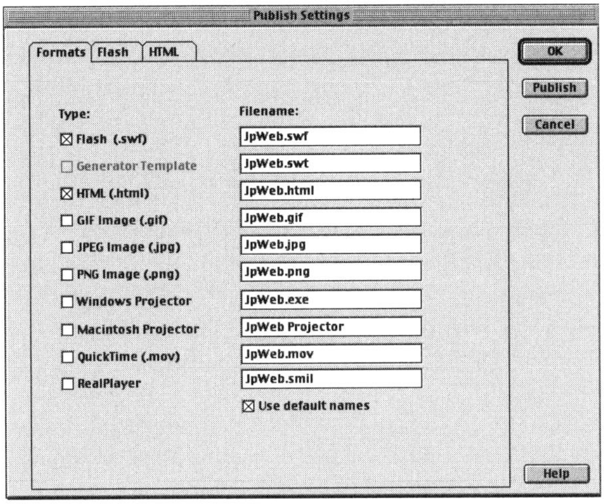

CHAPTER 8 • EXPORTING YOUR FILES FROM FLASH

Figure 8-3   Publish Settings window in the Formats section.

for the PC. I will cover this later in this section. First, I will cover the templates available in this menu.

Flash Only

The default setting is Flash Only. This will create the HTML needed to post your movie on the Web, but if your visitors do not have the plug-in, they will see a broken plug-in. This is not really what you want because most visitors will just click on to another site. This setting is good for using in a site where you already know that the user

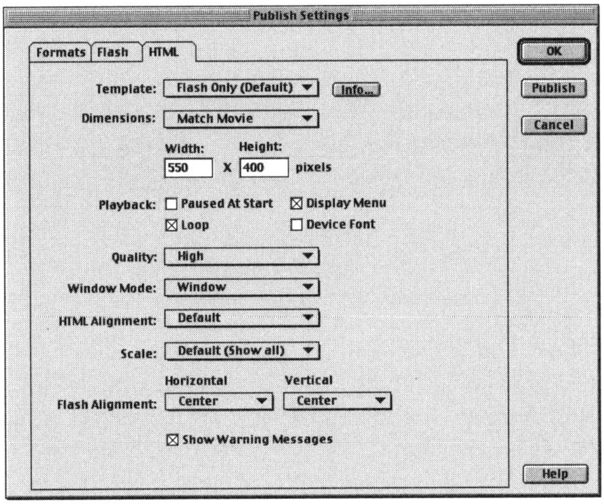

Figure 8-4   Publish Settings window in the HTML section.

has the plug-in for testing to see if the site works. I only use this setting when I am exporting SWF and HTML files to post them on a staging site so clients can look at the site.

Flash with FSCommands

This creates the HTML and code needed to complete FSCommands. The only drawback is that you will need to put the code for any FSCommands into the HMTL file. All the template does is add all the Javascript to prepare the browsers for the commands. The HTML page does have a comment in the space where you are to place your FSCommands. This makes it easy for you to insert your code.

Image Map

When you choose the Image Map template, you will have to pick an image to apply your map to. You can choose from the PNG, GIF, and JPEG file formats. Flash will automatically create an image map for any button using the "Get URL" action that is in the last frame of the movie file. To change the frame that Flash uses as the map, create a label and call it "#Map". This frame should be the same one that you selected as your static image to be saved out. I usually create my image maps and static images in other applications.

There are many programs that will allow you to create image maps. Two easy programs to use are Adobe ImageReady and Macromedia Fireworks. These programs will also export the code for your file, which you can then paste into the HTML file you have already created. I actually prefer to export an image out of Flash, then take it into ImageReady or Fireworks. This way, I can break the image apart and make a table and image maps as I need. This allows you to add a little more life to the page by adding rollovers. It will also make the file size smaller because you can slice the image and compress it better.

> **Tip**
> By default, Flash takes the static image from the first frame. To select a particular frame as the image to be exported, create a label in that frame and call it "#Static".

Java Player

To make this work, you will need to go into the Players folder that is in your Flash Program folder and grab copies of the Flash.jar and Flash.class files. These files need to be placed in the directory with the HTML and SWF files that are created when you publish. Also, you will need to make the SWF file Flash Version 2. The animation is slower when you use this, and I can say that I have never found a use for this option.

CHAPTER 8 • EXPORTING YOUR FILES FROM FLASH

Quicktime

This setting exports an HTML file and a streaming Quicktime movie file. This Quicktime movie should not be confused with the Quicktime video file. It is a streaming movie file that works much differently than a video file. The Quicktime streaming file allows some interactivity, but it is very picky with what frame actions you are allowed to use. It seems to allow you to do almost all of the basic button actions you would need to make an instructional piece or presentation. One bonus to exporting in the Quicktime movie format is that you will be able to include Quicktime video files. In addition to streaming over the Web, this file will also play locally in the Quicktime Player. Before you publish with this feature, you should take a look at the Quicktime section of the Publish Settings window. In this section, you will be able to control how the movie will play and behave when it is exported (Figure 8-5).

Some of the options in this window are self-explanatory, so I am only going to cover a few of them. The options I am going to cover are: Alpha, Streaming Sound, Playback, and File.

ALPHA

The Alpha option has three settings: Auto, Alpha-Transparent, and Copy.

- Auto makes the movie opaque unless there is another track behind the movie.
- Alpha-Transparent makes the movie transparent so tracks under the Flash movie are visible.
- Copy makes the movie opaque and blocks all tracks under the Flash movie from being seen.

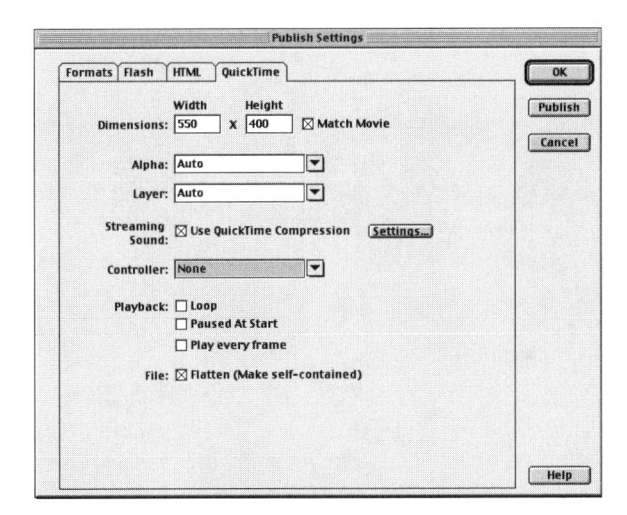

Figure 8-5 Quicktime menu in the Publish Settings window.

STREAMING SOUND

The Streaming Sound option allows you to convert the audio to Quicktime Compression, but only if you have Quicktime Pro 4 or higher (Figure 8-6).

PLAYBACK

The Playback section has three options: Loop, Paused At Start, and Play every frame. The Loop and Paused At Start features are self-explanatory, so I am only going to cover the Play every frame option. When you check this option, the movie will play every frame and will not play the audio. So it is best to leave this option unchecked if you have audio in your file. Streaming files will often skip frames to keep pace with audio files.

FILE

The File section only contains one option, which might seem strange if you are not familiar with how a streaming file is put together. If you are using video files, you can leave this unchecked. This will make the movie link to the files externally. The only downside to this is that you will have to make sure that you keep all the video files together with the main movie so it can link to them. If you check this box, the movie will flatten all the video files into the main movie file.

User Choice

This is a combination of User Choice and Javascript detection. The file will first detect if the person has Flash, then it will place a cookie, depending on the outcome of this finding. A cookie is a small, site-specific file that is placed on the user's machine. This file will save the particular settings for the site. If the person gets sent to the wrong page, they will be able to choose the right page from a menu that is placed at the bottom of the page.

When you run this template, you will need to select a GIF or JPEG so that the detection will have an image to display for people who do not have the plug-in. If you

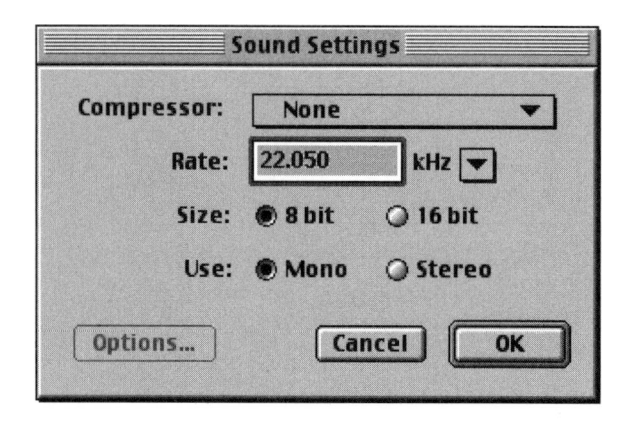

Figure 8-6 Sound Settings window, or setting the compression of the audio in a Quicktime movie file.

CHAPTER 8 • EXPORTING YOUR FILES FROM FLASH

know HTML, you might want to go into the file and move the position of the links that this template adds to the bottom of the page (Figure 8-7). These links change the setting of the cookie. This is where the User Choice comes from. For example, if a visitor to your site knows they have the plug-in but gets sent to the still page, they can choose to go to the Flash page. This will set the cookie so that the next time they come to the site, they will be sent to the Flash version right away. If you are really ambitious, you can go into the template file and make changes to these links. Then they will appear exactly how you want them to every time you use the template. The only downside to using this technique is that the user might have disabled cookies. This basically means that the user will have to go through the detection every time because their machine will not save the file.

Ad 3 Banner, Ad 4 Banner, Ad 5 Banner, and Ad Any Banner

These templates are basically the same in that they all check for the plug-in and are replaced with a file of your choice if the user does not have the plug-in. The only difference between the first three templates is which version of the Flash plug-in they are

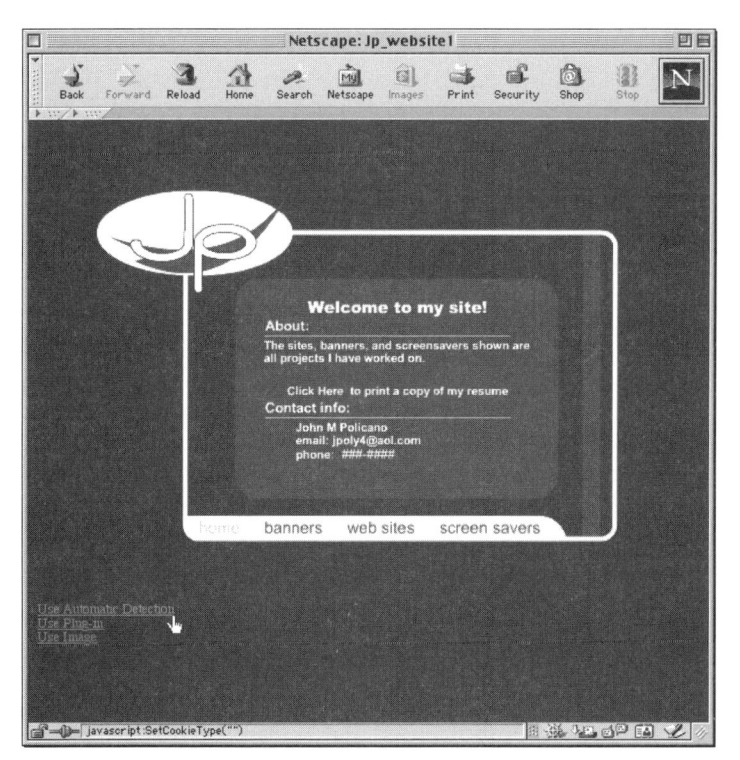

Figure 8-7 Screen shot of a Web site that has links at the bottom of the window as they appear when you use the User Choice temple.

trying to detect, Flash 3, 4, or 5. The Ad Any Banner looks for the Flash 3, 4, and 5 versions of the plug-in, making it more versatile.

Customizing or Creating Your Own Templates

To customize or create your own template, it is easier to start out by looking at one of the templates provided to you by Macromedia.

1. Go into the Macromedia Flash 5 folder on your computer.
2. Open the HTML folder.
3. Select the Default.html file and open it in an HTML or text editor.

    You should see the following:
    ```
    $TTFlash Only (Default)
    $DS
    Use an OBJECT and EMBED tag to display Flash.
    $DF
    <HTML>
    <HEAD>
    <TITLE>$TI</TITLE>
    </HEAD>
    <BODY bgcolor="$BG">

    <!— URL's used in the movie—>
    $MU
    <!— text used in the movie—>
    $MT
    <OBJECT classid="clsid:D27CDB6E-AE6D-11cf-96B8-444553540000"
    codebase="http://download.macromedia.com/pub/shockwave/cabs/flash/sw
    flash.cab#version=5,0,0,0"
     WIDTH=$WI HEIGHT=$HE>
     $PO
    <EMBED $PE WIDTH=$WI HEIGHT=$HE
     TYPE="application/x-shockwave-flash" PLUGINSPAGE="http://www.macro-
    media.com/shockwave/download/index.cgi?P1_Prod_Version=Shockwave-
    Flash"></EMBED>
    </OBJECT></BODY>
    </HTML>
    ```

Let's go over what is in this file so you will have a better understanding of how to build your own template file.

$TT

The first thing we see in our Default.html file, is "$TTFlash Only (Default)". This is the name of the template that shows up in the Template menu of the HTML section of the Publish Settings window.

$DS $DF

The next line we see is "$DS", followed by "Use an OBJECT and EMBED tag to display Flash". The "$DS" is the start of the description. The text that follows this tag is the description that shows up if you click the Info button next to the Template menu. The description is followed by "$DF", which means that this is the end of the description.

> **Note:** The OBJECT and EMBED tags are used to display Flash in a browser. The reason there are two tags is because we need to accommodate two browsers.

$TI

Next we have some basic HTML until we get to the TITLE tags. In the TITLE tags, you will see "$TI". This sets the name of the page to the name of the Flash file that you set up in the Format section of the Publish Settings window.

$BG

Inside the BODY tag you will see the background color equal to "$BG". This sets the HTML page's background color equal to that of the Flash movie.

$MU AND $MT

I am not really a big fan of these two tags; I think that they just clutter up your HTML. The "$MU" might be useful in some instances because it grabs the URLs used in the movie. The "$MT" tag, on the other hand, just grabs all the text that you entered into the movie and places it all in brackets in the HTML.

$WI AND $WE

These tags are pretty easy to figure out. They fill in the width and height that you set up in the Publish Settings window.

$PO AND $PE

This fills in parameters for the OBJECT and EMBED tags, which you selected in the HTML section of the Publish Settings window. For example, the Loop, Display Menu, Quality, and HTML Alignment options are provided, just to mention a few.

That is all there is to the Default.html template. It makes a very simple HTML file without a Javascript/VBScript for detection.

I have covered the basic tags that you would use to create your own page. If you would like to see more tags, check out the "Customizing HTML Publishing Templates" sections in the "Publishing and Exporting" section of the *Using Flash* guide that comes with Flash.

Dimensions

The Dimensions setting has three choices: Match Movie, Pixels, and Percent. I usually use the default, Match Movie. This way, the movie is locked to the exact size that you used when you designed it. For most movies, this is the best choice, as I discussed in Chapter 6. If you would like your movie to fill the browser, then you should choose Percent. This will make the movie fill the window to any percent you set, so setting the movie to 100 percent will fill the window completely. The Pixels setting is a good way to change the movie's size if you need it to be smaller or larger but you do not want it to scale. The only problem with this setting is there is no way to lock the aspect ratio of the width and height. With this setting, you could end up distorting the outcome of your movie if you are not cautious. A safe bet when you are not sure what to set the movie to is the Match Movie setting; at least this way, you can be sure the movie will look the same as it did when you were building it.

Playback

There are four items in this section that need to be looked at because they will affect how your movie plays on the Web. The settings are all built into the code and will not affect the SWF file unless you are looking at the movie in a browser using the HTML file.

Paused at Start

When you check this box, the movie will stop in the first frame until a user interacts with the movie. The problem with using this is that you will need to have a button set up that will tell the movie to play when the user clicks it.

Loop

This is pretty straightforward; if the box is checked, the movie will loop back to the beginning when it hits the last frame. When making an ad banner, you would want to check this box to make sure that the banner continually loops. This will not work if you have placed a stop action in the last frame of your movie. I never use this feature; instead, I make movies loop using actions and labels.

Display Menu

When this is checked, it allows visitors to affect the movie and how it looks and plays in their browsers. If you are looking at a movie on the Web and you Command + click on a Mac or right-click on a PC, you will see the menu (Figure 8-8). This menu contains Zoom In, Zoom Out, Show All, High Quality, Play, Loop, Rewind, Forward, Back, Print, and About Flash Player 5. You can stop people from accessing all of these settings by not checking on this box. This is a box that I always make sure is not checked when I am making my HTML files.

CHAPTER 8 • EXPORTING YOUR FILES FROM FLASH

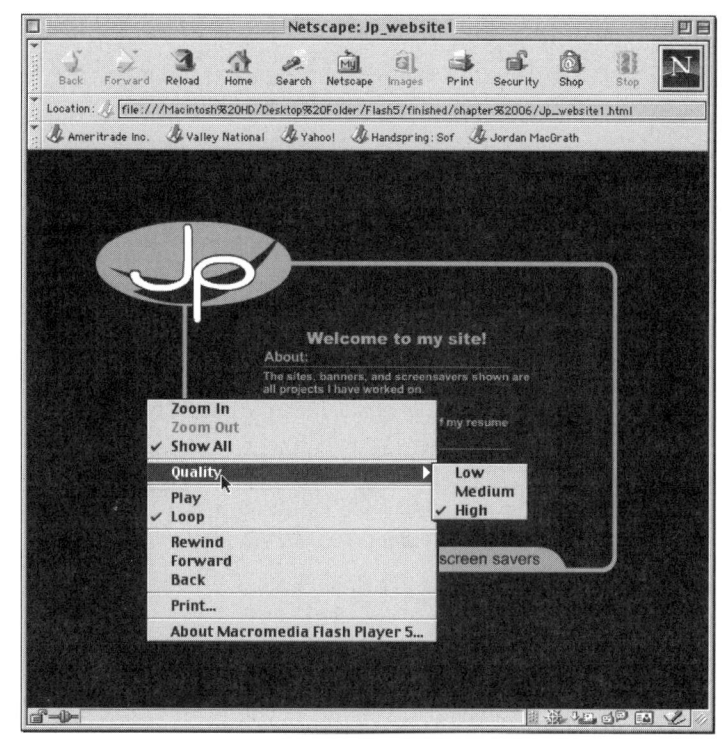

Figure 8-8 The display menu that can be accessed when control-clicking (right-clicking on a PC) on a Flash file while it is in the browser.

Device Font

This is a Windows-only setting that substitutes fonts that the user does not have with some from their system that are similar. I never check this box and it is off by default. There really is no reason to check this box since Flash embeds all the fonts except those that you specify not to in the text fields. It is also important to note that this feature only affects the text that you have created in Flash.

Quality

There are six settings to choose from in this menu, starting with Low and working up to Best. These all directly affect the way the movie looks and the way it plays back in a Web browser.

Low

Quality is compromised so the movie can play back faster.

Auto Low

Quality is compromised but will get better when it will not affect the playback of the movie.

Auto High

This will affect the quality and speed the same until the movie is not playing as intended. The first thing to go is the anti-aliasing so that the movie will play better.

Medium

The Medium setting only anti-aliases some graphics and text. This setting also does not smooth any bitmaps.

High

This is the default setting and the one I suggest that you use. The quality takes top priority. The only quality setting that is affected is the smoothing of the bitmaps. This setting is turned off when there is animation.

Best

Speed is compromised so that all of the graphics will look their best. If the quality of your appearance is your main concern, then this setting is for you.

Window Mode

This is a Windows-only setting that lets you use features that are only available in IE 4.0 and higher on a PC. What you can do is set the movie to play in its default Window, an Opaque Windowless state, or a Transparent Windowless state. The Transparent Windowless setting will let anything that is in the background show through. This would be better if it worked in all browsers and platforms. Then you could have background images outside of Flash and make the file sizes smaller. The Opaque Windowless setting will not show anything through the movie, just like default Window. I never use this feature because it limits the amount of viewers that can see the movie the same way.

HTML Alignment

This is a strange setting because what you think it does and what it actually does are two different things. You would think that it would allow you to position the movie in the Top, Bottom, Left, Right, or Center (default) of the browser window. But in actuality, it doesn't position the movie in the browser window. What this does is position the movie within the embedded file space. For example, if you have set the dimensions in the HTML file to be disproportionate to the movie, it will align the movie within this space. You are better off leaving this setting alone and aligning the movie yourself in another program like Dreamweaver.

Scale

There are three choices in this menu: Show All (default), Exact Fit, and No Border. This setting only needs to be used when you are setting your movie to 100 percent of the browser window.

Show All

The default setting, Show All, makes sure that all of the movie is visible at all times and that the movie is not distorted in any way. With this, you might see borders on the top and bottom or right and left sides when the movie does not fill the window completely. This is actually the best setting and the one that I always use.

No Border

This setting makes sure that there is no border for the movie. The problem with this is that parts of the movie might not be visible. This happens if the movie needs to be made larger to ensure there are no borders.

Exact Fit

This setting makes sure there is no border and the whole movie is seen all the time. At first this seems like the best choice, but what happens is that the movie will be distorted to fit the window no matter what the size of the window. It is actually a bad setting because you cannot control what size people have their browser windows open to.

Flash Alignment

In this menu, you will be able align the Flash movie within the Flash window that is embedded in the HTML page. This is best left to the default of Center for both Vertical and Horizontal. You should not have to use this at all, but sometimes you will have objects just off the Stage that you do not want to show, so you can align the movie to the opposite side.

Show Warning Messages

This setting will show you a message when you try to publish your movie and you have chosen a template that requires an image, but you have not selected one. You might want to turn this off if you are planning on making your image in another application.

USING DREAMWEAVER

The best scenario in which to use Dreamweaver is when you have a site where there is both an HTML version and a Flash version, or if you have a splash screen before an HTML site. This way, you can try to send all the visitors to the Flash version of the site, and if they do not have the plug-in, the code will send them to the HTML version of the site. Dreamweaver makes this process very easy, and you never even need to look at any HTML or Javascript. All you have to do is have an HTML version of your site created so that you can use this as the alternate HTML file that people get sent to if they do not have the Flash plug-in.

1. Open Dreamweaver.
2. Click the Insert Flash button from the Objects palette and select your Flash file (you can also choose Insert -> Media -> Flash).
3. Make sure the Flash file on the HTML page is not selected.
4. Open the Behaviors window by choosing Window -> Behaviors or by pressing F8.
5. Select the Check Plug-in behavior from the Plus menu. This will bring up the Check Plug-in window.
6. Choose Flash as the plug-in.
7. Enter the name of the alternate HTML site in the Otherwise, Go To URL field (Figure 8-9).

USING THE MACROMEDIA FLASH DEPLOYMENT KIT

First, you will need to download this kit from the Macromedia site (http://www.macromedia.com/software/flash/download/deployment_kit/). There are two ways that you can take advantage of this new download from Macromedia. You can either update Dreamweaver with a new behavior or you can use the files that are included in the download to help you create your own HTML files.

First, you can use the files included with the download to set up Dreamweaver with a new behavior. The new behavior is called the Macromedia Flash Dispatcher. When you open the Deployment Kit, you will find a folder called dreamweaver_behavior. In this folder, there is a Read Me file that will guide you through the setup and basic use of this

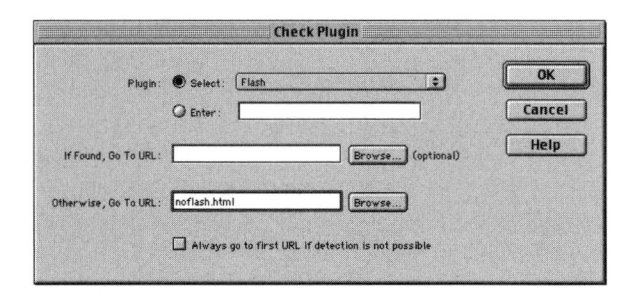

Figure 8-9 Check Plug-in window from Dreamweaver.

behavior. When following these instructions, you will be installing the file "Dispatcher Assets" into the Dreamweaver/Configurations folder and the file "Macromedia Flash Dispatcher.htm" into the Dreamweaver/Configurations/Behaviors/Actions folder. If you install the files in the correct spots, you should be able to choose the Macromedia Flash Dispatcher behavior from the Plus menu, which is located in the Behaviors window. This will open the Macromedia Flash Dispatcher Behavior window (Figure 8-10).

This window lets you choose what you want the code to do in certain instances. For example, if the person who is trying to look at your site does not have the Flash plug-in and the file cannot auto-install, then you can either send them to Macromedia's site to download the plug-in or you can send them to an alternate HTML file.

If you do not have Dreamweaver, you can try the other method, which starts by opening the enter.html file into an HTML or text editor. This file contains a bunch of scripts that you do not need to touch. All you have to do is change a few lines of code to customize the code to your needs. Look at the SCRIPT tag that is located in between the opening and closing BODY tags.

```
<SCRIPT LANGUAGE="JavaScript">
    MM_FlashDispatch(
  "fancy/",
  "4.0",
  false,
// Don't require latest rev. of plug-in
  "upgradeFlash.html",
  !MM_FlashUserDemurred(),
// Don't install if user said no once
  "installFlash.html",
  "plain/",
  false
    );
```

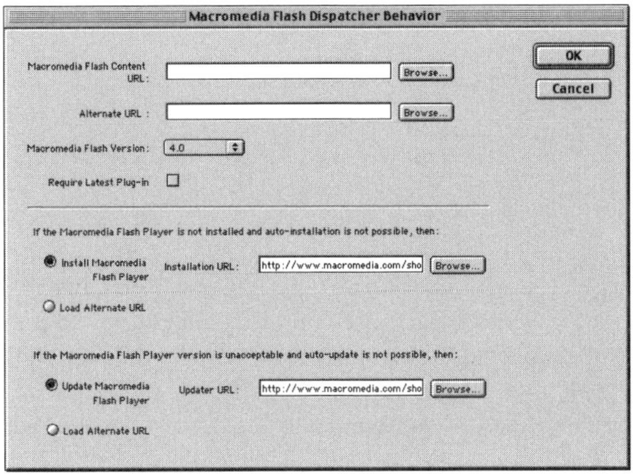

Figure 8-10   Macromedia Flash Dispatcher Behavior window from Dreamweaver.

```
</SCRIPT>

<SCRIPT LANGUAGE="JavaScript">

  MM_FlashDispatch(
 "flash/index.html",
 "5.0",
 false,
// Don't require latest rev. of plug-in
 "upgradeFlash.html",
 !MM_FlashUserDemurred(),
// Don't install if user said no once
 "installFlash.html",
 "noflash/index.html",
 false
   );

</SCRIPT>
```

Find the first line inside this tag that says "MM_FlashDispatch". The line you need to change is the second one that says "fancy/". Change this to the name of your HTML file. You can also change the line that says "false" under "4.0" to "true" if you want to require the user to have the latest version of the plug-in. You should also change the line that says "plain/" to your alternate HTML file if you have one.

You will encounter a few differences in the code when you are using the PC version. The code works the same, but the main difference is seen in the folder structure. The "plain" site on a Mac is placed in the "plain" folder; on a PC, it is placed in the "noflash" folder.

For your site to work, you will need to upload all of your files, plus the following files from the Deployment Kit:

- enter.html
- upgradeFlash.html
- installFlash.html
- Dispatcher.vbs
- Dispatcher.js

The last thing you might want to do to make this work better is to rename the enter.html file to either index.html or default.html, depending on what your server requires. Your server might require another name for the default Web page. If you do not know what this is, it is best to consult the company in charge of your server. This way, the file will be called automatically instead of your URL ending with "enter.html".

UNDERSTANDING THE HTML BEHIND YOUR MOVIE

This section shows you the code that is required for your Flash movie to play in a browser. I will show you how to create the basic HTML for a site, how to use Javascript to detect the Flash plug-in, and use how to use Flash to detect if the visitors to your site have Flash. You will see the bare minimum code you need for Flash to play in your browser. You can also take a close look at the Javascript and how it can send visitors to another page when they do not have the Flash plug-in. The last section will show you how a small Flash file and a META "refresh" tag can detect if the visitor to your site has the Flash plug-in.

CREATING BASIC HTML FOR A SITE

Flash requires a few HTML tags to play consistently on all browsers. The following example shows the basic code required for a Flash movie to play in browsers.

```
<HTML>
<HEAD>
<TITLE>FlashSite</TITLE>
</HEAD>
<BODY bgcolor="#FFFFFF">

<OBJECT classid="clsid:D27CDB6E-AE6D-11cf-96B8-444553540000"
codebase="http://download.macromedia.com/pub/shockwave/cabs/flash/swflas
h.cab#version=5,0,0,0"
 WIDTH=550 HEIGHT=400>
 <PARAM NAME=movie VALUE="flashsite.swf">
 <PARAM NAME=bgcolor VALUE=#FFFFFF>
<PARAM NAME=quality VALUE=high>
<EMBED src="flashsite.swf"
 bgcolor=#FFFFFF quality=high
 WIDTH=550 HEIGHT=400
 TYPE="application/x-shockwave-flash" PLUGINSPAGE="http://www.macrome-
dia.com/shockwave/download/index.cgi?P1_Prod_Version=ShockwaveFlash">
</EMBED>
</OBJECT>

</BODY>
</HTML>
```

The code for the Flash file starts with the OBJECT tag. This tag is followed by the "classid" tag. This is for Internet Explorer browsers using ActiveX. The "classid" code tells the browser what type of control is required by the object. The next line starts with the "codebase" tag. This tells the ActiveX-enabled browsers where they can automatically download the plug-in. The next part of the code has the WIDTH and HEIGHT tags. The tags in the example code are in pixels. If you want to have your page be a percentage of the entire page, you can change them to a number followed by a percentage (for example, WIDTH=100% HEIGHT=100%).

The next lines are PARAM tags. These are basic parameters needed by browsers to display the right movie correctly. The first tag, NAME=movie, needs to have its VALUE set to the name of your Flash SWF file. This is case-sensitive, so if the name of your movie has a capital in it, be sure that you type it into the code the same way. The second tag, Name=bgcolor, has its VALUE set to the background of the Flash movie. This is a great tag because if your client does not like the background color you have chosen, you can quickly change it with this tag. The next tag is Name=quality with its VALUE set to HIGH. This is the default for this setting, which we talked about earlier in this chapter.

The next line in the code starts the EMBED tag. You will notice that the OBJECT tag has not been closed. This is because the EMBED tag has to be placed inside the OBJECT tag. The first line in the EMBED tag is src="flashsite.swf". This needs to be in the code because the EMBED tag is required for the Netscape browser; that is why the movie's name is placed in the code again. This is also why the bgcolor, WIDTH, and HEIGHT tags are entered again. When you are making your site, you must be careful that all of these duplicate tags are entered correctly or the movie will not look the same on all browsers. Perhaps someday we will not have to worry about this if the competing companies would agree on standards.

The first unique tag that we see in the EMBED tag is the TYPE tag. This tag tells the browsers what type of file is being loaded into the page. The next line has the PLUGINSPAGE tag, which will make it so that if the user does not have the plug-in, they can click the broken plug-in on the page to download the plug-in.

After this, the EMBED tag and OBJECT tags are closed. This completes the code needed to display your Flash movie on the Web.

USING JAVASCRIPT PLUG-IN DETECTION

Using detection is very important because you do not want visitors seeing a broken plug-in. By using Javascript, you can send visitors to a still image if they do not have the plug-in. There is a drawback to using Javascript plug-in detection. If a person visits your site with Internet Explorer 4.5 or earlier on a Mac, they will automatically get sent to the still image instead of the Flash file. This is because Internet Explorer on a Mac did not have the ability to detect plug-ins until version 5.0.

The following code uses Javascript to point the visitor to either your HTML site or a still GIF image:

```
<HTML>
<HEAD>
   <TITLE>flashsite</TITLE>
```

```
</HEAD>
<BODY bgcolor="#FFFFFF">

<OBJECT classid="clsid:D27CDB6E-AE6D-11cf-96B8-444553540000"
codebase="http://download.macromedia.com/pub/shockwave/cabs/flash/swflas
h.cab#version=5,0,0,0"
  WIDTH=550 HEIGHT=400>
 <PARAM NAME=movie VALUE="flashsite.swf">
 <PARAM NAME=quality VALUE=high>
<PARAM NAME=bgcolor VALUE=#FFFFFF>

<SCRIPT LANGUAGE=JavaScript>
<!--
var plugin = (navigator.mimeTypes && navigator.mimeTypes["application/x-
shockwave-flash"]) ? navigator.mimeTypes["application/x-shockwave-
flash"].enabledPlugin : 0;
// Check for Flash version 4 or greater in Netscape
if ( plugin && parseInt(plugin.description.substring(plugin.descrip-
tion.indexOf(".")-1)) >= 4 ) {

document.write('<EMBED src="flashsite.swf" quality=high bgcolor=#FFFFFF
');
document.write(' WIDTH=550 HEIGHT=400');
document.write(' TYPE="application/x-shockwave-flash"
PLUGINSPAGE="http://www.macromedia.com/shockwave/download/index.cgi?P1_P
rod_Version=ShockwaveFlash">');
}
 else if (!(navigator.appName &&
navigator.appName.indexOf("Netscape")>=0 && navigator.appVersion.in-
dexOf("2.")>=0)){
// Netscape 2 will display the IMG tag below so don't write an extra one
document.write('<IMG SRC="flashsite.gif" WIDTH=550 HEIGHT=400 BOR-
DER=0>');
}
//-->
</SCRIPT>
<NOEMBED><IMG SRC="flashsite.gif" WIDTH=550 HEIGHT=400 BORDER=0></NOEM-
BED>
<NOSCRIPT><IMG SRC="flashsite.gif" WIDTH=550 HEIGHT=400  BORDER=0></NO-
SCRIPT>
</OBJECT>

</BODY>
</HTML>
```

If you look at this code, you will see that it only checks for the Flash plug-in of the Netscape browser. This is because the OBJECT tag outside the Javascript takes care of Internet Explorer on a PC. It will use ActiveX to install or update the plug-in. Since the earlier versions of Internet Explorer on the Mac do not support checking for the plug-in, this browser will always get the image file running this code. The only browser left to test for is the Netscape browser, which reacts basically the same across both platforms. If you are using this code, just make sure that when editing the Javascript that each "document.write" line has a close to it. If you look at the code, you will see that each line of code following the "document.write" command has an open " (' " and a close " '); ".

PLUG-IN DETECTION USING FLASH

This is one of the most fool-proof detection methods that I have seen. All you have to do is create a one-frame Flash SWF file and embed it into a page. All that needs to be in this document is a "Get URL" action that calls the main site. You can use the code from the basic HTML section for your HTML file or you can use the default setting from the Publish feature in Flash. Once you have created your HTML file, all you have to do is place the following META tag in the HEAD tag of your HTML page:

```
<META HTTP-EQUIV="refresh" CONTENT="2;
    URL=noflash.html">
```

The META "refresh" tag is set to two seconds, then it will call another page. This other page can either be a version of the site without Flash or a page alerting the visitor that they need Flash to view your site. The reason we are using a META "refresh" tag is because if the Flash file does not load, then the tag will automatically send the person to the other site and we do not have to worry about Javascript and VBScripts not working properly. I give the META "refresh" tag two seconds because I do not want to hastily send someone to the wrong site because their Iternet connection slowed down.

Looking at the tag above, the area that you should be concerned with is after CONTENT. The number right after the equals sign is how long the page will wait before refreshing to a new page. Then you have the URL, where you enter the page you want to send people to that do not have Flash. This is all you need to do to detect if a person has the Flash plug-in with Flash.

chapter 9

SHRINKING YOUR FILE SIZE

This chapter covers techniques that will help you to shrink the file size of your movie. The first section shows you how to pinpoint where in your movie the file size is the largest. This will also show you which symbols, bitmaps, and sounds are causing problems. The rest of the chapter covers how to optimize your files so you will have the smallest file sizes possible. You will learn how to optimize imported bitmaps, how font use affects your movie, how to optimize shapes, and how audio files can be compressed better without a great loss in quality.

FINDING TROUBLE SPOTS

There are a few things you can do to find out what files or frames are causing the biggest problems in your file. By problems I mean the files that have the largest file sizes and the frames that will affect the streaming playback of your movie because they are too bulky. One thing you can do to check on the playback is to look at the Bandwidth Profiler. You can also export a Size Report to check out the problem areas. If you use these features together, they will help make your movie playback smoother and you will have a smaller file size, which means visitors to your site will be happier because they will not have to download a 400K file just to see your site.

BANDWIDTH PROFILER

The Bandwidth Profiler can be looked at in two ways. One way is in Streaming Graph mode, which shows the "KB" for the frames as they affect the playback of the movie when it is streaming. The second way to look at the Bandwidth Profiler is in Frame by Frame Graph mode, which shows the total "KB" for each frame.

1. Open a Flash file.
2. Choose Control -> Test Movie.

> **Note:** You can also use Command + Enter (Control + Enter on a PC) to test a movie. The Test Movie function opens a movie in a new window so you can test your site. This function actually exports the file as an SWF file, which is what you are viewing in the new window within Flash.

3. Choose View -> Bandwidth Profiler to open the Bandwidth Profiler. You can also press Command + B (Control + B on a PC).

This will place the Bandwidth Profiler in the window with your movie. You will be able to test the playback of your movie in this mode. You will also be able to view the Bandwidth Profiler in two different modes, Streaming Graph and Frame by Frame Graph.

Streaming Graph

The Streaming Graph mode is great for viewing how your movie will play back while it is streaming over the Web (Figure 9-1). To make sure that you are looking at the Streaming Graph mode while in the Bandwidth Profiler, you can choose View to see if the Streaming Graph option has a check next to it. You can also press Command + G (Control + G on a PC) to open the Streaming Graph mode.

In the Bandwidth Profiler, you have the ability to see how your movie will play over any type of connection. Under the Debug menu, you can set the Profiler to stream as if it were playing back over a 14K, 28K, or 56K modem. You also have three customizable settings that you can set to any bit rate you want. Follow the instructions from the previous section to open your file with the Bandwidth Profiler so you can test how your movie plays back over the Web.

Choose View -> Show Streaming, or you can press Command + Enter (Control + Enter on a PC), to make the movie stream while it is in the Test Movie mode.

It is best to show a movie streaming while you are viewing the movie with the Bandwidth Profiler open. This way, you can see the frames and graphics that are

CHAPTER 9 • SHRINKING YOUR FILE SIZE

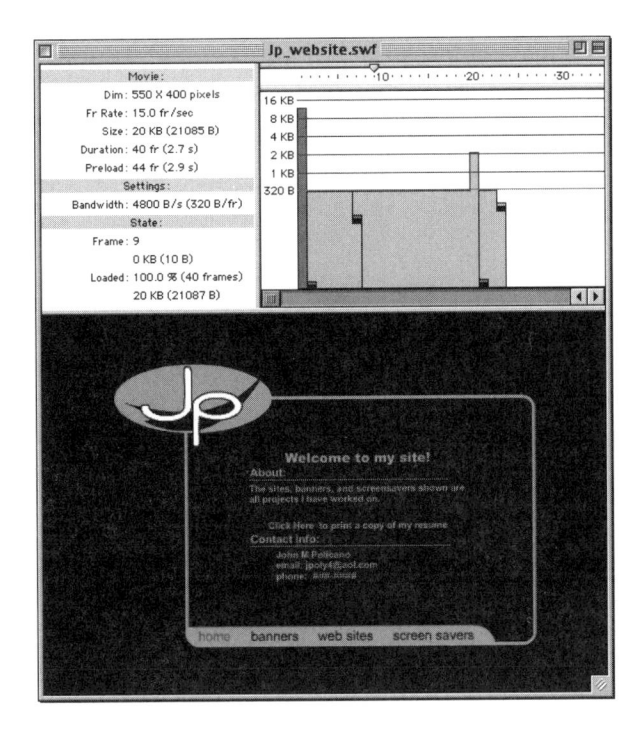

Figure 9-1 Streaming Graph mode in the Bandwidth Profiler.

causing the most problems. You can also tell how much they have to change to be able to stream properly. There is a red line that runs across the Bandwidth Profiler that shows you where your graphics should be if you want them to stream correctly. This is the maximum size that will stream over the Web to a person's computer with the connection you have selected in the Debug menu. If a bar on the graph goes above the red line, the animation will stop and hold on this frame until it is completely loaded. This can be both helpful and harmful to your movie while it is playing back. If you watch the Profiler and look into which frames are causing problems, you can rearrange your files and frames. You will want to arrange them so that if they have to stop, they stop in a frame that looks good, not one that is in the middle of an animation. Also, they should preferably stop with enough content so that people will have something to read while they are waiting for the movie to play again. The trick is to not let the viewer know that the movie has stopped.

Frame by Frame Graph

The Frame by Frame Graph mode shows a detailed breakdown of all frames (Figure 9-2). To switch to the Frame by Frame Graph mode from the Streaming Graph mode, choose View -> Frame by Frame Graph. You can also press Command + F (Control + F on a PC). Unlike the Streaming Graph mode, the Frame by Frame Graph mode

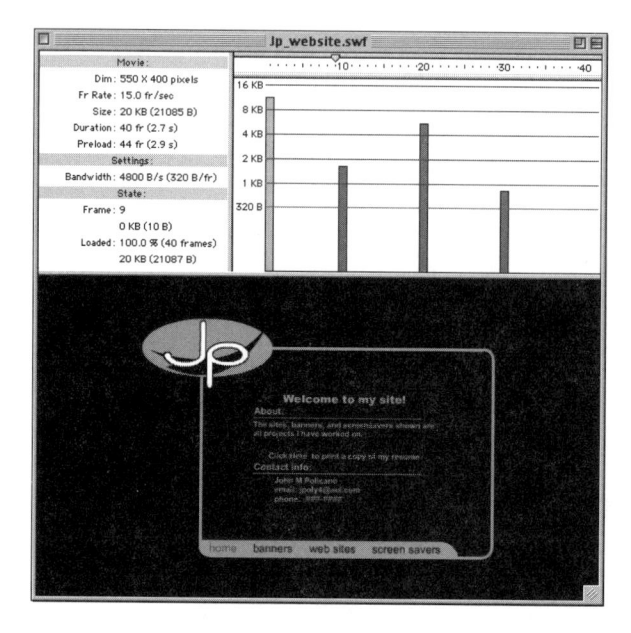

Figure 9-2 Frame by Frame Graph mode in the Bandwidth Profiler.

shows the actual amount of KBs per frame. If you compare the graphs in Figures 9-1 and 9-2, you will notice that the graphs both illustrate that the first frame is really heavy.

A great way to work around having a very heavy first frame is to make the page build piece by piece. This will spread all the graphics over multiple frames, instead having them all in the first frame. One thing you need to look out for is that symbols, especially movie clips, load completely before they play. This is the same for audio clips that have their Sync set to Event. This is something that you should keep in mind when you are building and troubleshooting your sites. What I like to do is hide the audio clips or symbols that are really heavy, so I can preload them before they have to be used.

1. Open a new file.
2. Rename "Layer 1" to "Animation 1" and create an animation that starts at Frame 1 and ends at Frame 10. For this example, you can keep it simple and make a circle move across the screen.
3. Insert a new layer and call it "Animation 2".
4. Create an animation in this layer that starts at Frame 5 and ends at Frame 15.
5. Insert a new layer and call it "audio".
6. Insert a keyframe in the new layer at Frame 10.
7. Choose Window -> Common Libraries -> Sounds.

8. Select Beam Scan and drag it onto the Stage while you are in Frame 10.
9. Choose Control -> Test Movie.
10. Choose Control -> Bandwidth Profiler and set the Profiler to Frame by Frame Graph (Figure 9-3).
11. Choose Debug -> 14.4 (1.2KB/s), setting the download speed to 14.4.
12. Choose View -> Show Streaming.

You will notice that the movie gets hung up while it is loading the audio clip. This is something that we want to avoid. If we rearrange the animations, we can place the clip in between them so that it does not affect the animation.

1. Use the file from the previous example.
2. Drag the audio clip keyframe from Frame 10 to Frame 8.
3. Change "Animation 1" so that it goes from Frames 1 - 7 instead of Frames 1 - 10.
4. Change "Animation 2" so that it goes from Frames 8 - 15 instead of Frames 5 - 15.
5. Choose Control -> Test Movie.
6. Choose View -> Show Streaming.

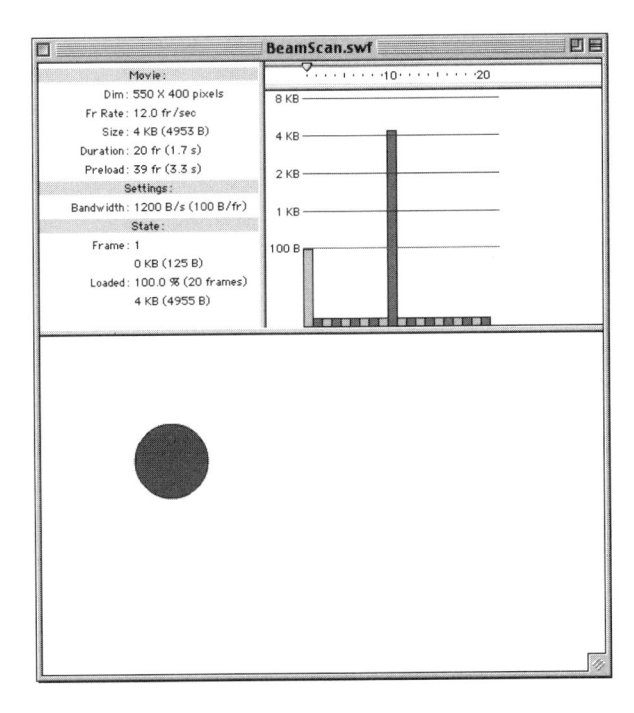

Figure 9-3 Frame by Frame Graph showing how an audio clip can affect the download of your site.

Now our example shows how the audio clip does not affect the animation. You can also use this example to preload symbols or audio clips. For example, you can set a symbol so that its Alpha is zero, or you can edit an audio clip so that its volume is all the way down. Then, you can place it in between animations, so that it does not affect the playback of the site. This way, the file will load while in the background and will be completely loaded by the time it is supposed to show up in the site. By strategically placing symbols and audio clips throughout your site, you can spread out the download time. This will allow the rest of the site to play back smoother because the symbols and audio clips will have been loaded already.

SIZE REPORT

The Size Report is one of the best features available in Flash. This feature will allow you to check everything about a file, from which fonts are used to the file size of a particular graphic or sound. The following is an example of a Size Report:

```
Movie Report
------------
Frame #    Frame Bytes     Total Bytes     Page
-------    -----------     -----------     ----------------
     1         53790           53790       Scene 1
     2             2           53792       2
     3             2           53794       3
     4             2           53796       4
     5             2           53798       5
     6             2           53800       6
     7             2           53802       7
     8             2           53804       8
     9            10           53814       9
    10            32           53846       10
    11             2           53848       11
    12             2           53850       12
    13             2           53852       13
    14             2           53854       14
    15             2           53856       15
    16             2           53858       16
    17             2           53860       17
    18             2           53862       18
    19            10           53872       19
    20           105           53977       20
    21             2           53979       21
    22             2           53981       22
    23             2           53983       23
    24             2           53985       24
    25             2           53987       25
Page                           Shape Bytes     Text Bytes
----------------------         -----------     ----------
Scene 1                                  0              0
```

CHAPTER 9 • SHRINKING YOUR FILE SIZE

```
Embedded Objects              420               0
Symbol                   Shape Bytes      Text Bytes
----------------------   -----------      ----------
BackToMenu_web                 40              51
banners                         0              49
banners_button                 37              84
banner_anim                   486               0
banner_outline                486               0
bckgrnd1                      127               0
boxes                           0               0
boxsm                           0               0
client1_ban                    50               0
client1_screen                  0              49
client1_web                     0              50
client2_ban                    50               0
client2_screen                  0              49
client2_web                     0              68
client3_ban                    50               0
client3_screen                  0              49
client3_web                     0              35
client4_ban                    50               0
client4_web                     0              51
client5_ban                    50               0
client5_web                     0              55
client6_ban                    50               0
jp                            508               0
screen outline                847               0
screen_anim                   841               0
screen_button                   0             104
sections                       82               0
websites button                37              90
websites_outline              532               0
website_anim                  530               0
web_sect                      100               0
welcome_header                  0              67
welcome_text                    0             229
Bitmap              Compressed  Original   Compression
-------             ----------  ---------- -----------
client1a.gif              883      41760    Lossless
client1b.gif             3281      41040    Lossless
client2a.gif             4698      44400    Lossless
client2b.gif             9518      40080    Lossless
client3a.gif             3900      40080    Lossless
client3b.gif             3655      41280    Lossless
client4a.gif             3571      38640    Lossless
client4b.gif             6097      35040    Lossless
client5.gif              4767      40800    Lossless
Event sounds: 11KHz Mono 16 kbps MP3
Sound Name               Bytes              Format
----------------        --------      ---------------------
Visor Hum Loop            2407        11KHz Mono 16 kbps MP3
```

```
Font Name                      Bytes      Characters
---------------------          -------    ----------
Arial                          919         abceinrstvw
Arial Bold                     2048        ,.123Itabcdefghi
                                           Jklmnoprstvw
Arial Black                    2296        !.ABCNOPSVWAbcdeh
                                           Iklmnoprstuwxy
```

The Size Report shows the number of bytes in each frame, as well as a running total of bytes for the whole file. It also breaks scenes down, showing how many bytes are used by shapes and text. The next section shows every symbol that you have used in the movie. This section is broken down to display how many bytes are in each symbol. The Bytes section shows how many bytes are from both shapes and text for each symbol. The next section covers bitmaps, and it gives a breakdown of what the file is after it has been compressed, what it was originally, and what compression you have chosen. The next section covers audio. This section shows the name of each clip used, its file size, and the compression used on the clip. The last section covers fonts. The fonts are listed by name, bytes, and which characters are used.

OPTIMIZING IMPORTED BITMAP FILES

Bitmap files can make your movie's file size very large. One way to make your file size smaller is to replace some of your bitmaps with vector art. If the project calls for a lot of bitmap images and you cannot substitute vector art, you will have to compromise some image quality to really decrease the movie's file size. The best way to keep image quality as high as possible and make the file size smaller is to compress each file individually. To do this, go to the library of your movie and select one of the graphics.

1. Choose Window -> Library to open the Library window.
2. Double-click on a graphic to open the Bitmap Properties window (Figure 9-4).
3. Go to the Compression pull-down menu and select Photo (JPEG), if it is not selected already.
4. Uncheck the Use document default quality box.
5. Now, set the image to a quality level that you feel is a good trade-off of quality and file size.
6. To see how the file is affected by the quality setting, click the Test button.

The Test button shows the quality, original file size, compressed file size, and percentage of the original file. You will also see the image in the upper left-hand corner of the window update with the compression. It is always good to test a file while it is set

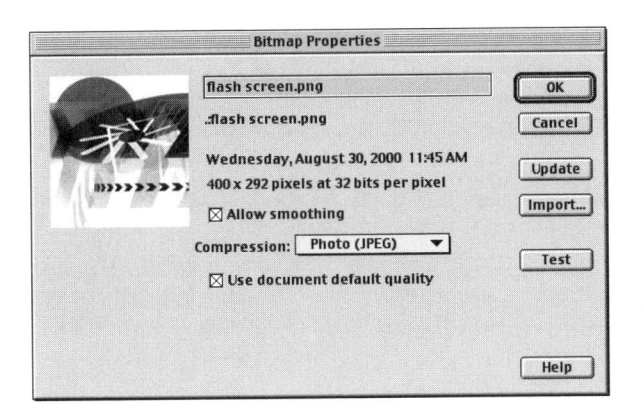

Figure 9-4 Bitmap Properties window, where you can set the compression for a bitmap image.

to Lossless (PNG/GIF). Some files are just compressed better under this setting. The setting you choose in this window will override the setting that the movie has in the Export Flash Player window unless you leave the Use document default quality box checked. Then, the file will use the compression that is set in the Export Flash Player window when the movie is exported.

Another way to shrink the file size of your movie is to not animate your bitmap images. The more you animate and scale your bitmap images, the larger the file size gets. You can use masks to cover the images and animate the masks to bring the bitmaps onto the screen. This will save a little file size, and this way, the image does not move at all.

AFFECTING FILE SIZE WITH FONTS

Fonts are the key to getting your message across. If you cannot use fonts, then how will you let your clients or visitors know what you are about? The same fonts that are the key to your site can also be your biggest problem. All the characters of a font that you have used in Flash are stored in the final movie. If you look at the previous Size Report, you will see that it lists three types of the Arial font and all the characters that each one used next to it. If I had used all of one type of Arial, I could have saved around 2K. Also, the more complicated the font, the higher the file size. The reason for this is that the shape is more complicated. So if you are using a font with fancy serifs, it will be larger than a standard font like Charcoal or Geneva. Another way to make the file size smaller when working with fonts is to make sure that you leave the fonts intact. What I mean by this is whenever possible, do not break fonts down to basic shapes. Another great way to make the file size smaller is to use text fields that do not embed a font. This will make your movie's file size a lot smaller. Text fields are gone over in greater detail in Chapter 10.

STREAMLINING SHAPES

The best way you can make your file size smaller is to use symbols whenever possible. Like I have said in previous chapters, it does not matter how many instances you use of a symbol, it will not add to the file size. Once that symbol is used, it has been loaded for all the future uses. If you have to use shapes, you might want to try and use some that are less complicated. Because of how the vector information is stored, the more points, curves, and angles a file has directly affect the file size. You can trim some of those curves by using the Optimize Curves tool on your graphics.

1. Select the shape you want to optimize.
2. Choose Modify -> Optimize (Figure 9-5).
3. Move the slider to a position of your discretion.
4. Click OK.

> The Optimize Curves tool can distort your graphics. You will have to test it on each graphic individually to find the setting that works best. To see how much each shape is being changed, make sure the Show totals message box is checked. I suggest that you start closer to the None side of the slider and work your way up to the Maximum side. You can also choose a lower setting and check the Use multiple passes box.

I have a couple of examples of a graphic that has been optimized with the Optimize Curves tool. I have pictures of the graphic in three different stages.

The first picture shows the graphic before it was optimized (Figure 9-6).

The second picture shows the graphic after it was optimized at a low setting (Figure 9-7).

Figure 9-5   Optimize Curves window.

CHAPTER 9 • SHRINKING YOUR FILE SIZE

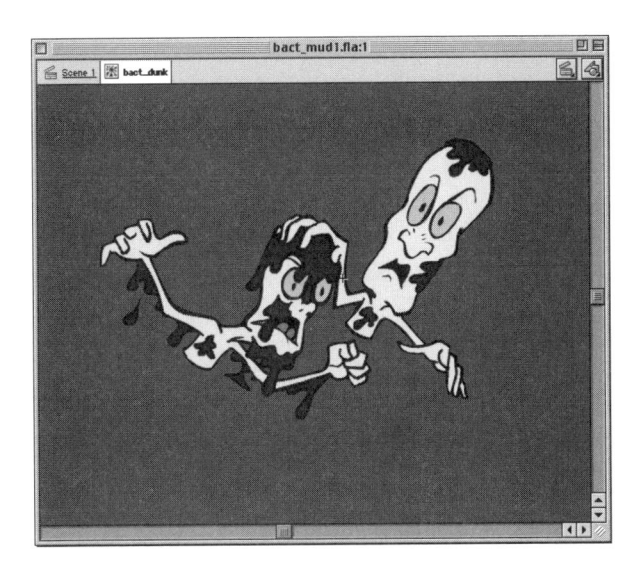

Figure 9-6 A graphic before using the Optimize Curves tool. Visuals provided courtesy of Oxy® © 2000 SmithKline Beecham.

The third picture shows the graphic with the maximum optimization level applied (Figure 9-8).

These pictures are to show you the ways that the Optimize Curves tool will change your image. You should notice the big difference between the graphic in Figure 9-6 and the one in Figure 9-8. The image in Figure 9-8 has lost a lot of its round corners and has become a little boxy.

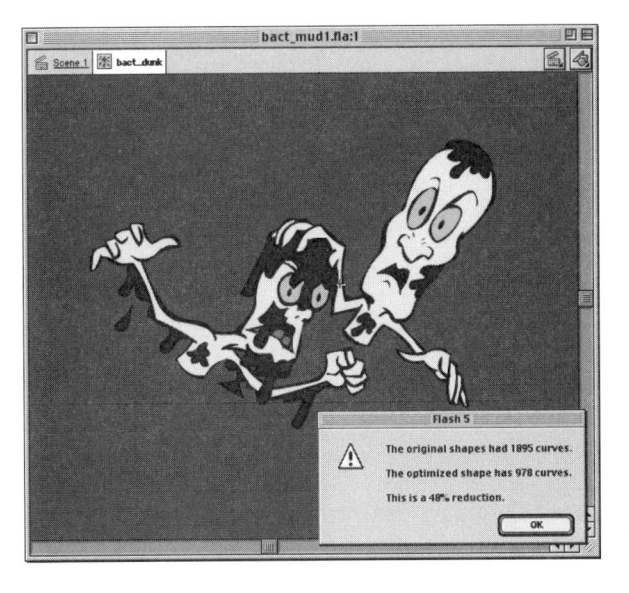

Figure 9-7 The same graphic as in Figure 9-6, but after using the Optimize Curves tool at a fairly low setting. Visuals provided courtesy of Oxy® © 2000 SmithKline Beecham.

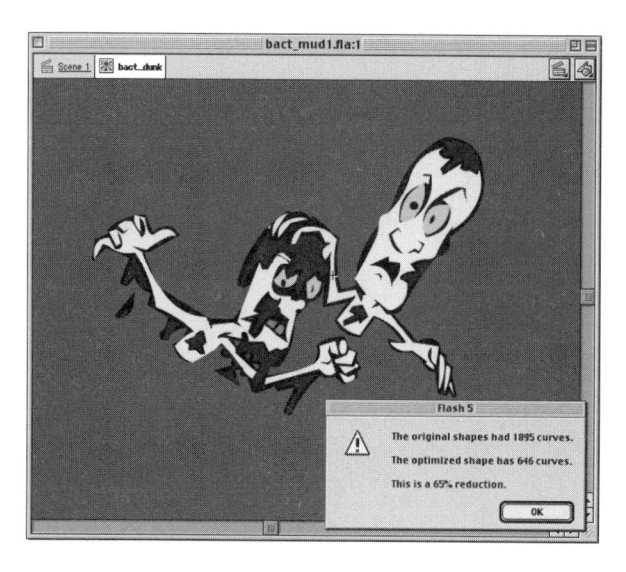

Figure 9-8 The same graphic as in Figure 9-6, but after using the maximum setting in the Optimize Curves tool. Visuals provided courtesy of Oxy® © 2000 SmithKline Beecham.

USING MP3 AUDIO COMPRESSION

Audio is really tricky. It can double or triple your file size. You should always try to limit the amount of audio used if you are really concerned about file size, which I assume you are because you are reading this section. You can also use the MP3 Compression feature. This will help you keep some of the quality of the clip while making the file size much less than traditional compression. You can also optimize audio clips individually, just like bitmaps. All you have to do is select the sound clip you want to work with in the Library.

1. Choose Window -> Library to open the Library window.
2. Double-click the audio clip you want to compress. This brings up the Sound Properties window.
3. Change the Compression menu from Default to MP3. This reveals the compression options for MP3 compression (Figure 9-9).
4. Set the Bit Rate and Quality settings so that they work best with your sound.
5. Click Test to make sure the sound still sounds good.
6. Click OK when you have finished testing.

This will override any settings that you set in the Export Flash Player window, unless you checked the Override sound settings box. The MP3 compression setting

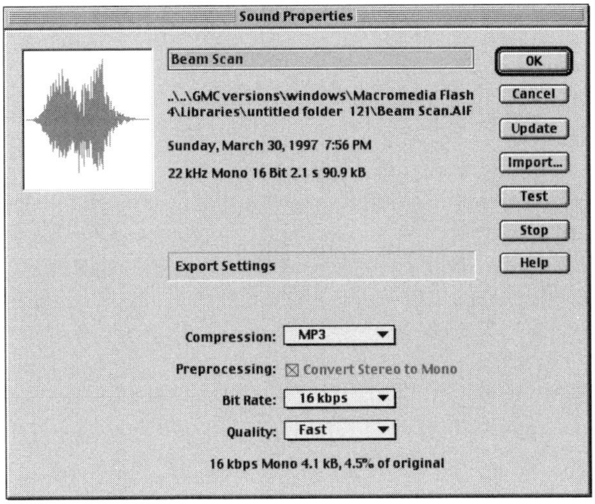

CHAPTER 9 • SHRINKING YOUR FILE SIZE

Figure 9-9 Sound Properties window with the Compression set to MP3.

allows you to have smaller file sizes with better audio quality than the other types of compression. The Sound Properties window automatically updates the size of the file and its percentage of the original file. This will aid you while you are trying to find a compression level that has the quality and file size you want.

chapter 10

TIPS AND TECHNIQUES

This chapter uses combinations of the lessons from previous chapters to show you how to better control your movie, add better functionality, and make files other than Web sites. The first sections of this chapter will cover using JavaScript to open and close browser windows and take an in-depth look at text fields. The second group of sections will cover topics like creating projectors and screen savers. Flash has come a long way, which is why I felt the need for a chapter like this one. I get to showcase some specific features and uses for Flash that you will be able to use directly and indirectly to spark your imagination and allow you to create something totally new.

USING JAVASCRIPT TO OPEN AND CLOSE BROWSER WINDOWS

This is a pretty popular request. I have been asked to do this a number of times, and I have been asked an even greater number of times to show people how it's done. There is one downside to using JavaScript commands to call out a new window; this technique is not supported by Internet Explorer 3.0. Unfortunately, this is the only way to call out a window that is a specific size with whatever window options you want like no scrollbars, a certain width, height, etc. You can use the Get URL action to call a new window, but you cannot set the size of the window, and it would have all the toolbars that you do not need, cluttering up the new window. The next section talks about closing windows using JavaScript and Flash. This example is straight from a project I did for one of my clients. The client had a Flash demo that popped up in front of the HTML site and requested that people be able to get back to the HMTL site from the demo. The best way to do this was to close the window that the Flash movie was playing in to reveal the HTML site.

OPENING A WINDOW

If you know JavaScript, this is a pretty simple task. If not, I will explain it in enough detail so that you will be able to use this technique. There are two steps: First, you will need to set up the Flash file; then you will have to set up the HTML file. I start by covering what to do to the Flash file, then I show you the code that needs to be placed in the HTML file for the site so that the script will work.

1. Open a new Flash file.
2. Create a button.
3. Add the Get URL action to this button.
4. Type "javascript:winOpen()" in the URL section of the action window (Figure 10-1).

> **Make sure that when you are filling in the Get URL field that you do not check the Expression box next to the URL field.**

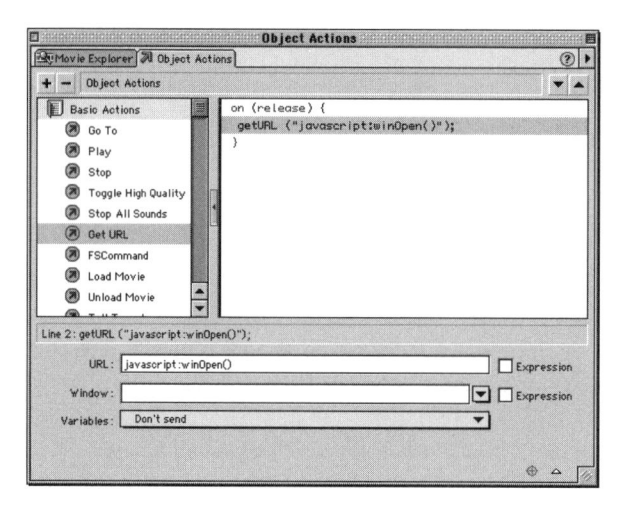

Figure 10-1 Get URL action for opening a new browser window.

We are halfway there; now we need to add the JavaScript to your HTML file. If you have not created an HTML file, create one now and follow the instructions below.

1. Open your HTML file into an HTML or text editor.
2. Add the following JavaScript into the "HEAD" section of the HTML document:
   ```
   <SCRIPT LANGUAGE="JavaScript">
   function winOpen() {
   window.open("demo.html","","height=520,width=640,,toolbar=no,
   status=no,scrollbars=no,resizable=no,location=no,menubar=no");
   }
   </script>
   ```

If you already have JavaScript in your HTML document, you do not need to use the SCRIPT tags. All you need to do is copy the code in between the SCRIPT tags into the existing SCRIPT tags. The place you will need to concentrate on is the code inside the brackets. You will want to replace "demo.html" with the HTML file that you are using. Next, you will see the height and width sections. This code calls out a window that is 520 pixels tall by 640 pixels wide. You will then see that this code opens the window without the toolbar, status bar, location bar, menu bar, and scrollbars, and makes the window not resizable. You can change any one of these settings by changing them so that they say "yes", or "1", instead of "no". This wraps up our script for opening a window, so let's move on to closing the window with JavaScript.

CLOSING A WINDOW

This feature works just like the technique for opening a new window. This example shows how to close any window. The thing that changes most is the JavaScript. Again I will show you how to set up the Flash document, and then I will show you what to do to the HTML file.

1. Open a new Flash file.
2. Create a button.
3. Add the Get URL action to this button.
4. Type "javascript:winClose()" in the URL section of the action window (Figure 10-2).

Next, we need to add the JavaScript to our HTML file. Take the following code and place it into the HEAD section of your HTML document:

```
<SCRIPT LANGUAGE="JavaScript">
function winClose() {
```

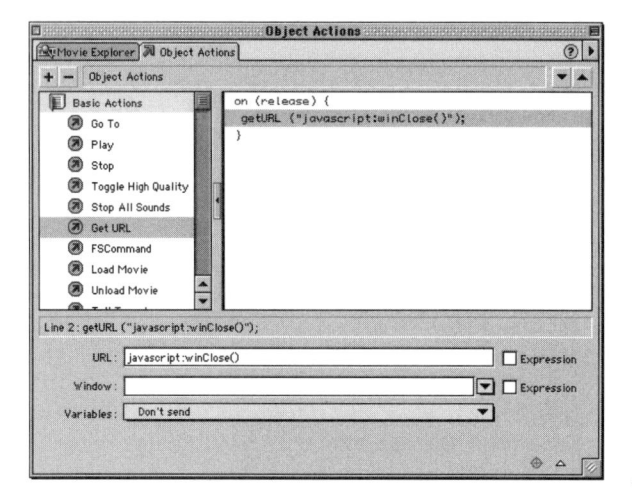

Figure 10-2   Get URL action for closing a browser window.

```
window.close("demo.html");
}
</script>
```

This code is very simple, but there is one section that you need to worry about. You need to replace "demo.html" with the page that you want to close. If you want to close the HTML page that you have this code on, then you need to place the name of the HMTL file in this spot. This wraps up the code for closing an HTML page using Flash and JavaScript.

WORKING WITH FRAMESETS

This is actually very easy in Flash, but you have to understand how Framesets work to use them. I am not a big fan of Framesets, but some people still use them and find them necessary for their sites. This is why I have included this example in the book. To control framesets, we will be using the Get URL action. The example is for a site that has two frames, one called "menu" and the other called "main" (Figure 10-3).

1. Create your HTML files for the Frameset.
2. Open your Flash file.
3. Create a button.
4. Apply the Get URL action to this button.

CHAPTER 10 • TIPS AND TECHNIQUES

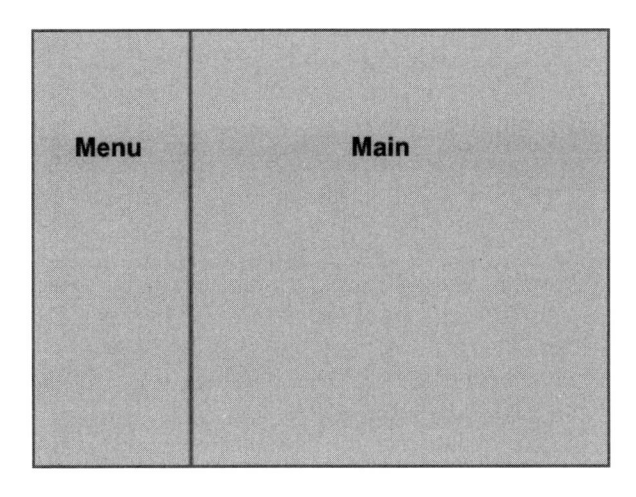

Figure 10-3 Diagram of how the Frameset is broken up for this example.

5. Fill in the HTML file you are calling with the button in the URL field of the Actions window.
6. Change the Window menu to read "main" (Figure 10-4).

Setting the Window menu to "_main" will call the HTML file and place it in the Frame called "main".

You can also control more than one frame with Flash. To change two frames, place two Get URL actions in the button, one calling each of the frames that you want to change (Figure 10-5). If you are having trouble calling the frames, check to see that

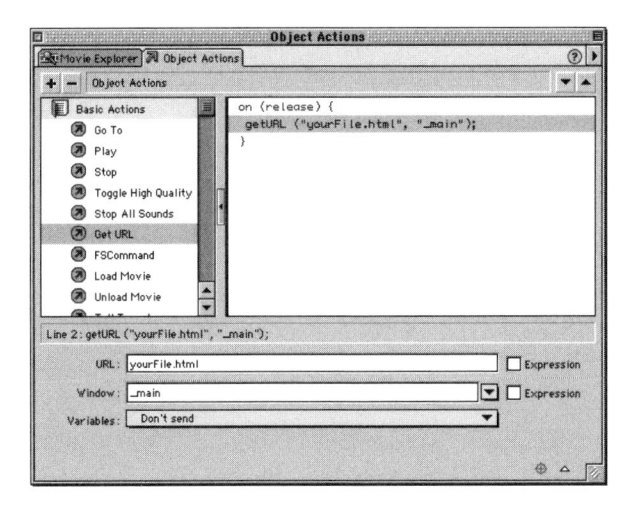

Figure 10-4 How the Get URL action should be set up to call to a frame called "main".

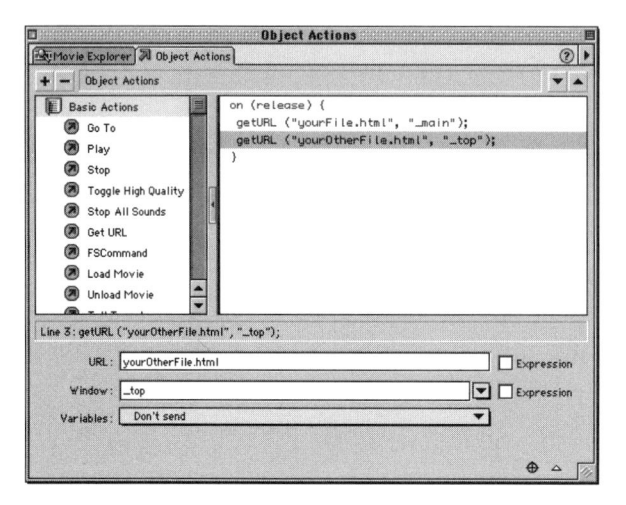

Figure 10-5 A button used to call two frames in a Frameset must have two Get URL actions.

the name of the frame you are calling from the Flash movie is the same as the name specified in the HTML file.

LAYERING MOVIES

This is a really great feature that is hard for some people to understand. You can actually load separate SWF files on top or in place of the main SWF file. There are so many things that you can do with this, some being very simple to those that are a little more complicated. For example, you can use separate movies to hold the sections of your site. This way, you can change certain sections without having to edit the whole site file. Another reason why you might want to keep the sections in other movies is that it will keep the file size of the main movie down. This way, people will only have to wait for the sections they are visiting to load. If you have sections of your movie that are too large or that people do not visit too often, then you should consider this approach of breaking down the site into separate movies. But, if you have a small site, it is easier to keep all the sections in one movie.

The next two sections show examples of this feature. The first shows how to load your audio track into a layer above the main movie and the second shows how to create a fake video file that someone can download if they want to see it.

AUDIO IN A LEVEL

This is best for an audio track that is looped beneath the main movie and does not need to be synchronized with any animation. I use this for most of my sites, but especially when I have a site that crosses multiple scenes. To load the audio in a level above the main movie, first create a separate movie that has the audio file in it. This movie can be any size you want it to be, but if you want to put any graphics in this file, it is best to keep it the same size so that you will have a better idea where the graphics will show up over the main movie.

1. Open a new Flash file.
2. Import your audio clip.
3. Place the audio clip into the Timeline.
4. Set this clip to loop in the Sound panel.
5. Export the movie as an SWF file.
6. Open the movie you want to load this file above.
7. Set a Frame action in the first frame that loads the "audio.swf" file into your main movie (Figure 10-6).

When you are working with levels, you do not want to load movies into Level "0" because that is where the main movie is playing. If you load a movie into Level "0", it will unload the main movie and load in the new one.

This will load the audio movie into Level 1, above the main movie. The only problem with this is that now your main movie will pause here, waiting for the audio movie to load. The best solution for this is to preload the audio so that it is ready to play right

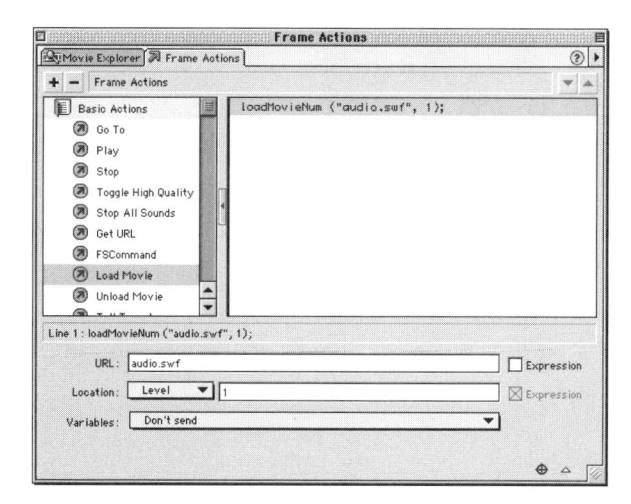

Figure 10-6 Action for loading the "audio.swf" file into a level above the main movie.

away when you need or want it to. Loading screens is covered in a section later in this chapter.

There is another problem you might encounter when loading an audio clip into the first frame of the Timeline. If your movie has a label in the first frame that gets called to from another part of the movie, the audio clip will be reloaded every time you jump to this label, causing it to sound like it is skipping when it reloads.

I am actually a big fan of adding music to animations and sites. Some people find the music loops monotonous, so you will want to have a way for those people to turn the music on and off.

Turning that Audio On and Off

This is a great feature for people who are trying to read something or for frequent visitors so they will not have to listen to the same audio loop every time they visit a site. We are going to make a button that will turn the audio on and off whenever it is clicked. If your audio is in a separate movie, this is a very easy task. This example uses the audio movie that was created in the previous example.

1. Open your movie with the looping audio file.
2. Insert two new layers.
3. Call one "actions" and the other "labels".
4. Extend all the layers out to Frame 15.
5. In the first frame of the "labels" layer, create a label that says "on".
6. Insert a keyframe in Frame 10 of the "labels" layer.
7. Create a label in this keyframe that says "off".
8. Insert keyframes in Frames 9 and 15 of the "actions" layer.
9. Add stop actions to these keyframes.
10. Add a keyframe in Frame 10 of the "audio" layer.
11. Open the Sound panel.
12. Set this new keyframe to use the same audio clip, but set the Sync menu to Stop (Figure 10–7).
13. Insert a new layer.
14. Insert a new symbol with its Behavior set to Movie Clip.
15. In Frame 1 of this new movie clip, make a graphic that says "off".
16. In the same layer, insert a new keyframe in Frame 5.
17. In this keyframe, make a graphic that says "on".
18. Insert two new layers.
19. Call one "actions" and the other "labels".

CHAPTER 10 • TIPS AND TECHNIQUES

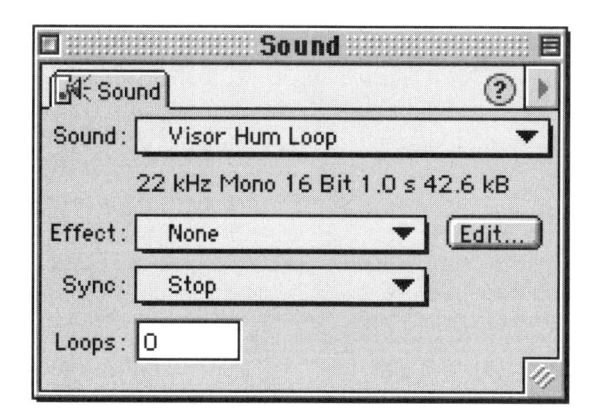

Figure 10-7 Setting an audio clip to stop playing via the Sound panel.

20. Create a label in Frame 1 that says "on".
21. Create a label in Frame 5 that says "off".
22. Insert keyframes in Frames 4 and 9 on the "actions" layer.
23. Add stop actions to these keyframes (Figure 10-8).
24. Go back to the main Timeline.
25. Set the instance Name for the movie clip to "on/off".
26. Insert a new layer above the "on/off" movie clip.
27. Draw a square over the "on/off" movie clip in the new layer.
28. Convert the square to a button (press F8).
29. Double-click the new button to go into Symbol Editing mode.
30. Move the square to the Hit state of the button. There should be nothing else in this button but the square in the Hit state.
31. Go back to the main Timeline.

> **Note:** You will see a translucent light blue square as the button. It does not appear like this when you export the movie. It only appears this way on the Stage so you can work with it.

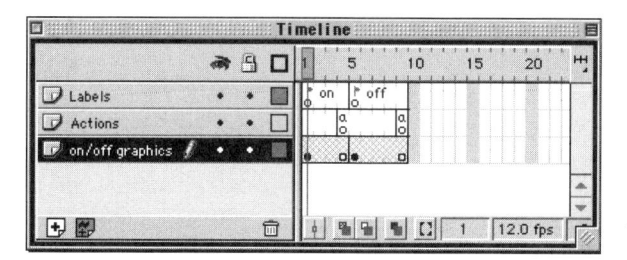

Figure 10-8 Timeline of the "on/off" movie clip.

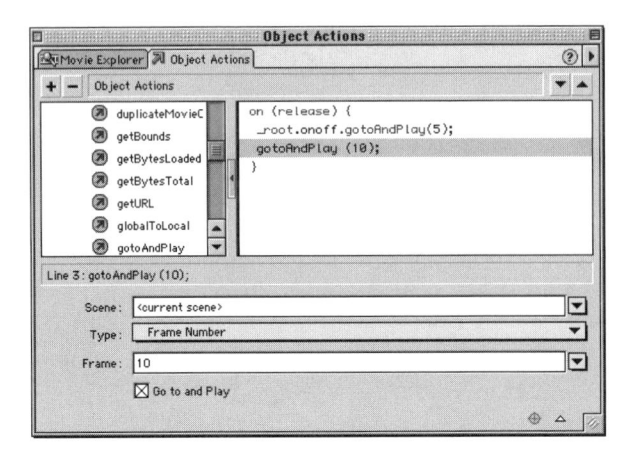

Figure 10-9 Actions are applied to the button in Frame 1 to make it turn the music off.

32. Apply the action from Figure 10-9 to the button in Frame 1.
33. Insert a keyframe in Frame 10 of the button's layer.
34. Apply the action from Figure 10-10 to the button in Frame 10.

These actions tell the movie to jump to the frames that control whether or not the movie is playing or stopped. They also control the "on/off" movie clip so that the right graphic is displayed when you click the button. When this movie is loaded into a level above the main movie, you will see the buttons to turn the movie on or off (Figure 10-11). Now you can add music to any site and you will be able to control it easily.

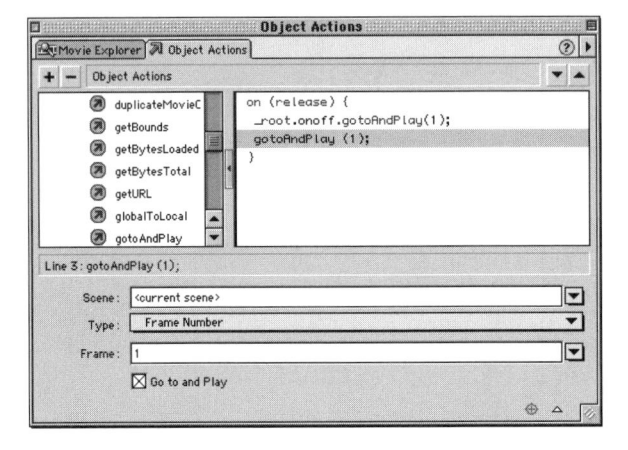

Figure 10-10 Actions are applied to the button in Frame 10 to make it turn the music on.

CHAPTER 10 • TIPS AND TECHNIQUES   231

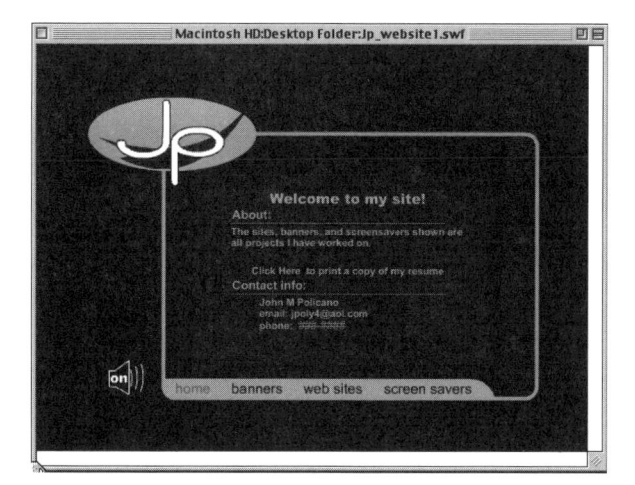

Figure 10-11   Screen shot of the site with the "on/off" button from the audio movie loaded on top.

FAKING VIDEO IN FLASH

If you cannot have the real thing, at least have something close. What I mean by this is you can have movies that look like they are video. The best way to do this is to create your video clip just as you would if you were going to place it into an HTML site. Use a program like Adobe's After Effects or Apple's Quicktime Pro to save the movie out in an image sequence. I would use JPG or PNG file formats for this because they will keep the file size down. This is a two-step process: first, we need to prepare the movie for the image sequence; then we need to prepare the main movie.

1. Open a new Flash movie.
2. Insert a new symbol with the Behavior set to Movie Clip.
3. Import your image sequence into this movie clip.
4. Add a new layer above the image sequence in the movie clip.
5. Create a label called "begin" on the new layer in Frame 1.
6. Go back to the main Timeline.
7. Place the sequence movie clip on the Stage.
8. Set the instance Name of this movie to "clip".
9. Insert a new layer behind the movie clip.
10. Draw a rectangle behind the clip that makes it look like the clip is in a window. You should leave enough room under the clip to accommodate buttons that will control the clip (Figure 10-12).
11. Insert a new layer in front of the movie clip.

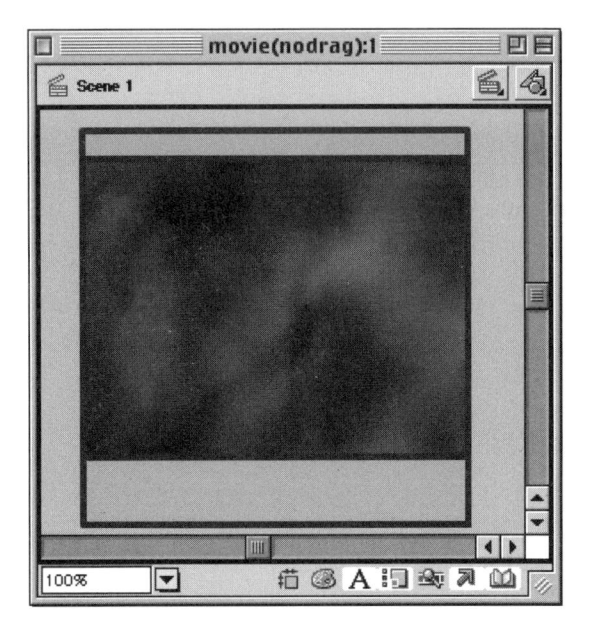

Figure 10-12   Movie "clip" with window around it.

12. Create three buttons in this layer: Play, Stop, and Rewind (Figure 10-13).
13. Modify your movie's Dimensions to match the size of the window you created around your movie.
14. Set the action for the Play button to tell the movie "clip" to play (Figure 10-14).

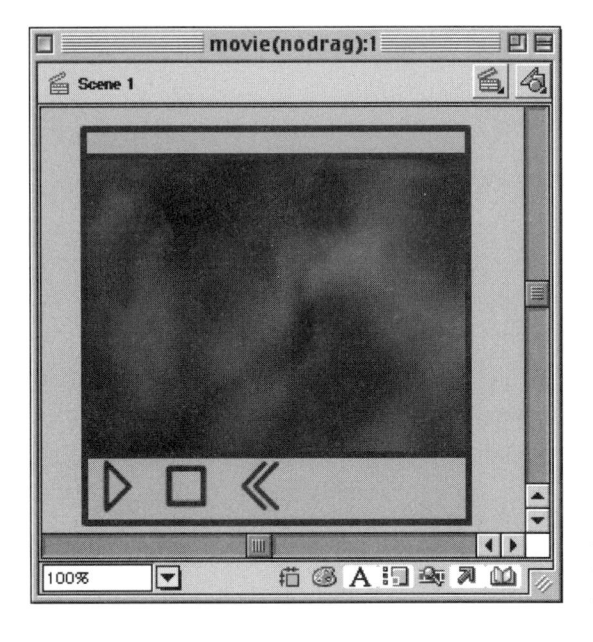

Figure 10-13   Movie "clip" with the controls added to the bottom of the window.

CHAPTER 10 • TIPS AND TECHNIQUES

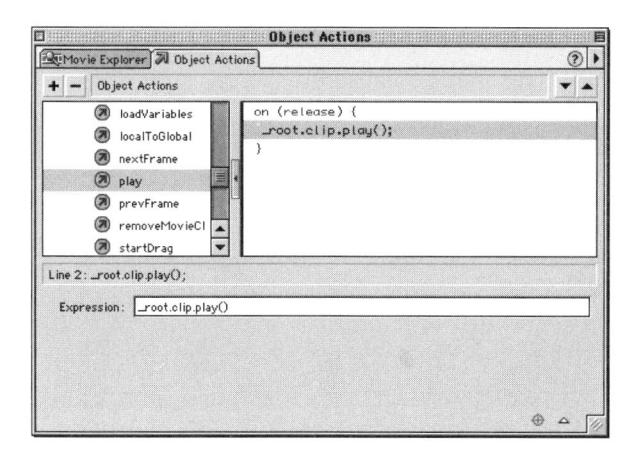

Figure 10-14 Action in the Play button to target the movie "clip" and play it.

15. Set the action for the Stop button to tell the movie "clip" to stop.
16. Set the action for the Rewind button to tell the movie "clip" to go to the label "begin" (Figure 10-15).

When you test the movie, you should be able to control it with the controls we added to the bottom of the window.

We have finished the first part of our project, now we need to set up the main movie to load and position our clip when it is loaded.

1. Open a new Flash movie.
2. Create a button that will be used to load the movie.
3. Add two actions to this button, one that loads "movie.swf" into "_level1" and another that plays the main movie (Figure 10-16).

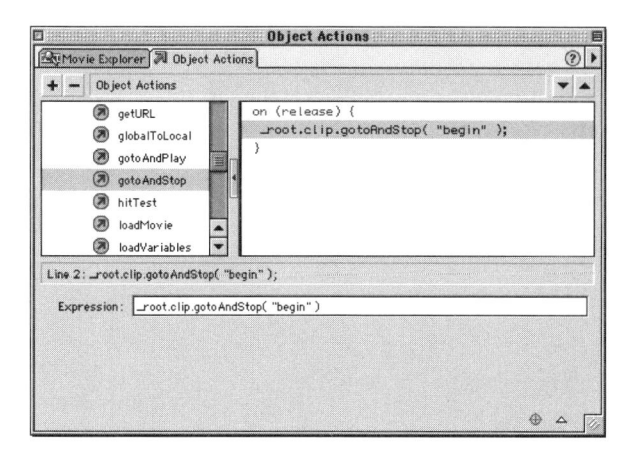

Figure 10-15 Action that tells the movie to rewind by jumping to the label at the beginning of the movie "clip".

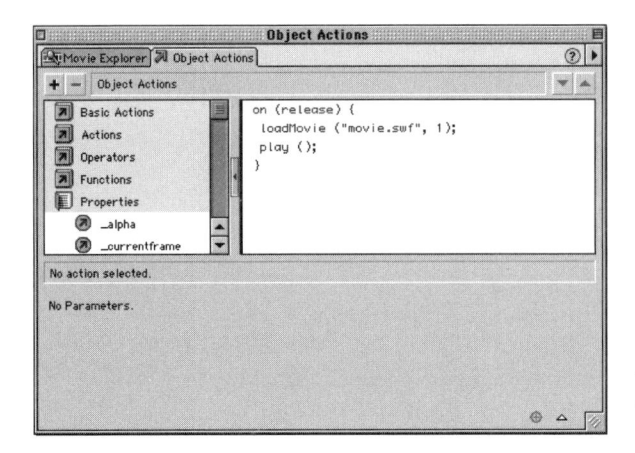

Figure 10-16 Action that loads "movie.swf" into "level1".

4. Add a new layer and call it "actions".
5. Add a stop action in Frame 1 of the "actions" layer.
6. Add Frame actions that will change the X and Y positions of the movie so it will be placed where you want it in the "actions" layer in Frame 3 (Figure 10-17).
7. Add a stop action in Frame 4.

If you test this movie while it is in the same directory or folder as "movie.swf", you will notice that the movie file will appear where you have set up the coordinates. The coordinates are for the upper left-hand corner of the movie. So, if you choose 0 for x and y, the movie clip will appear in the left-hand corner of the main movie.

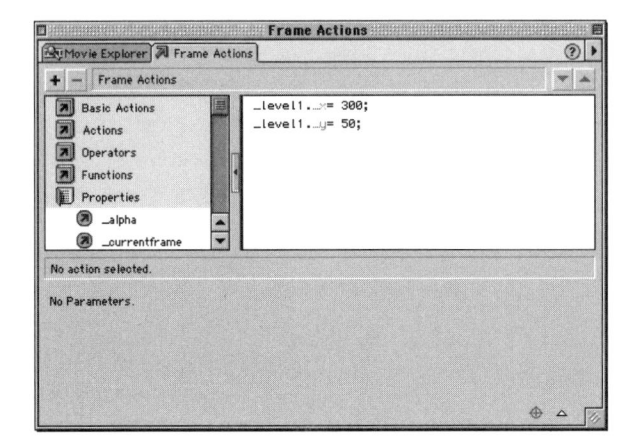

Figure 10-17 Actions that change the position of the loaded clip.

LOADING SCREENS

This section covers a topic that is very important for movies that are used on the Web. If you put together a site and place it on the Web, it will try to stream. Most of the time, the movie will hang on frames while they are loading and this causes them to not play smoothly. I use loading screens all the time on sites that I build. It helps the overall look and feel of the site. This is something you can add to your file once it is completed, or you can create it first. I like to make the movie first, then I check to see if I am going to need a loading screen. This example uses the Web site we have been working with throughout the book. The loading screen uses a combination of scenes, actions, and layers to keep track of the loading movie.

1. Open your Flash file.
2. Open the Scene panel.
3. Add a new scene to this movie.
4. Change the name of this scene to "intro" and move it above the original scene in the Scene panel (Figure 10-18).

> **Warning:** It is important to move the scene ahead of the first scene in the list because Flash plays the first scene that is in the Scene panel.

5. Go to the "intro" scene.
6. Add two new layers, one called "actions" and the other called "labels".
7. Place a label called "loop" in Frame 5.

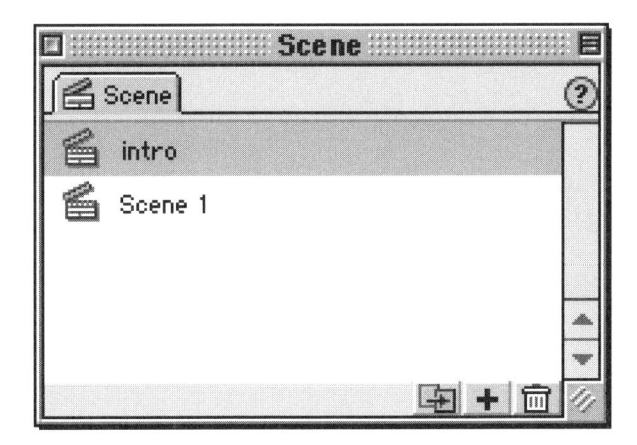

Figure 10-18 Scene panel showing the "intro" scene in front of "Scene 1".

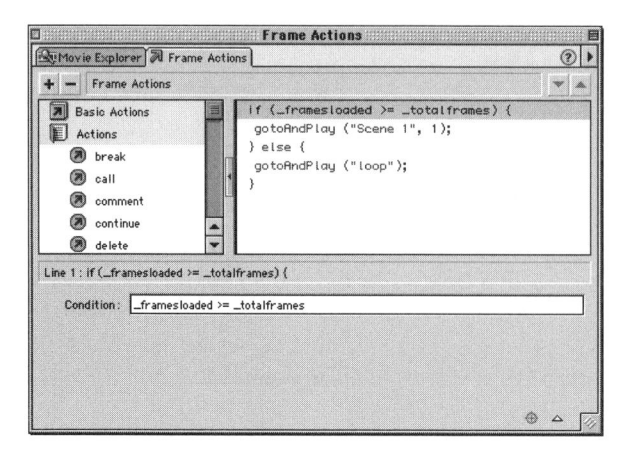

Figure 10-19 Frames Loaded action, checking to see if the whole movie is loaded.

8. Add an action in Frame 15 that checks to see if the frames loaded are equal to the total frames in the movie (Figure 10-19).
9. Create a graphic that says "Loading" in Layer 1.
10. Insert three new layers.
11. Call these new layers "Dot 1", "Dot 2", and "Dot 3".
12. Insert a keyframe in Frame 7 of the "Dot 1" layer.
13. Create a dot in this keyframe.
14. Copy the dot from the "Dot 1" layer.
15. Insert a keyframe in Frame 10 of the "Dot 2" layer.
16. Paste the dot into the new keyframe.
17. Insert a keyframe in Frame 13 of the "Dot 3" layer (Figure 10-20).
18. Paste the dot into the new keyframe.

> **Note:** I usually use a sequence of images or dots to create the loading animation. The reason why I like to have an animation is because it shows visitors that something is happening and the site is loading.

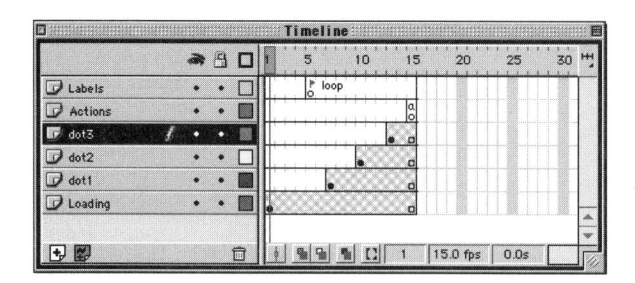

Figure 10-20 The Timeline for the loading screen that shows how all the components are placed for the loading screen to work.

CHAPTER 10 • TIPS AND TECHNIQUES   237

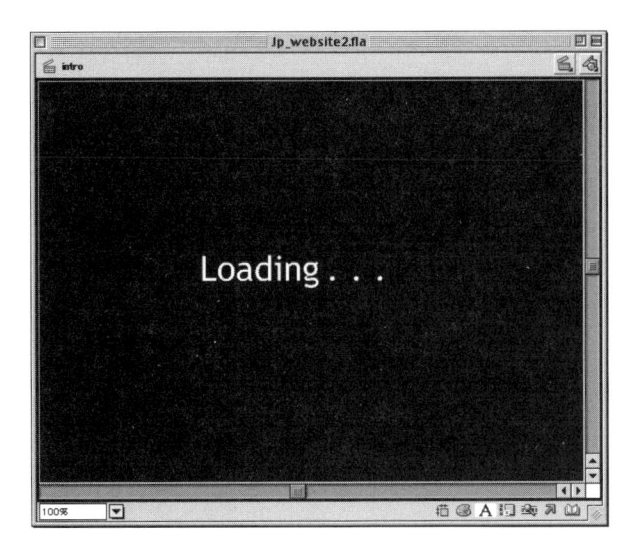

Figure 10-21 "Loading" graphic with all the dots next to it.

You can test the loading screen on the Web or by using the Test Movie feature of Flash. This example illustrates a very simple, but effective loading screen (Figure 10-21). You can add more graphics and animation to this screen to keep your visitors entertained. Just remember to keep checking how the file streams because by adding more graphics, you might be doing more harm than good.

PAUSING YOUR MOVIE

Sometimes you will need to pause a movie so that people will be able to read something or take in what is happening. This is most useful when you are making a demo or animation that just plays without user interaction. To do this, you can use the GetTimer action to set the movie to pause for a specific amount of time. One good reason why you would want to pause your movie like this is because it keeps your Timeline shorter. All you need to do is have three frames that you can work with.

1. Open a new file.
2. Insert a keyframe in Frame 5.
3. Set a variable in this new keyframe that has "time" equal to the GetTimer action.
4. Also in this keyframe, set a variable that has "length" equal to "time" plus two seconds (Figure 10-22).
5. Insert a keyframe in Frame 6.
6. Set a variable in this new keyframe that has "time" equal to the GetTimer action.
7. Insert a keyframe in Frame 7.

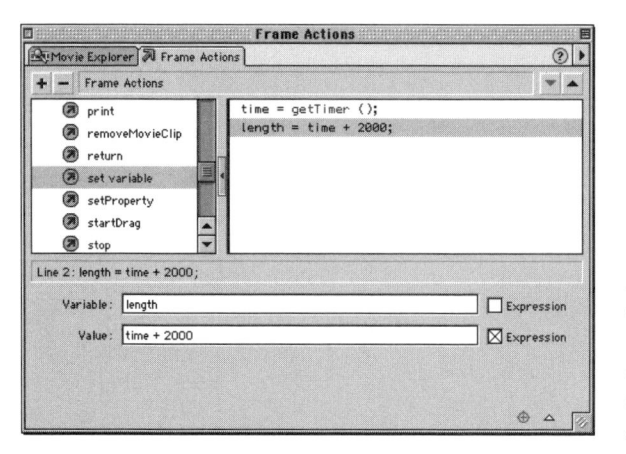

Figure 10-22   An action that checks the "time" of the main Timeline and an action that sets the variable "length" equal to "time" plus two seconds.

8. Set up an If statement that checks to see if the variable "time" is less than or equal to the variable "length". If this is true, the action should be set to go to the previous frame, which is 6 in this example (Figure 10-23).
9. Add a stop action to Frame 10.
10. Insert a new layer.
11. Add a graphic in Frame 10 so that you will know that the movie has hit this frame.

When you test the movie, it should pause for two seconds, then play until it reaches the graphic you placed in Frame 10. You can change how long you want the movie to pause by changing the "length" variable. Remember that the GetTimer action works in milliseconds, so to pause for 3 seconds, you need to put 3000 in the "length" variable. If this is not working properly, it might be because the GetTimer action only works for the main Timeline. This is the one downside to using this function.

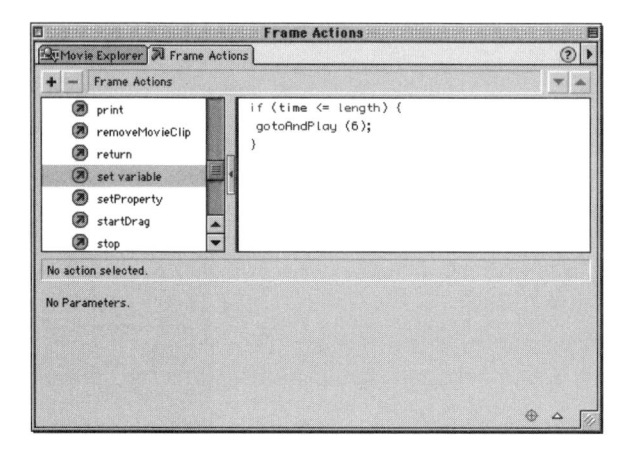

Figure 10-23   Action that checks to see if the movie has paused for two seconds.

CHAPTER 10 • TIPS AND TECHNIQUES

A work-around for this is to use a series of variables and a movie clip to determine your pause. All you have to do is set the movie clip up with one more frame than the frame rate of the movie. For example, this example is using a movie that has its Frame Rate set to 15, so the movie clip will have 16 frames.

1. Open a new movie file.
2. Set the movie's Frame Rate to 15 frames per second.
3. Create a new symbol with its Behavior set to Movie Clip.
4. Open the movie clip in Symbol Editing mode.
5. Set a Frame action in the first frame of this movie clip to stop.
6. Also in this first frame, set Variable "n" = 1.

> **Warning:** Make sure that when you are setting a variable equal to a number that the Expression box is checked next to the number's field. If you do not do this, you will not be able to add another number to this number. It will be treated as a string and Flash will set all the numbers you add to this into a string. For example, if you add 1 to the number one while the Expression box is not checked, it will show up as "11" instead of "2".

7. Insert a keyframe in Frame 16.
8. Set up an If statement that checks to see if n < _root.length.
9. If it is, then have the movie go to Frame 2 and play and set n += 1.
10. Set up an Else in part of this statement and have it make the main movie play (Figure 10-24).

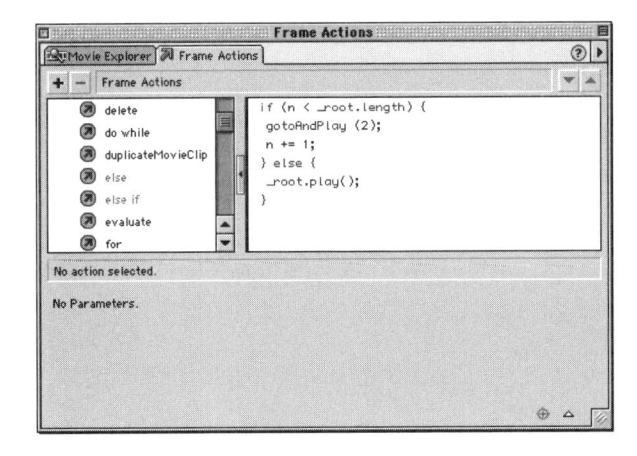

```
if (n < _root.length) {
    gotoAndPlay (2);
    n += 1;
} else {
    _root.play();
}
```

Figure 10-24   Action that is set up in Frame 16 of the movie clip.

11. Go to the main movie.
12. Drag the movie clip from the Library window onto the Stage.
13. Set the instance Name of the movie clip to "timer".
14. Insert a new layer and call it "actions".
15. Insert a keyframe in Frame 5.
16. Set the variable "length" = 5.

> **Note:** You can use the "next" variable to set the "pause" clip to jump to any label you have created. The movie clip is set up to jump back to the main movie and check the "name" variable. The "L" variable is very important in this example. It equals the amount of time in seconds you want the movie to pause. This is a very approximate number because older machines will play back slower than newer machines.

17. Set an action that makes the movie clip "timer" play.
18. Also set a stop action so the movie does not go beyond this frame while it is pausing (Figure 10-25).
19. Add a stop action in Frame 10.
20. Insert a new layer.
21. Add a graphic in Frame 10 so that you will know that the movie has hit this frame.

When you test your movie, it should pause for about five seconds before moving on to the graphic you have placed in Frame 10. You can change how long the movie will pause by changing the "length" variable.

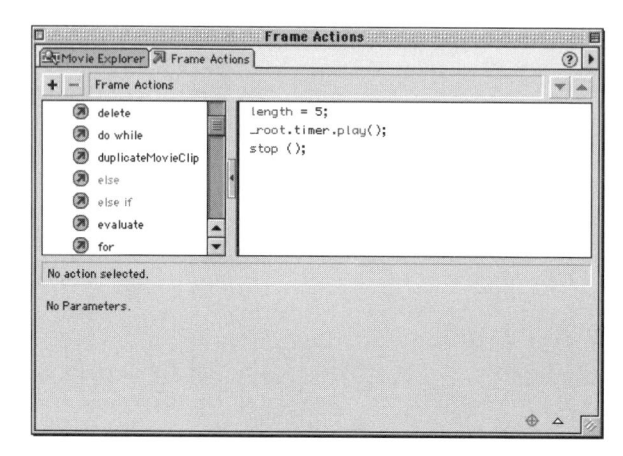

Figure 10-25 Action that needs to be set up in the main movie to call to the movie "clip" to start working.

ALL YOU NEED TO KNOW ABOUT MASKS

The Mask feature is great, but it tends to be too much for slower processors. This also depends on what you are trying to do with your mask. There are many things you can do with the Mask feature. I am going to show two uses in this section. First, I am going to show you how to make a spotlight effect, then I will show you how to use a mask to make a wipe.

SPOTLIGHTING EFFECT

1. Open a new movie.
2. Set the movie's background color to black.
3. Type in any text you want. For this example, I used the word "spotlight".
4. Add a new layer above the text.
5. Draw a circle in this layer.
6. Convert the circle to a symbol.
7. Change the layer Type to Mask.
8. Change the layer Type of the text to Masked.
9. Animate the circle across the text and back (Figure 10-26).

Test your movie and you should have a Spotlight effect that only reveals part of the text at a time (Figure 10-27). To view what the mask will look like on the Stage, you have to lock the mask and masked layers.

BUILDING A WIPE WITH A MASK

The next type of mask you can use is a reveal, or wipe. I have used this one a few times. Most of the time, you will be doing this for screen savers or longer cartoonlike animations. The example I have chosen for illustrating a wipe was a project I built for

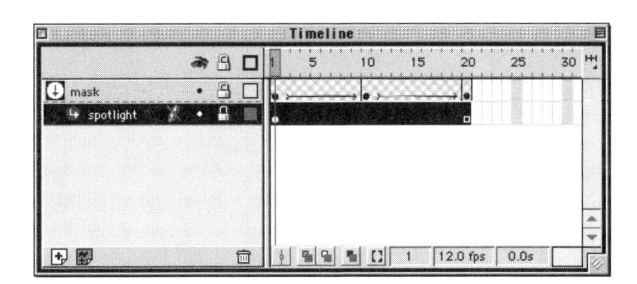

Figure 10-26   Timeline of the circle mask with the circle animated from side to side.

Figure 10-27   Picture of text that has a Spotlight effect applied to it.

Oxy. You can see this animation on the Oxy Web site, http://www.oxyoxygen.com. The animation required that the bacteria be wiped off the screen with a pad. You will see the Timeline has more than one layer set up as masked layers (Figure 10-28).

The mask layer in this animation is a shape that is shape tweened as the arm swipes across the screen (Figure 10-29). The arm actually is not part of the wipe, it is just a layer that has been placed above the mask to make it look like the arm is actually wiping the bacteria and mud off the screen.

The ability to shape tween the mask layer can make for some very cool and interesting wipes. The one drawback is when you try to mask using multiple animated images in a movie clip. Flash will select the top-most layer as the mask and disregard the rest of the layers.

Figure 10-28   Timeline of the Oxy bacteria animation, showing more than one layer being masked.

Figure 10-29 Picture of the wipe from the Timeline in Figure 10-28. Visuals provided courtesy of Oxy® © 2000 SmithKline Beecham.

TEXT FIELDS AND FORMS

Using text fields and actions, you can create some very complex Web applications. This is because Flash can interact with many of today's popular languages like Cold Fusion, Perl, and ASP. People use this feature for everything from email applications through fields that calculate anything you want.

You can use text fields to make your movie's file size smaller by having the text field get its information from an external text or HTML file. This might seem like a lot of information, so I have broken this section down into smaller sections that cover specific techniques.

USING EXTERNAL TEXT FILES

Believe it or not, you can have your text field call to an external text or HTML file that has all your copy for that section. You can even set up the text field to scroll. I am going to show you an example of how to make your Flash movie pull up the text from a text file, then I am going to show you how to make the text scroll.

1. Open a new file.
2. Select the Text tool.
3. Set the type to Input Text in the Text Options panel.
4. Draw a text field on the Stage.

> **Note:** One way to tell the difference between Static, Dynamic, and Input Text fields is by where you can scale the window. Dynamic and Input Text fields can be scaled from the bottom right-hand corner, and Static Text fields can be scaled from the top right corner.

5. Select the text field.
6. Set the Variable for the text field in the Text Options panel. This should be something that is easy to remember because we will be referencing the field by this name later in this example.
7. While in the Text Options panel, select Multiline, Word wrap, disable editing, and do not include font outlines (Figure 10-30).
8. Add the Load Variables action in the first frame of the text field or the first frame from which you want the text to be called.
9. Place the name of the text file into the URL field (Figure 10-31).

This is all you need to do to your Flash movie. Now you need to create your text file. You have to make sure that the filename is exactly how you input it in the Load Variables action. I find that it works best if you let Flash take care of the wrapping of the text. This way, you can be sure that the text will look similar on all the different machines on which it will be viewed. The very first line of the text field needs to have the name of the text field with an equals sign. So, for this example, the first line of our document would read "welcome=". This tells Flash that everything after the equals sign is for the "welcome" text field. You can start typing your text right after the equals sign if you do not want any space at the top of your text field.

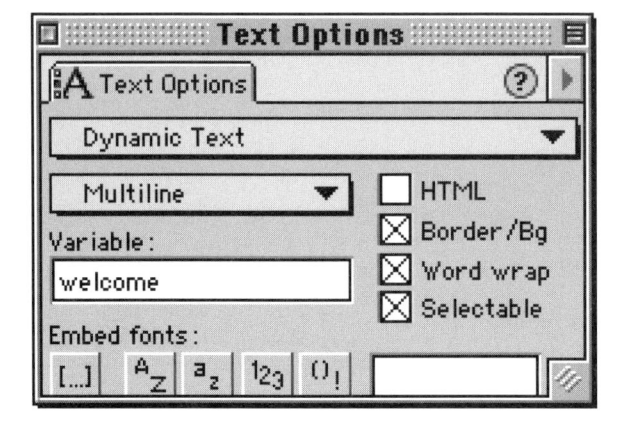

Figure 10-30 Text Options panel with the settings used in this example.

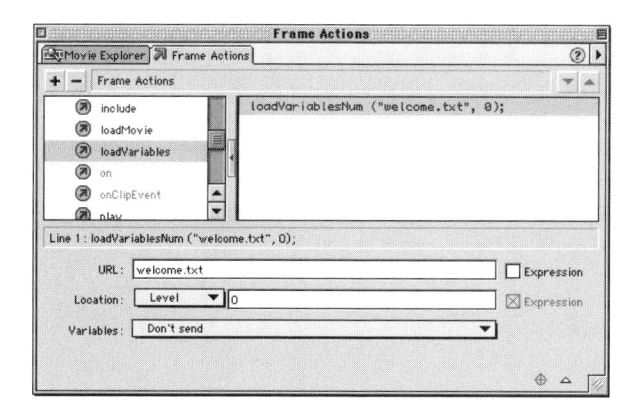

Figure 10-31 Load Variables action that loads text from a text document into a level of our Flash movie for us to use.

HTML TEXT IN FLASH

To use HTML text in Flash, do everything the same as the previous example. The main difference is you will have a lot more control over your text if you are using an HTML file. The only drawback to this is that Flash only supports some tags from HTML 1.0 (Table 10-1).

You can take your HTML file and add "variable=" right before the HTML tag and Flash will read the file. I would clear out all the unnecessary tags so they do not confuse Flash. Flash will actually read the text from the <TITLE> tag, but there is really no use for this because you cannot control the look of the font in the TITLE tag.

Flash does not support tables. Also, there is no support for images.

SCROLLING TEXT

To make your text scroll, all you have to do is add a simple action script that will allow you to scroll your text.

Table 10-1 HTML Tags Supported in Flash

Tag	Explanation
<P>	The align attribute of the P tag is supported.
<A>	The href attribute of the anchor is supported.
<U>	The underline tag is supported.
<I>	The italics tag is supported.
<B>	The bold tag is supported.
<FONT>	The color, face, and size attributes of the FONT tag are supported.

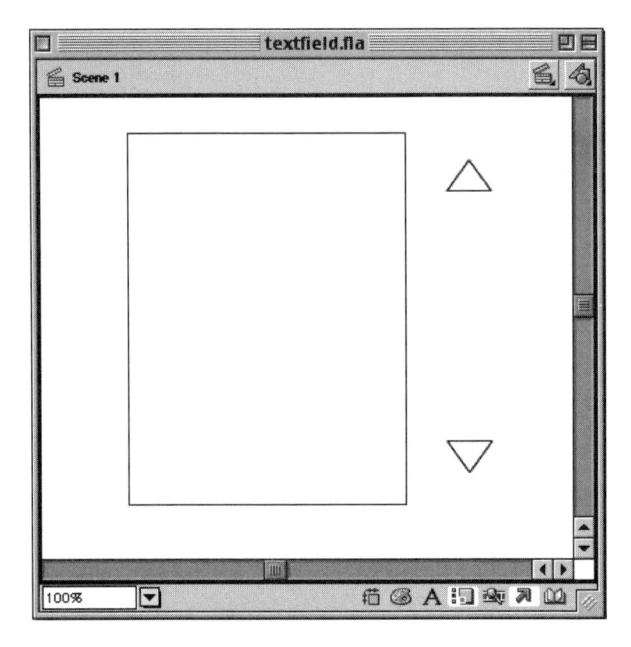

Figure 10-32   Text field with the arrow button next to it.

1. Open the file from the previous example.
2. Insert a new layer and call it "actions".
3. Create an arrow that will be used as our up and down arrows.
4. Convert the arrow to a button.
5. Place two instances of the arrow button in the new layer next to the text field, one pointing up and the other down (Figure 10-32).
6. Add an on Release action to the top arrow that will set the variable "welcome.scroll" equal to "welcome.scroll" - 1 (Figure 10-33).

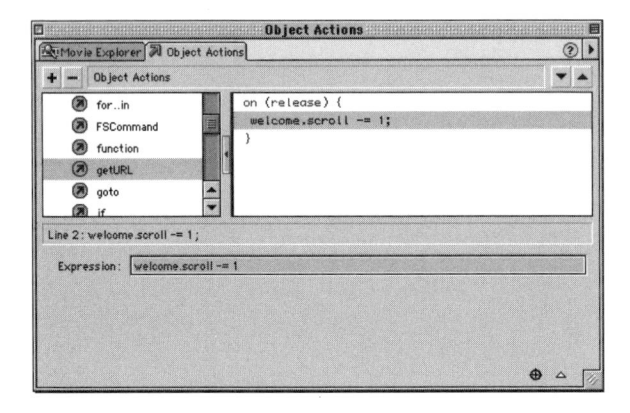

Figure 10-33   Action applied to the top arrow, which makes the text scroll up.

CHAPTER 10 • TIPS AND TECHNIQUES

7. Add the same action to the bottom arrow, except set "welcome.scroll" to + 1 instead of −1.

This is all you need to do to scroll your text files. If you are using this for your own files, place the name of your text field in the variable name instead of "welcome".

USING TEXT FILES TO HOLD YOUR URLS

Sometimes you create a movie and you cannot remember the name of one or more of the links. Maybe someone has changed the file structure of the Web site. I have run into this problem before and it always seems to happen when you have finished the movie and it is posted to the server. This example is a work-around for this so that you can have your Flash movie access an external text file to grab the URL or URLs you are using in your movie. This is a two-step example: first, we have to create or change the actions of the buttons so that they will call the text file; then, we are going to need to create the text file.

1. Open a new Flash file.
2. Create a button.
3. Add an action to this button that on Release will Get the URL of "but1". Make sure that this field is set to Expression (Figure 10-34).
4. Place an action in the beginning of the movie that loads the variables from the text file into the movie (Figure 10-35).

> **Tip:** It is easier to load the variables into Level 0 because this is where the main movie is. So, calling to the variables will be easier.

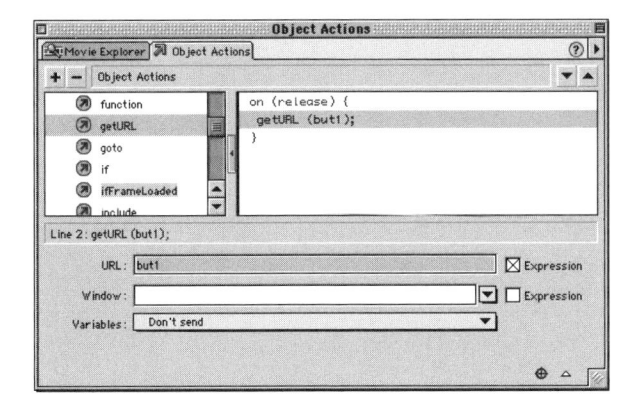

Figure 10-34 This action is applied to the button and it allows the button to grab the URL from variables that have been loaded into the movie.

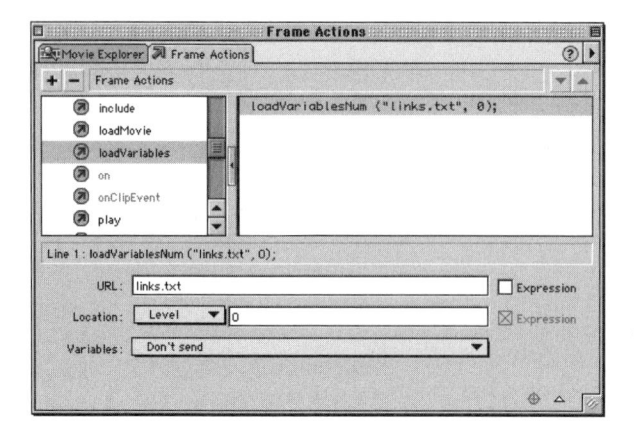

Figure 10-35 This action is placed at the beginning of the movie so that it will load the variables needed by the buttons.

This completes our movie. Now we need to set up the text file. This is treated pretty much the same as the external text file for a field. The difference is that this file is more likely to contain multiple variables. To separate the variables, all you have to do is place the "&" symbol between them, like the following code. Remember that when you place your movie onto the Web, the text file must be placed in the same directory as the movie unless you have set up the load variable to pull the file from another directory.

```
but1=http://www.phptr.com&but2=http://www.flash.com&
```

USING FORMS FOR CALCULATIONS

Some sites will require a form that has the ability to calculate certain numbers. For example, you might be working on a site that has a couple of questions for the visitors to answer, then they will get results based on their input. Most sites that do this now use HTML in conjunction with some other program that will calculate the fields and return a result on a new page. With Flash, we can set up the fields to automatically update as soon as the person has completed them. I got the idea for this example from a site with a form that calculated how much money a person spent on cigarettes per year.

1. Open a new file.
2. Create a text field and set it to Input Text.
3. Set Max Chars to 4 and the Variable to "list".
4. Create static text above this text field that says "Enter the price per pack".
5. Create a text field and set it to Input Text.

6. Set Max Chars to 2 and the Variable to "packs".
7. Create static text above this text field that says "Enter the number of packs you smoke a day".
8. Create a text field and set it to Input Text.
9. Set the Variable of the text field to "total".
10. Create static text above this field that says "The total cost of Smoking for you per year" (Figure 10-36).
11. Extend your movie out to Frame 3.
12. Insert a layer and call it "actions".
13. Insert a keyframe in Frame 3 of the "actions" layer.

    Insert the following code into this new keyframe. This is a series of variables and expressions that will allow us to achieve our answer.

    ```
    peryear = list * packs;
    allyear = peryear * 365;
    x100 = allyear * 100;
    howlong = mblength(x100);
    allyearWdec = mbsubstring(x100, 1, howlong-2) add "." add mbsubstring(x100, howlong-2, 2);
    total = "$" add allyearWdec;
    ```

14. The first variable finds out the total of the two fields multiplied together.
15. The second variable multiplies the total by 365 so that we get the total expense per year for the cigarettes.

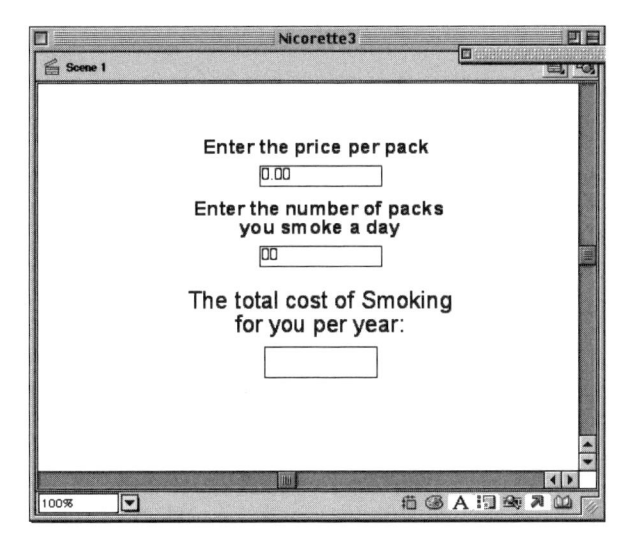

Figure 10-36 Layout of the text fields and text for this page.

16. The next three variables make sure that the final expense will have a decimal point and two zeros if the price works out to an even dollar amount.
17. The third variable multiplies the total expense per year by 100.
18. The fourth variable uses the Mblength string function to find out how many characters are in the number after it was multiplied by 100.
19. The fifth variable separates the characters out to the numbers before the decimal point and those after the point. This variable makes use of the MBSubstring string function.
20. The sixth and final variable takes the answer after the decimal point has been added and sticks the dollar sign on the front. By naming this variable "total", it also sends this to the text field with the same name.

This completes our calculating form. This movie has to constantly loop for it to check and update the answer. If the movie stops, it will not calculate the answer. As with any movie that uses variables and ActionScripting, you need to be careful with the naming of the variables.

Dragging Items

This feature is really cool and it is geared for e-commerce sites that are looking to do things a little differently. You can also use this feature for other things like allowing visitors to drag popup menus and windows. I have two examples for this section, one uses the movie clip from the "Faking Video in Flash" section and the other is a mocked-up e-commerce site that has products that can be dragged into the shopping cart.

Dragging a Movie Clip

1. Open the Movie file from the "Faking Video in Flash" example.
2. Insert frames for all the layers out to Frame 20.
3. Add two new layers, one called "labels" and the other called "actions".
4. In Frame 1 of the "labels" layer, add label "no drag".
5. In Frame 10 of the "labels" layer, add label "drag".
6. In Frames 9 and 20 of the "actions" layer, add stop actions.
7. Add a new layer called "x for drag".
8. Create an "X" at the top of the window and make it into a button.

CHAPTER 10 • TIPS AND TECHNIQUES

> **Tip:** The Hit area of the "X" button should be large. This will help when you are trying to stop the dragging of the object. If the Hit area is too small, you might be dragging the box from an area that is not in the Hit area. If this happens, you will not be able to stop the dragging of the box.

9. Add a new layer called "click to drag".
10. Create text next to the "X" that says "click X to drag" (Figure 10-37).
11. Add a Drag action to the "X" button in Frame 1.
12. The target for this action should be whatever level you plan to place this clip in. For this example, the target has been set to "_level1".
13. Check the "Lock mouse to center" box.
14. Add go to and Play action to this button that goes to the "drag" label. The code from Steps 11 - 14 is shown here:

```
on (release) {
    startDrag ("_level1", true);
    gotoAndPlay ("drag");
}
```

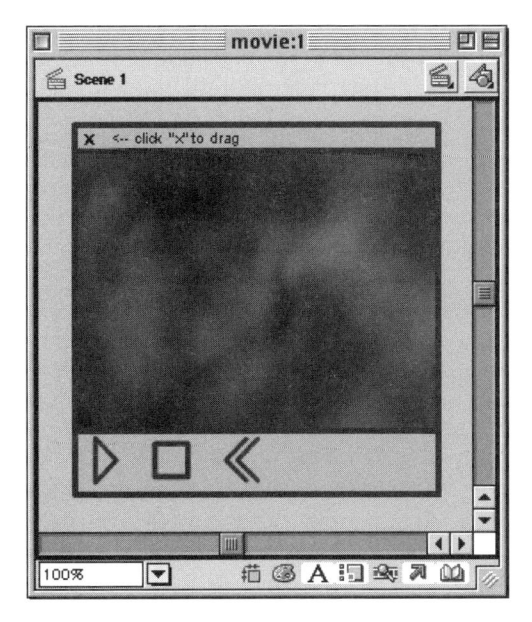

Figure 10-37 Picture of the movie window with the "X" button in the upper left-hand corner.

15. Create a keyframe in Frame 10 of the "X" button layer (Figure 10-38).
16. Change the Drag action in this button to a stop drag.
17. Change the go to and Play action to go to the "no drag" label, as shown below:

```
on (release) {
   stopDrag ();
   gotoAndPlay ("no drag");
}
```

This completes the movie clip and will allow it to be dragged when it is loaded into Level 1 of another movie. The great thing about having the Drag action loaded into the movie clip is you do not need to worry about programming it in the final movie. You can use the Drag action on movie clips as well as the movies that are loaded into a level above the main movie. The next example will show how you can have multiple movie clips use this feature in an e-commerce example.

DRAGGING PRODUCTS TO A SHOPPING CART

This example will use a combination of a few scripts to allow people to be able to drag products into a shopping cart. The first thing we will need to do is set our store page. Then we will set up the products and the shopping cart. This page will have a list under the shopping cart that will be able to tally all the items that have been dropped into the cart. Figure 10-39 shows the screen for this example.

1. Open a new file.
2. Insert a new movie clip symbol called "var_control".
3. Go into Symbol Editing mode for this clip if you are not there already.
4. Set this clip up with two layers, one called "actions" and the other called "labels".
5. Add a label in the first frame called "start".
6. Add labels across the next four frames called "1", "2", "3", and "4".

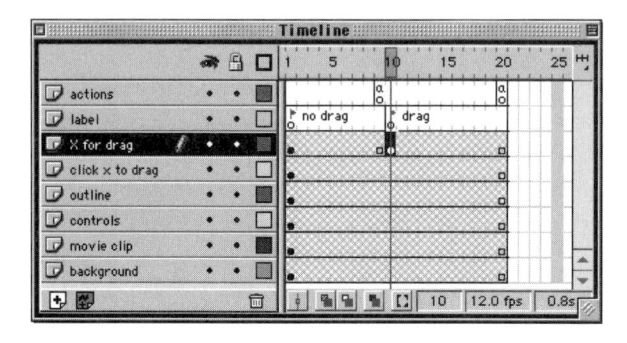

Figure 10-38 Picture of the Timeline showing where to place the keyframe for the second instance of the "X" button.

CHAPTER 10 • TIPS AND TECHNIQUES

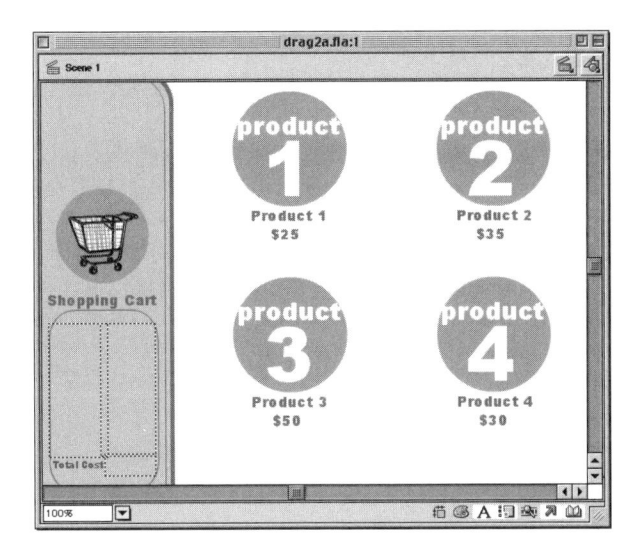

Figure 10-39 Screen shot of the site used for the product-dragging example.

7. In the "actions" layer of the first frame, set two variables and a stop action (Figure 10-40).
8. We need to add the same action and variables to the other frames, except the names of the item variable will be "Product 1" through "Product 4", coinciding with the labels in the layer above them.
9. The "price" variable can be set to anything you want for this example. I used 25, 35, 50, and 30 for "Product 1" through "Product 4", respectively.

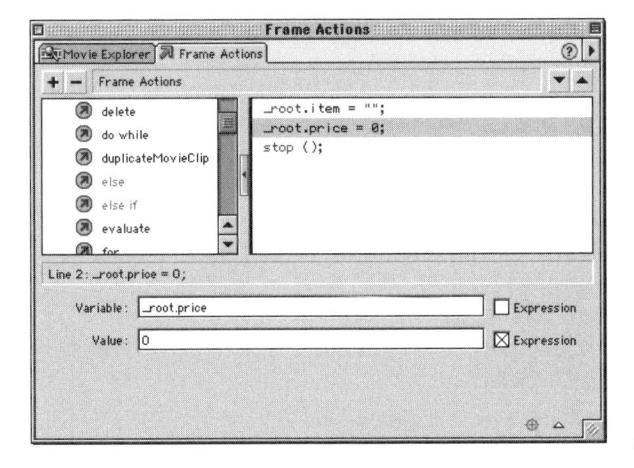

Figure 10-40 Action and variables added to the first frame of the "vars" movie clip.

> **Note:** We have to set two variables in each frame of the clip so that we can pass the correct variables depending on which product we are dragging. The first variable is "item" and the second is "price". We set these variables to be stored in the main Timeline so that it is easier to access them later. To set up a variable to be stored in the main Timeline from a movie clip, we will need to place "_root" in front of the variable name. For example, our first variable name will be "_root.item". You will notice in Figure 10-40 that the "item" variable is blank and the "price" variable is set to "0". This is important and you will see why later in this example.

10. Go back to the Stage and place this movie clip off the Stage in the upper left corner.
11. Set the instance Name of the movie clip to "vars".
12. Insert a new symbol with the Behavior set to Movie Clip.
13. Go into Symbol Editing mode for this symbol if you are not there already.
14. Create your product and how you want it to look. For this example, I just used a number.
15. Add a new layer to this movie clip and call it "actions".
16. Add stop actions to Frames 1 and 2.
17. Inset a new layer above your product.
18. Create a button that is the same size as your product.
19. Set this button up so that there is only the graphic in the Hit state. Make the button transparent.
20. Add the following actions to the button:
    ```
    on (release) {
        _root.item1.startDrag( lockCenter );
        _root.vars.gotoAndStop(2);
        gotoAndStop (2);
    }
    ```
21. The startDrag action is targeting the name of the movie clip. This button is inside, so we can drag the product into the cart.
22. The next action targets our "vars" movie clip so that we know we are dragging "Product 1" and how much it costs.
23. Insert a keyframe (press F6) in Frame 2 of this movie clip so we can set up another instance of the button.
24. Clear the actions from the button in the new keyframe in Frame 2.
25. Add the following actions to the button:

CHAPTER 10 · TIPS AND TECHNIQUES

```
on (release) {
   call ("_root.position");
   gotoAndStop (1);
}
```

26. This instance of the button uses a call action that calls an action we will be setting up a little later. The action in the frame we are calling makes the clip stop dragging and it also sends it back to its place on the screen.

27. Drag the "products" movie clip onto the Stage.

28. Set the instance Name to "Item1".

29. Repeat Steps 12 - 28 for the next four products.

Be careful to change the variables and actions that are specific to each product. For example, the item targeted in the Drag action will need to change for each button and the frame that the "vars" clip needs to go to also coincides with the number of the product you are working on.

The next step for this example is to set up the main Timeline. Then we will be able to set up our shopping cart and finish our site.

1. Go to the main Timeline.

2. Add two layers, one called "actions" and the other called "labels".

3. In the first frame of the "actions" layer, add the following actions:
```
n = 1;
while (n<5) {
    set ("_root.Item" add n add "X", getProperty("_root.Item" add n
,_x));
    set ("_root.Item" add n add "Y", getProperty("_root.Item" add n
,_y));
    n+=1;
}
```

4. This example uses the while action to loop through these variables to record each product and its position. This is important because we will want to be able to send the products back to their starting position when the Drag action is stopped.

5. Add a stop action to Frame 5.

6. Add the following actions to Frame 10:
```
n = 1;
while (n<5) {
   setProperty ("_root.Item" add n, _x, eval("_root.item" add n add
"X"));
   setProperty ("_root.Item" add n, _y, eval("_root.Item" add n add
"Y"));
    n+=1;
    stopDrag ();
}
_root.vars.gotoAndStop( "start" );
```

7. This example again uses the while action, but this time it is setting the products to the position they should be in as well as stopping the Drag action. The last action also sets the "vars" movie clip back to start because if we have reached this point, the "product" movie clip is no longer being dragged and the variables need to be 0 in case the shopping cart gets clicked.

8. Add the following actions to frame 11:

```
if (Price == 0) {
} else {
    if (Total == 0) {
        Prices = Price;
        Items = Item;
    } else {
        Items = Items add newline add Item;
        Prices = Prices add newline add Price;
    }
}
Total = Total+Price;
```

9. To be able to target or call to these actions we have just added to the movie, we need to add labels to the frames above them. In Frame 10, add a label called "position", and to Frame 11, add the label "cart".

10. Insert a new layer and call it "Shopping Cart".

11. Insert a new symbol with the Behavior set to Button.

> **Note:** The previous actions use the "Price" and "Item" variables to build a list of items that are in the shopping cart. The list for the shopping cart will be built later in the example. It consists of three text fields. These text fields are "Items", "Prices", and "Total". If you look closely at the previous actions, you will see that the If statement first checks to see if "Price" is set to "0". If you remember from the setup of the "vars" movie clip, we had the price set to "0" when no items were being dragged. This is why the If statement tells the movie to do nothing when "Price" is "0". The Else part of the If statement triggers another If statement that determines whether there has been an item already entered into the list or not. If the "Total" equals "0", then the "Price" and "Items" variables are added straight into the list. If the "Total" is not equal to "0", then the Else statement makes the "Items" and "Price" variables get added to the end of the existing lists. After the If statement is closed, we have a variable that updates "Total" each time a new "Price" variable is introduced to the equation.

12. Go into Symbol Editing mode for this button if you are not there already.
13. Build your shopping cart how you want it to look. The Hit state for this button should be smaller than the actual size of the image you are using.
14. Go to the main Timeline and place the shopping cart in its place.
15. Add the following actions to the button:
    ```
    on (rollOver) {
        call ("_root.position");
        call ("_root.cart");
    }
    ```
16. This example calls to the actions that were added to Frames 10 and 11. These actions determine which clips to add to the list and how much they cost.
17. Next we need to add two text fields under the shopping cart. These will be our list of what has been added to the shopping cart and how much it costs. The fields should be the same size and placed like columns next to each other.
18. Call the text field on the left "Items" and the field on the right "Prices".
19. Add a small text field under the "Prices" text field that is called "Total".

This completes the example, so all we need to do now is test the movie to make sure that it performs the way it should. If you run into any problems, you should double-check that the labels and variables have all been named correctly and all the movie clips have been targeted correctly.

SWISH: A PC-ONLY TEXT ANIMATOR

Swish is a really cool program, but unfortunately right now it is only available for the PC. The good news is that a Macintosh version is currently under development. There are six tabs along a window in the program that let you choose from General, Content, Timeline, Scene, Actions, and Export. The General tab lets you control the settings of your Flash movie (Figure 10-41). This program is pretty easy to pick up and start working with, especially since it uses a Timeline very similar to the one in Flash.

1. Open Swish.
2. Choose Modify -> Insert Text.
3. Click the Text tab.
4. Change the text to "www.JpGraphics.net".
5. Click the Timeline tab.
6. Highlight the "JpGraphics" layer.

258 CHAPTER 10 • TIPS AND TECHNIQUES

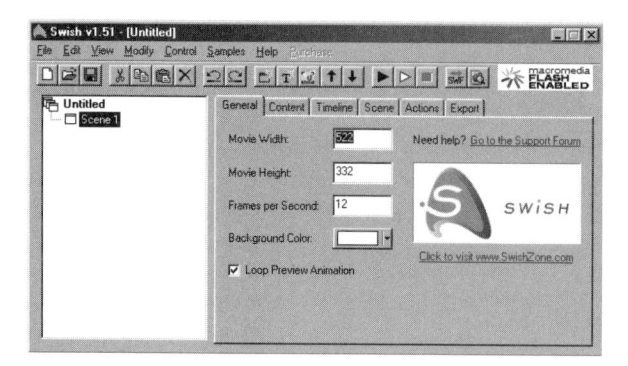

Figure 10-41 Main screen of Swish, showing all the menus and options available.

7. Click the Add Effect button in the Timeline window.
8. Choose Wave Effect (Figure 10-42).
9. Set the Wave Effect window as shown in Figure 10-42 and click OK.
10. Choose File -> Export To SWF.

That is all you need to do to create animated text with this program. If you preview the Wave effect, you should get something that looks like Figure 10-43. There are nine different effects that you can choose from with this program: Squeeze, Explode, Typewriter, Wave, Scale Characters, Alternate Characters, Revert Characters, 3D Spin, and Vortex. All of these are customizable and can be combined to create different-looking effects. Using this program will allow you to create text effects that look like it took you hours, but in fact took only a few minutes. You can find out more about this software from http://www.swishzone.com.

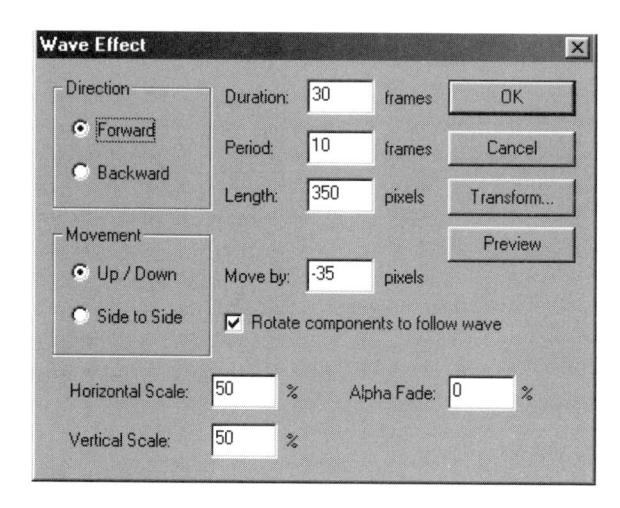

Figure 10-42 Wave Effect window.

Figure 10-43   One frame of the Wave effect generated from the Swish text animation program.

PROJECTORS

There are a few uses for projectors that you export out of Flash. Since these files are executable files, or program files, you can send them to anyone and they will be able to use the files without needing a browser and plug-ins. The one good feature of making projectors in Flash is the ability to export both the Mac and PC versions. This can be done from either platform, unlike Director, where you need to own a Mac or PC version of the software to make the executable files for both platforms. A common use for Projectors is for creating CD-ROMs. This is good because with Flash, you can make a really animated file that has a much smaller file size than most other applications. There are five FSCommands that are specific to the standalone player or projector: fullscreen, allowscale, exec, showmenu, and quit. These Projector files will work for the most part like the movie files in a browser. For example, these files can call to external text files and will load SWF files on top of themselves.

SCREEN SAVERS

Building a screen saver is really one of the easiest things to do in Flash. All you have to do is create the animation that you like and save out the file as a Projector file. The hardest choice is picking how to make the installer and final product. There are a few programs that are out there specifically designed to work with Flash to make screen savers. One of them that I used and had a lot of luck with is ScreenTime for Flash. This program is so easy to use it almost seems wrong that you get to charge clients so much for converting the file. The only thing I have to warn you about with screen savers is to know the limitations of your users' computers. You can design this awesome screen saver, but if it will just not play back on the system for which it was intended, it is virtually useless.

INDEX

A

About Flash, Apple menu, 43
ActionScripts, 12, 21, 92, 97–121
    ActionScript window, 98–103
        Actions section, 99–101
        Basic Actions, 99
        Colored Syntax feature, 99
        Functions section, 102
        Objects section, 103
        Operators section, 101–2
        Properties section, 102
    compared to Javascript, 97
    debugger, 106–9
        features, 108–9
        local vs. remote debugging, 107–8
        Properties List, 108
        Variables List, 109
        Watch List, 109
    defined, 97
    Frame Actions, 98
    Object Actions, 98
    samples, 109–21
        changing the cursor, 113–14
        controlling the volume, 114–18
        date script, 110–13
        email and ASP, 118–21
    syntax, 103–6
        targeting movie clips, 104–5
        writing/using variables, 105–6
    writing, 98–121
ActionScript Reference Guide, 97
Actions window, 14–15
    Check Syntax option, 15
    Expert mode, 15
Active Server Pages (ASP), 20, 110, 118–21, 243
Add Guide Layer button, Timeline window, 72

Add Motion Guide button, 72
Adobe After Effects, 185, 231
Adobe Illustrator, 27, 31, 46, 47, 125, 145, 187
    preparing files for Flash, 50–51
Adobe Illustrator Sequence, 182
Adobe ImageReady, 190
Adobe Photoshop, 27, 43, 47
    exporting from, 54–55
Adobe Streamline:
    Conversion Setup window, 52
    and vector-based images, 51–53
ADPCM (Advanced Differential Pulse Code Modulation), 95
Advanced color combinations, and Effect panel, 42
AIFF, 82
AI file format, 50
Align panel, 6–7
Alpha, and Effect panel, 42
Alpha effect, 69
Animated GIF, 47, 150, 182
Animation, 57–80
    frame-by-frame, 79–80
    keyframes, 57–59
    morphing a circle into an "A," 61–65
    Motion Tweening, 67–76
    of position and scale, 67–68
    of the shape of letters, 65–66
    Shape Tweening, 59–66
    timeline, 57–59
    using movie clips to add to buttons, 130–32
Anti-aliasing, 198
Art Explosion, 55
Artwork, 27–55
    grouped objects, 38, 40
    imported bitmaps, 42–46

261

Artwork (*cont.*)
  importing from other applications, 46–55
    from FreeHand to Flash, 46–49
  path, following, 71–74
  shapes, 38–40
  symbol, fading the instance of, 69
  symbols, 41–42
ASP, *See* Active Server Pages (ASP)
Assistant menu, 3
Audio, 81–96
  adding to project, 81–84
  audio files:
    importing, 83–84
    setting up, 82–83
    using shared libraries for, 93–94
  compression, 95–96
  controlling, 84–94
  Event Sound option, 89–91
  file formats, 82
  in a level, 226–28
  Looping feature, 87–89
  MP3 compression, 218–19
  sound editing controls, 84–89
    Envelope Handles and Lines, 86–87
    Time In/Out controls, 85–86
  Streaming Audio option, 91–93
  turning on/off, 228–31
Audio clips, looping, 87–89
Audio files, using shared libraries for, 93–94
AutoCAD DXF, 47, 187
AVI, 182, 185

B

Bandwidth Profiler, 208–12
  Frame by Frame Graph mode, 209–12
  Streaming Graph mode, 208–9
Banners section, Web site, 139–41
Basic Actions, ActionScript window, 99
BBedit, 188
Behaviors:
  of buttons, changing, 135–36
  symbols, 41

Bezier points, drawing with, 31
Bitmap files, imported, optimizing, 214–15
Bitmap Properties window, 43, 44
Bitmaps, 47, 187
  imported, 42–46
BMP, 27, 185
BMP Sequence, 182
Bouncing ball, 75–76
Break Apart feature, 34, 40
Brightness, and Effect panel, 42
Browser windows, and Javascript, 221–24
Button Actions, applying, 134–35
Button behavior, symbols, 41
Buttons:
  changing behaviors of, 135–36
  creating, 127–30
  using movie clips to add animation to, 130–32
Buttons library, 17
Button symbol, 27

C

Calculations, using forms for, 248–50
Character panel, 8, 14
  Kerning checkbox, 8
Checkbox option, Smart Clips, 21
Check Plug-in window, Dreamweaver, 200
Check Syntax option, Actions window, 15
"classid" tag, 203
Clipboard tab, Preferences window, 2–3
Clip Parameters panel, 10, 19
  for the Menu clip, 22
CMYK, 48
Cold Fusion, 243
Colored Syntax feature, ActionScript window, 99
Command + B, 33–35, 40, 44, 62, 66, 78
Command + Enter, 208
Command + F8, 41, 77, 89
Command + F, 60
Command + G, 40
Command + L, 126

INDEX

Command + M, 124
Command + R, 43
Command + Return, 61
Command + Shift + H, 63
Command + X, 131
Common Libraries menu, 17–18
Compression, 95–96
   ADPCM (Advanced Differential Pulse Code Modulation), 95
   default setting, 95
   MP3, 96
   Raw compression, 96
Control + Alt + C, 78
Control + Alt + V, 79
Control + B, 33–35, 40, 44, 66, 78
Control + Enter, 61, 208
Control + F8, 41, 77, 89
Control + F, 60
Control + L, 126
Control + M, 124
Control + R, 43
Control + Shift + H, 63
Control + X, 131
Control ->Test Movie, 61
Conversion Setup window, Adobe Streamline, 52
Cookie, 192
Corner Radius text box, 30
Customize Shortcuts window, 3

D

Debugger:
   ActionScript, 106–9
      features, 108–9
      local vs. remote debugging, 107–8
      Properties List, 108
      Variables List, 109
      Watch List, 109
Debugger window, 12
Device Font checkbox, 197
Dimensions setting, Publish feature, 196
Display Menu checkbox, 196

Distributive Blend Type, 60
Dot syntax, 104–5
Dragging, 250–57
   movie clips, 250–52
   products, to a shopping cart, 252–57
Dreamweaver, 188, 199–200
   Check Plug-in window, 200
   Macromedia Flash Dispatcher Behavior window, 201
Duplicate Symbol button, 10
Duplicate Symbols, 42
DXF Sequence, 182
Dynamic Text option, Text Options panel, 8–9

E

Edit Actions, 42
   button, 10
Edit Envelope window, 85, 88
Editing tab, Preferences window, 2–3
Edit Multiple Frames button, 58
Edit Symbols, 42
Effect menu, 84
Effect panel, 9–10, 42
Electronic Cosmo, 83
EMBED tag, 204
EMF Sequence, 182
Envelope Handles and Lines, 86–87
EPS 3.0, 187
EPS 3.0 Sequence, 182
EPS, 50
Eraser Mode button, 37
Eraser tool, 27–28, 36–38
   Faucet option, 37
Event Sound option, 89–91
Event Sync option, 89
Exact Fit setting, 199
Expert mode, Actions window, 15
Export Flash Player window, 146, 215
Exporting movies, 181–86
   Dreamweaver, 188, 199–200
   file formats, 182

Exporting movies (*cont.*)
   Macromedia Flash Deployment Kit, 200–202
   Publish feature, 188–202
      dimensions setting, 196
      HTML Alignment setting, 198
      playback settings, 196–97
      quality settings, 197–98
      scale, 199
      template menu, 188–95
      templates, customizing/creating, 194–95
      Window mode, 198
   single frame Video, 187–88
   SWF file format, 182–85
      Audio Stream and Event settings, 185
      Debugging Permitted, 184
      Generate size report, 184
      JPEG Quality setting, 184
      Load Order menu, 184
      Omit Trace actions, 184
      Override sound settings check box, 185
      Password field, 184
      Protect from import box, 184
      Version setting, 185
   video, 185–86
      exporting a single frame, 187–88
      Quicktime Movies, 185–86
External text files, using, 243–45
Eyedropper tool, 45

F

Faucet option, Eraser tool, 37
File formats:
   audio, 82
   for exporting movies, 182
   graphics, 47
File organization, 125–26
File size, shrinking, 207–20
   Bandwidth Profiler, 208–12
      Frame by Frame Graph mode, 209–12
      Streaming Graph mode, 208–9
   finding trouble spots, 207–14

   and fonts, 215
   imported bitmap files, optimizing, 214–15
   MP3 audio compression, 218–19
   shapes, streamlining, 216–18
   Size Report, 212–14
Fill panel, 4–5
Fireworks, 27, 46
   PNG Import Settings window, 54
   preparing files with, 53–54
Flash 5:
   ActionScript, 97–121
   animation, 57–80
   artwork, 27–55
   audio, 81–96
   compression, 95–96
   dragging, 250–57
   exporting movies, 181–86
   faking video in, 231–34
   file size, shrinking, 207–20
   Flash Tennis game, 168–80
   game creation, 153–68
   HTML text in, 245
   Keyboard Shortcuts, 3–4
   layering movies, 226–34
   Libraries, new features, 17–24
   masks, 241–43
   movie clip, creating, 77–80
   new features, 1–26
   panels, 4–12
      Align panel, 6–7
      Character panel, 8
      Clip Parameters panel, 10, 19
      Effect panel, 9–10, 42
      Fill panel, 4–5
      Frame panel, 11, 60
      Generator panel, 12
      Info panel, 4
      Instance panel, 9–10, 42
      Mixer panel, 7
      Paragraph panel, 8
      Scene panel, 11–12
      Sound panel, 11
      Stroke panel, 4–5, 6, 29–30

INDEX

Swatches panel, 7–8
Text Options panel, 8–9
Transform panel, 6, 67
plug-in detection using, 206
Preferences window, 2–3
Print feature, 145–49
Publish feature, 188–202
   dimensions setting, 196
   HTML Alignment setting, 198
   playback settings, 196–97
   quality settings, 197–98
   scale, 199
   template menu, 188–95
   templates, customizing/creating, 194–95
   Window mode, 198
ShapeMatch game, 153–67
sound editing controls, 84–89
text fields, 243–48
video, 185–86
for video, 185–86
video:
   exporting a single frame, 187–88
   Quicktime Movies, 185–86
   using in, 80
Web site, 123–52
windows, 12–17
and XML, 25
Flash Alignment menu, 199
Flash Enterprise Kit for IE 5.5 (Macromedia), 25
Flash Export window, 49
   Freehand, 48–49
Flash with FSCommands template, 190
Flash/FutureSplash Player, 47
Flash movie, preparing, 126
Flash Only (Default) template, 189–90
Flash Player, 182, 187
Flash SWF Export Options window, 54
Flash SWF Format Options window, 51
Flash Tennis game, 168–80
   adding the code, 175–80
      to the ball, 176–80

      to the computer paddle, 175–76
      to the player paddle, 175
   background, 171
   ball, 173–74
   graphics creation, 168–75
   paddles, 174–75
   score bar, 171–73
   walls, 169–70
Flash Writer export window, 50
Fonts, affecting file size with, 215
Font Symbol Properties window, 24
Font symbols, making, 24–25
Forms, using for calculations, 248–50
Frame Actions, 98
Frame Actions window, 92
Frame-by-frame animation, 79–80
Frame panel, 11
   opening, 60
Frames button, 88
Framesets, working with, 224–26
Freehand, *See* Macromedia Freehand
FSCommands, 190
Functions section, ActionScript window, 102
FutureSplash, 182, 187

G

Game creation, 153–68
   Flash Tennis game, 168–80
      adding the code, 175–80
      background, 171
      ball, 173–74
      graphics creation, 168–75
      paddles, 174–75
      score bar, 171–73
      walls, 169–70
   ShapeMatch game, 153–67
      adding the code, 161–67
      background, 155
      graphics creation, 154–61
      grid, 157–58
      reset button, 156
      scoreboard, 155–56

Game creation (*cont.*)
   ShapeMatch game (*cont.*)
      ShapeMatch graphic, 157
      tiles, 158–61
      "You win!" text, 161
General tab, Preferences window, 2–3
Generator panel, 12
Generator Template, 182, 187
GIF, 27, 55, 187
GIF Sequence, 182
Graphic behavior, symbols, 41
Graphics:
   finding, 55
   spinning, 70–71
Graphics library, 17
Grouped objects, 38, 40
Guides, 14

H

HEIGHT tag, 204
Hit state:
   creating for text, 129
   defined, 90
Home page section, Web site, 137–38
Homesite, 188–89
HTML, 203–6
   basic, creating for a site, 203–4
   Flash plug-in detection, 206
   Javascript plug-in detection, 204–6
HTML Alignment setting, 198
HTML site, adding Flash animations to, 150–51
HTML text in Flash, 245

I

Illustrator, *See* Adobe Illustrator
Image Map template, 190
Imageready, exporting from, 54–55
Importing:
   bitmaps, 42–46
      optimizing the file, 214–15
   libraries, 17–19

Info panel, 4, 14
Ink Bottle tool, 27–28, 34–35
Input Text option, Text Options panel, 8
Insert -> Convert to Symbol, 41
Insert ->Moton Guide, 72
Insert Layer button, 65
   Timeline window, 72
Instance panel, 9–10, 14, 42
Interface, creating, 127–32

J

Java Player template, 190
Javascript, 97, 200
   and browser windows, 221–24
      closing, 223–24
      opening, 222–23
Javascript plug-in detection, 204–6
JPEG, 27, 47, 55, 187
JPEG Sequence, 182
JRVisuals Web site, 150–51

K

Kerning checkbox, Character panel, 8
Keyboard Shortcuts, 1, 3–4
   defined, 4
Keyframes, 57–59
Keywords Identifier, 99
Knowledge Track button, 20

L

Lasso tool, 27–28, 32–33
   Magic Wand option, 33
Launcher Bar, 14
Layering movies, 226–34
   audio in a level, 226–28
   faking video, 231–34
   turning audio on/off, 228–31
Layers, creating, 65
Learning Interactions, 1, 17, 19–20
Letter, breaking apart, 34

INDEX

Letter shapes, animating, 65–66
Libraries:
   importing, 17–19
   importing movies as, 18
   Learning Interactions, 1, 19–20
   library files, sharing across multiple movies, 18–19
   new features, 17–24
   permanent, creating, 18
   sharing, 17–19
   Smart Clips, 1
Library, 41
Library window, 14
List menu, Smart Clips, 21
Lock/Unlock All Layers button, 57–58
Loop checkbox, 196
Looping feature, 87–89

M

MacPaint, 47
Macromedia Fireworks, 190
Macromedia Flash Deployment Kit, 200–202
Macromedia Flash Dispatcher Behavior window, 201
   Dreamweaver, 201
Macromedia FreeHand, 3, 27, 31, 46, 125, 145
   Flash Export Window, 48–49
   Import window in Flash, 48
Macromedia Web site, 50
Magic Wand option, Lasso tool, 33
Masks, 241–43
   spotlighting effect, 241
   wipe, building with, 241–43
Match Movie setting, 196
META "refresh" tag, 203
Miletsky, Jason, 55
Mixer panel, 7, 14
Modify Onion Markers button, 58
Morphing:
   circle into an "A," 61–65
   circle into a square, 59–61
Motion Guide layer, 72–76

Motion Tweening, 67–76
Movie Clip behavior, symbols, 41
Movie clips:
   adding animation to buttons with, 130–32
   creating, 77–80
   dragging, 250–52
   pulsing circle, 77–79
   targeting, 104–5
Movie Clips library, 17
Movie Clip symbol, 27
Movie dimensions, 123–24
Movie Explorer window, 12, 14, 16
Movie print, making, 147–49
Movie Properties window, 126
Movies:
   layering, 226–34
      audio in a level, 226–28
      faking video, 231–34
      turning audio on/off, 228–31
   pausing, 237–40
MP3 audio compression, 218–19
MP3 files, 82, 96
   importing, 25
MPecker Drop Decoder, 83
Musicmatch Jukebox, 83

N

Navigation, Web site, 132–36
No Border setting, 199
No Color icon, 29–30
Normal mode, Actions window, 15

O

Object Actions, 98
Objects section, ActionScript window, 103
Onion Skinning buttons, 58
Onion Skinning mode, 58, 64–65
Opaque Windowless setting, 198
Operators section, ActionScript window, 101–2
Optimize Curves tool, 216–18
Optimize Curves window, 216

Option + Command + C, 78
Option + Command + V, 79
Output window, 16
Oval tool, 27–28, 29
Override sound settings box, 218
Oxy Web site, 242

P

Paint Bucket tool, 27–28, 36, 45
   Don't Close Gaps option, 36
Panels, 4–12
   Align panel, 6–7
   Character panel, 8
   Clip Parameters panel, 10, 19
   Effect panel, 9–10, 42
   Fill panel, 4–5
   Frame panel, 11, 60
   Generator panel, 12
   Info panel, 4
   Instance panel, 9–10, 42
   Mixer panel, 7
   Paragraph panel, 8
   Scene panel, 11–12
   Sound panel, 11
   Stroke panel, 4–5, 6, 29–30
   Swatches panel, 7–8
   Text Options panel, 8–9
   Transform panel, 6, 67
Panel Sets menu, 4
Paragraph panel, 8
PARAM tag, 204
Path, following, 71–74
Paused at Start checkbox, 196
Pausing movies, 237–40
Pencil tool, 72
Pen tool, 3, 13, 27–28, 31–32
Percent setting, 196
Perl, 20, 118, 243
Permanent libraries, creating, 18
Photoshop, *See* Adobe Photoshop
PICT, 27, 47, 55, 185, 187
PICT Sequence, 182

Pixels setting, 196
Playback settings, 196–97
   Device Font checkbox, 197
   Display Menu checkbox, 196
   Loop checkbox, 196
   Paused at Start checkbox, 196
PLUGINSPAGE tag, 204
PNG, 27, 47, 54–55, 187
PNG Import Settings window, Fireworks, 54
PNG Sequence, 182
Polygon option, Lasso tool, 33
Position and scale of an object, animating, 67–68
Predefined Identifier, 99
Preferences window, 1, 2–3
   Clipboard tab, 2–3
   Editing tab, 2–3
   General tab, 2–3
Pre-production techniques/hints, 123–26
   file organization, 125–26
   movie dimensions, 123–24
   storyboarding, 125
Print feature, 145–49
   movie print, making, 147–49
   printable document, setting up, 145–46
Products, dragging to a shopping cart, 252–57
Projectors, 259
Properties, defined, 102
Properties section, ActionScript window, 102
Publish feature, 188–202
   Dimensions setting, 196
   template menu, 188–95
      Ad 3 Banner/Ad 4 Banner/Ad 5 Banner/Ad Any Banner, 193–94
      Flash with FSCommands setting, 190
      Flash Only (Default) setting, 189–90
      Image Map setting, 190
      Java Player setting, 190
      Quicktime setting, 191–92
      User Choice setting, 192–93
   templates, customizing/creating, 194–95
Pulsing circle, 77–79

INDEX *269*

Q

Quality settings, 197–98
  Auto high, 198
  Auto low, 198
  Best, 198
  High, 198
  Low, 197
  Medium, 198
Quicktime 4, 46
  files accepted by, 47
  Pro version, 82, 231
Quicktime Image, 47
Quicktime Movies, 47, 82, 182, 185
  exporting, 185–86
Quicktime template, 191–92
  Alpha option, 191
  File section, 192
  Playback section, 192
  Streaming Sound option, 192
QuickTime for video, 182

R

Radio Button option, Smart Clips, 21
Raw compression, 96
Rectangle tool, 27–28, 30–31
RGB, and FreeHand, 48
Rodriguez, Jose, 151
Round Rectangle Radius option, 30–31

S

Samples:
  ActionScript, 109–21
    changing the cursor, 113–14
    controlling the volume, 114–18
    date script, 110–13
    email and ASP, 118–21
Save Panel Layout menu, 4
Scale, 199
Scene panel, 11–12
Screens, loading, 235–37

Screen savers, 259
Screen savers section, Web site, 144
Screen shots, Mac vs. PC, 43
SCRIPT tag, 201
Scrolling text, 245–47
Shape Hints, 63–64, 66
  creating, 63
ShapeMatch game, 153–67
  adding the code, 161–67
  background, 155
  graphics, creating, 154–61
  grid, 157–58
  reset button, 156
  scoreboard, 155–56
  ShapeMatch graphic, 157
  tiles, 158–61
  "You win!" text, 161
Shapes, 38–40
  streamlining, 216–18
Shape Tweening, 59–66
Shared libraries, using for audio files, 93–94
Shared Library feature, 93
Sharing libraries, 17–19
Shift + Command + 4, 43
Shift + Command + G, 40
Shift + Command + H, 63
Shift + Command + V, 66, 131
Shift + Control + G, 40
Shift + Control + V, 66, 131
Shopping cart, dragging products to, 252–57
Show All Layers as Outlines button, 57–58
Show All setting, 199
Show Deprecated Syntax option, Actions window, 15
Show/Hide All Layers button, 57–58
Show Warning Messages setting, 199
Shrinking file size, 207–20
  Bandwidth Profiler, 208–12
    Frame by Frame Graph mode, 209–12
    Streaming Graph mode, 208–9
  finding trouble spots, 207–14
  imported bitmap files, optimizing, 214–15
  Size Report, 212–14

Silicon Graphics file type, 47
Single frame, exporting, 187–88
Size Report, 212–14
Smart Clip, 10
Smart Clips, 1, 17, 19, 21–24
   Checkbox option, 21
   and variables, 21
Smooth button, 72
Snap to Grid feature, 3, 73
_soundbuftime, 92
Sound Designer II, 82
Sound editing controls, 84–89
   Envelope Handles and Lines, 86–87
   Looping feature, 87–89
   Time In/Out controls, 85–86
Sound panel, 11
Sound Properties window, 219
Sounds library, 17
Splash screen, adding to Web site, 151–52
Spotlighting effect, 241
Stage window, 14
Static Text option, Text Options panel, 8
Storyboarding, 125
Streaming Audio option, 91–93
Stroke panel, 4–5, 29–30
   strokes available in, 6
Style menu, 23
Subselect tool, 13, 39–40
Sun AU, 82
SWA file format, 46
Swap Symbols, 42
Swap Symbols button, 10, 139–40
Swatches panel, 7–8
SWF file, 48–51
   exporting from Freehand, 48
SWF file format, 182–85
   Audio Stream and Event settings, 185
   Debugging Permitted, 184
   Generate size report, 184
   JPEG Quality setting, 184
   Load Order menu, 184
   Omit Trace actions, 184
   Override sound settings check box, 185
   Password field, 184
   Protect from import box, 184
   Version setting, 185
Swish, 257–59
Symbol Editing mode, 41, 89, 128, 140, 143, 147, 252
Symbol Linkage Properties window, 18–19, 24, 94
Symbol Properties window, setting up for "home" button, 128
Symbols, 18, 41–42
   behaviors, 41
   fading the instance of, 69
Syntax:
   ActionScript, 103–6
      targeting movie clips, 104–5
      writing/using variables, 105–6
System 7 sounds, 82

T

Template menu, 188–95
   Publish feature, 188–95
      Ad 3 Banner/Ad 4 Banner/Ad 5 Banner/Ad Any Banner, 193–94
      Flash with FSCommands setting, 190
      Flash Only (Default) setting, 189–90
      Image Map setting, 190
      Java Player setting, 190
      Quicktime setting, 191–92
      User Choice setting, 192–93
Templates:
   customizing/creating, 194–95
      $BG, 195
      $DS $DF, 195
      $MT, 195
      $MU, 195
      $PE, 195
      $PO, 195
      $T1, 195

INDEX

$TT, 194
$WE, 195
$WI, 195
Test Movie function, 208
Test Movie mode, 16, 23
Text fields, 243–48
   external text files, using, 243–45
   HTML text in Flash, 245
   scrolling text, 245–47
   using text files to hold URLs, 247–48
Text Options panel, 8–9
TGA, 47
TIFF, 47
Time In/Out controls, 85–86
Timeline, 57–59
   organizing, 132–34
Timeline window, 57
   Insert Layer button, 72
Tint, and Effect panel, 42
Tint Color setting, 69
Tint effect, 69
Toolbar, 13
   Eraser tool, 27–28, 36–38
   Eyedropper tool, 45
   Ink Bottle tool, 27–28, 34–35
   Lasso tool, 27–28, 32–33
   Oval tool, 27–28, 29
   Paint Bucket tool, 27–28, 36
   Pen tool, 27–28, 31–32
   Rectangle tool, 27–28, 30–31
   Subselect tool, 13, 39–40
Transform panel, 6, 67
Transparent Windowless setting, 198
Troubleshooting, Web site, 150
Tweening, 11
TYPE tag, 204

U

Ungroup feature, 40
URLs, using text files to hold, 247–48

V

Values window:
   defined, 23
   for the Menu clip, 22
Variables, ActionScript, 105–6
Vector-based images, and Adobe Streamline, 51–53
Video, 80, 185–86

W

WAV, 82, 182
Web Photoshop 6 Primer (Miletsky), 55
Web site, 123–52
   buttons, creating, 127–30
   Flash movie, preparing, 126
   HTML site, adding Flash animations to, 150–51
   interface, creating, 127–32
   movie clips, using to add animation to buttons, 130–32
   navigation, 132–36
      applying Button Actions, 134–35
      changing behaviors of buttons, 135–36
      organizing the Timeline, 132–34
   pre-production techniques/hints, 123–26
      file organization, 125–26
      movie dimensions, 123–24
      storyboarding, 125
   printing from Flash, 145–49
      making a movie print, 147–49
      setting up a printable document, 145–46
   sections:
      banners section, 139–41
      home page section, 137–38
      organizing, 137–44
      reusing elements, 138–44
      screen savers section, 144
      using movie clips for, 137–38
      Web sites section, 141–44

Web site (*cont.*)
   splash screen, adding, 151–52
   troubleshooting, 150
WIDTH tag, 204
Window mode, 198
Windows, 12–17
   Actions window, 14–15
   Debugger window, 16–17
   Movie Explorer window, 16
   Output window, 16
   Stage window, 14
   Toolbar, 13
Windows AVI, 182, 185
Windows Metafile, 47, 187
Wipe, building with a mask, 241–43
WMF Sequence, 182

X

XML, and Flash 5, 25

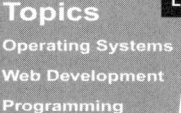

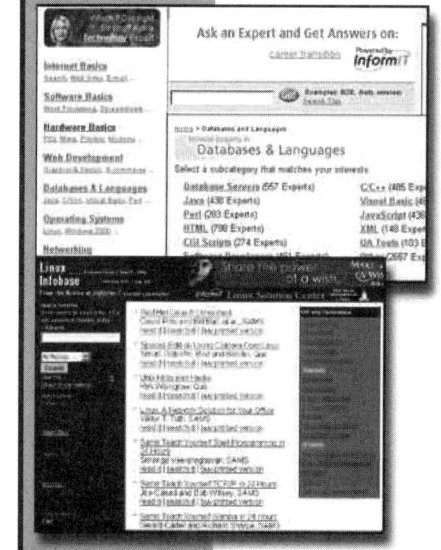

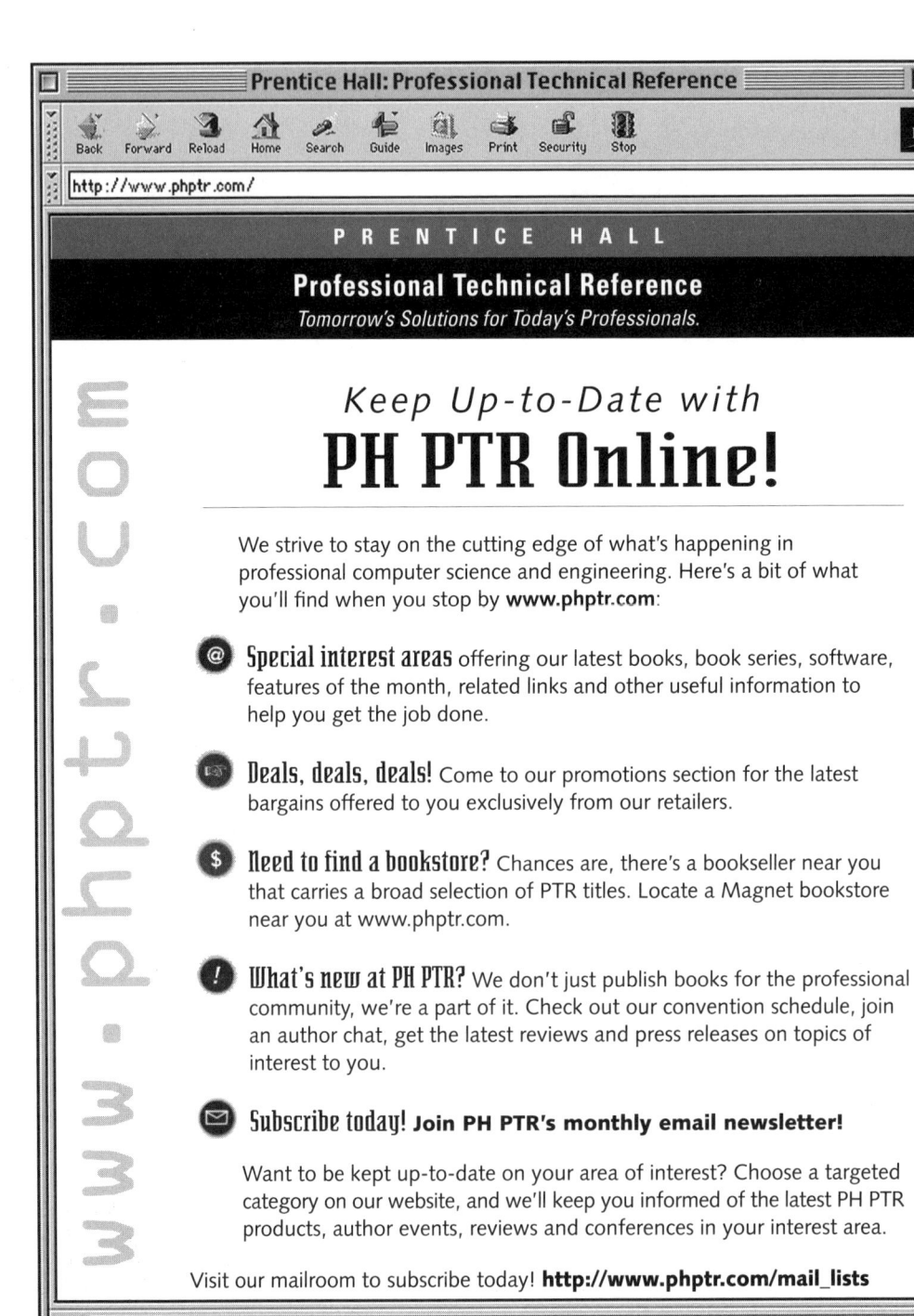

PRENTICE HALL
Professional Technical Reference
Tomorrow's Solutions for Today's Professionals.

Keep Up-to-Date with
PH PTR Online!

We strive to stay on the cutting edge of what's happening in professional computer science and engineering. Here's a bit of what you'll find when you stop by **www.phptr.com**:

- **@ Special interest areas** offering our latest books, book series, software, features of the month, related links and other useful information to help you get the job done.

- **Deals, deals, deals!** Come to our promotions section for the latest bargains offered to you exclusively from our retailers.

- **$ Need to find a bookstore?** Chances are, there's a bookseller near you that carries a broad selection of PTR titles. Locate a Magnet bookstore near you at www.phptr.com.

- **! What's new at PH PTR?** We don't just publish books for the professional community, we're a part of it. Check out our convention schedule, join an author chat, get the latest reviews and press releases on topics of interest to you.

- **Subscribe today! Join PH PTR's monthly email newsletter!**

Want to be kept up-to-date on your area of interest? Choose a targeted category on our website, and we'll keep you informed of the latest PH PTR products, author events, reviews and conferences in your interest area.

Visit our mailroom to subscribe today! **http://www.phptr.com/mail_lists**